A SONG TO SING AND A TALE TO TELL

A SONG TO SING AND A TALE TO TELL

JEAN BROWN

THULE
PRESS

First published 1979

© Jean Brown

ISBN 0 906191 43 2

Designed by Anthony B Ainley MSIA

Photoset in 10/12pt Plantin by Hanson Typesetting Services Ltd

Illustrated by Jennifer Sharp

Printed by The Scolar Press, Ilkley

Published by The Thule Press, Shetland, for the author.

For Vivienne

who has always wanted me to write about our camping days

in the Hebrides

and in memory of

my father

Who are these? Sitting around the fire.
They'll be happy to have your company
If that is your desire,
And the evening will be gay,
At the sunset hour of day,
With a song to sing and a tale to tell
And many a tune to play.

ACKNOWLEDGEMENTS

I am grateful to the following authors, literary executors and
publishers for permission to use quotations from their songs.

Roberton Publications for the 'Uist Tramping Song' and 'Westering Home'
by Hugh S. Roberton
Stainer and Bell Ltd for 'Lord of the dance' by S. Carter
The Society of Authors for 'Wind, wind, heather gypsy'
by John and Ada Galsworthy
for 'Summer Holiday' by Welch/Bennett © 1963 by Elstree Music Ltd
for 'The Road to the Isles' reprinted from 'Songs of the Hebrides'
by permission of the Trustees of the Estate of Marjorie Kennedy-Fraser
and Boosey and Hawkes Music Publishers Ltd
The Girl Guide Association for 'The Guide Marching Song' by Mary Chater
and several Camp-Fire Songs and Graces.
I trust I have not unwittingly used copyright material without permission
and acknowledgement.

1

We have campfire here,
By the deep, blue sea,
And the slender tree
On the lonesome isle.

All that we hold dear,
In the north or south,
Can we see so clear
In the evening glow.

Norwegian campfire song
set to Ole Texas.

When the sun goes down
Everything is still
And the campfire song
Echoes from the hill.

1

Chapter One

WE HAD just been introduced to an island man, in a small, crofter's cottage on Tiree in the Inner Hebrides. His handshake was warm and welcoming.

'And have you the Gaelic?' he wanted to know.

'I'm sorry,' I said, 'I'm afraid we have no Gaelic at all.'

His merry eyes twinkled. 'Och!' he said, 'and how are you going to get into Heaven when it is the only language the Lord knows?'

Perhaps this is so. If it is I must grumble less than most people for I have had more than my fair share of Heaven already and with that I must try to be satisfied.

That was many years ago and between then and now a great many Atlantic rollers have broken on the beach, crushing a great many delicate shells into sand and a great many children have left their footprints on the shore.

Perhaps it was the perfect fire which brought back the flood of memories. It was large and square and manageable and it burst into flame with the first match. The early smoke soon gave way to a steady flame and a crimson glow appeared on the crown of native peat. The wood for it had been collected that afternoon in the undiluted sunshine which poured down on us every hour of every day we have just spent at Luskentyre.

Linda, Peter, Craig and I had crept under the fence above our campsite. There was an easy place, worn by much use, near to our double bowled washing up stand. Wriggling underneath it I had seen for a moment the fluttering of our sun bleached tea towels against the blue of a cloudless sky. Barefoot and bronzed by long hours in the open air we had followed the line of the fence, picking up the fallen, rotten posts which had remained ungathered since their replacement many years ago. Now they burned cheerfully on the shore, not six yards from the Atlantic.

It was late August and by ten o'clock the sun had dropped behind Taransay leaving the mountains of North Harris clear and well defined. The sea and the hills formed a perfect backcloth for the fire on the beach and the children perched like gannets on the rocky ledges around and above it. They clustered together in friendship, their faces recently browned by the sun, now reddened by the fire, their lusty voices lifted to compete successfully with the din of the long line of surf breaking on the shore.

I do not sing well at the best of times and many would say that is an understatement and it would be far more accurate to say that I sing badly at all times. Nevertheless I always sing and I have grown used to the laughter and the teasing. They are not unkind. Nor does the presence of visitors silence me and there were many round the fire just four evenings ago. How many I could not tell. All our children had bare knees and pompom hats but among them were the broad shouldered silhouettes of island men and women and it was obvious that our numbers had risen well above the fifty we counted at every meal.

I should say that I always sing unless I am deeply moved. On these occasions I cannot raise even one untuneful note for some pebble from the beach seems lodged in my vocal cords and a sea mist seems to blow up from nowhere.

The fire needed no attention. The peat secured the logs and kept the sparks confined. The children were singing the 'Harris Song,' bequeathed to us by Catherine, many years ago and it seemed to me that I could hear the two hundred voices of the other children, down the years, who have camped with me on this and other beautiful shores. The songs they have sung and the things they have written are imprinted on my memory as indelibly as my own name, address and telephone number.

'Hello, Skipper, your favourite camper speaking,' announced tomboy Linda everytime she phoned me.

'Don't be scared,' Joan whispered to Jennifer in the doctor's surgery. They were both covered in sun spots. 'I'm not! Not when Skipper's here!' We could hear the pills he had prescribed being stamped out and then the almost inaudible patter as he accidentally spilled them on the floor. Through the half open door we could see him bend to pick them up.

'My idea of freedom,' wrote Julie, 'is to be in camp in the Hebrides!'

These are my rewards. Such simple, little things to remain with me so long.

It had been Jonathan's first camp and I wasn't sure how he rated me until he came to me on the long journey home and admitted me into his friendship by saying, 'Play cards with me, Skipper.'

Six camps later he paid me the compliment of driving over to show me his new, day old motor bike.

'I've just driven nearly a hundred miles,' he announced.

'Goodness, you must be starving,' I said. He was. He was ravenous!

They are all so unforgettable. Viv came to camp as a very independent eight year old and has matured into one of our much loved seniors.

'They've got a carpet an inch thick,' was her comment after visiting a Mainland home one day.

'Never mind, when you marry your millionaire with the double barrelled name,' I reassured her, 'you'll have a carpet just as thick.'

'She'll not want anything to do with us then!' laughed Margaret, my sister.

'Of course I will,' said Viv, 'I'll want you to take my children to camp.'

And there was Barbara, an active, very excitable child who did not always have the knack of being happy. One day, crossing the Tiree machair, she confided, 'I've found out how to be happy in camp, Skipper. You just work all the time!'

Very few have written letters but we have one from Joanna, written when she went to be a nurse a few months ago. It says, 'I remember everything, every chat we've had and every chocolate bun.' She had camped with us eight years on islands in the Hebrides.

I was remembering her especially in the close proximity of the fire. Darkness had fallen almost imperceptibly or perhaps the bright flames accentuated the curtain of night which was being wrapped about us. Many have looked back on similar campfires and known that they have shared an experience they'd have been the poorer to have missed. Many have felt the need to put their thoughts into words and the words into song.

'Now the Harris Camp is over,' sang the Riddlesden Lot,
    "And it's time to say 'Goodbye,'
    We must leave the fields of clover
    And I feel like I could cry."

Most of our children have had Yorkshire voices, many rich in the dialect of their homes and villages.

'Hod on,' Ken would call a hundred times a day. 'Ah'll do it!'

But there were Canadian girls who, when asked if they were enjoying camp, drawled, 'Gee, we're having a Ball!' There was Ulla, from Sonderborg, who said everything was 'vunderful' and taught us how to make our oven and, for three weeks at Budle Bay, there were the eight little refugees from a Displaced Person's Camp who called me Aunty Yan and taught us we were not so clever as we thought we were. There were Marie and Dominique, Faffy and Brigitte from France who continually used the adjective 'formidable' by which they meant 'terrific',' Margy from America who presented us with our most sensitive piece of poetry and from Jamaica had come Rebecca who gave us oatcakes because she'd had such a lovely camp and Hilary who wished all Jamaican children could come to camp with us.

'The sea's not as blue as this in the Mediterranean!' Toots had observed emphatically. I am not qualified to make a comparison but I know of no bluer sea than that which surrounds Tiree when it reflects a cloudless sky.

'This sea's clearer than the sea round the Bahamas,' well-travelled Mandy told us. Some have seen more than I but I know that the water in which we bathe on the Hebridean shores is as crystal clear as the spring water which bubbles up from deep in the earth at home.

Coming back from Ibiza Kathleen said, 'The sea maybe warm but it isn't clean like Tiree.'

'It's the first time I've seen the sea!' said ten year old Rosie.

So many of them have had no previous experience of a natural shore and a clean, unpolluted ocean and all return home with their memory of it so vivid that other beaches suffer in comparison, other places disappoint.

Normally I stoke the fire, feeding it frequently to keep the heat and the dancing flames but this fire was extremly well-behaved. There was no fickle wind to blow the smoke into unexpected quarters, no troublesome logs to drop suddenly and danger-ously into the fire sending a shower of sparks among the singers. Sometimes, too, I have to lead the singing in my unique and incompetent way. But on this happy evening, just four days ago, I was 'de trop' so I sat silent and I remembered.

There were funny things to recall. A wide-eyed Jill who had announced to a shocked table that she was sure she had eaten Fred on a lettuce leaf. All snails, big or small, are called Fred. Lesley and Sheila were incorrigible. They kept us amused all fortnight with their antics. They had two imaginary little people they kept now in the palm of their hand, now on their shoulder.

'Don't do that. It's not nice!' Lesley would reprimand the invisible offender in a way reminiscent of Joyce Grenfell.

'You're sulking again,' Sheila would say. 'Just because I told you to put your raincoat on!'

There was another Sheila who, having heard that there were adders on the Ben, suddenly asked in awe, as we neared the summit, 'And there really wild cats up here, Skipper?' and then in near panic when I nodded, 'Aw heck, wild cats and wild snakes!'

I remembered Vanda who was perpetually looking for plastic bags because she had an obsession about tidiness and Jenny who wanted to clean my shoes and used a whole tin of shoe polish in her enthusiasm to please, Denise who ran half a mile to tell Calum that the Tresnish Isles had just appeared out of the sea as if they were some strange phenomena just making their debut from the waves and Eleanor who was found sitting on her cabin bunk with her fishing rod protruding through the porthole into Oban harbour.

For many years a Glasgow boy used to spend his summer holiday with relatives on Tiree. From the age of four he would come to our camp and he was still coming ten years later. His first visit will be remembered for ever by Miriam for he bent down and peeped under the lat saying innocently, 'I can see you.'

Some, I recollected, had found the camp toilets very strange at first. Runa had fallen in because no one had told her to stride the trench and she had hung precariously over the edge with both feet on one side.

Gillian had become very constipated. 'Don't worry,' she'd said bravely when we were on our way to see if a crofter's bathroom would work any magic. 'I was like this once at home. That time we got the new toilet put in!'

Judith had wondered how near the centre of the 'town' we camped at Luskentyre, Pauline had burst into tears when Calum's aged mother sang the Eriskay Love Lilt one last evening on Tiree and Nellie had been covered in confusion that day when she suddenly realised she had eaten two teas.

'My stomach can digest anything,' remarked a full and contented Jane. 'Can I be cheeky and ask to come again next year?' wondered a happy and grateful Shirley.

'Hilary, Pamela, Janet, Sue, Gwen, Marta, Glenys, Irene whose help one stormy year had been indespensible. Fiona, Sylvia . . .

How very many of them there had been! Christian names had recurred again and again. How many Amandas, Rachels, Susans, Christines? One Chris had worried because she'd been told earwigs crawled into ears and ate out brains. There are millions of earwigs on Tiree! Another Chris announced joyfully when the post arrived, 'I'm an aunty for the eighth time!' (Baby Elizabeth is now old enough to come to camp). Another Chris rolled over in her sleeping bag on the morning of her departure and moaned, 'I don't wanna go home.'

And there had been boys. Stuart, David, Ian, Stephen, Duncan . . . Peter . . . Peter with the smiling face. Finding the youngsters particularly agreeable one day I promised, 'If you hear anyone grumbling about modern children send them to me.

I'll tell them a thing or two!'

'Okay,' said Peter. 'Expect mi gran'ma ev'ry Sat'day!'

There had nearly always been Paul. He came with us at ten, too embarrassed to swim because he complained his sunburn was all in stripes. He was still with us as an adult who had been teaching several years.

And there was Howard who imitated Danny La Rue to perfection in Fancy Dress, complete with panscrub ear rings; Howard who made a date to play 'Hangman' with Mrs Belsey on the boat home and naively believed everything we told him. He had been next in a long queue outside a crofter's 'loo' one day. It was a lovely 'loo' but the tank took ages to fill. 'If you're only spending a penny,' I'd called to the present occupier, 'don't pull the string.'

Howard had felt his empty pockets with despair. 'Aw heck,' he'd said, ''Ave yer ter pay?'

Memories were as multitudinous as the midges who alone seem to resent our summer invasion of the Hebrides. Memories, not only of children, though they surround me continually, but of islanders and their humour, their lively tolerance and their unequalled hospitality; of céilidh and dance and custom, of wind and rain, hot sunshine and blue skies, of flowers and birds and animals and of friendship, struggle, serenity and fun.

When I get home, I mused, intoxicated by the firelight and the singing, I'll organise all these unique souvenirs of twenty years with children in the Hebrides. I'll sort and sift them and put them in order and record them so that they'll not be forgotten. But even as the thought came I trembled to think what order and sifting would do to events as spontaneous as those which I remember so well and I knew then, that to be sincere, I would have to let them tumble onto the page in whatever way they would.

I am home now. In a little while the six wicker skips, with their white tents and kitchen equipment, will return to be collected from the local station. They will be unloaded and packed away in the camp store behind the old farmhouse in which I live. We will try to do it methodically ready for another year when, I hope, there will be another incredible journey to a land where there are no streets, or shops, or traffic; no amusements, no pavements, no concrete. Nothing but sea and sand, flowers and kindly people.

It pleases me to know that I am not alone. The work and the joy and the affection of so many children are shared. I have never taken a camp without either my sister, Margaret, or Hazel Belsey and I know that what we have given and what we have received has been so infinitely more valuable because we have given and received together. The whole has been so much greater than the sum of the parts. Only once have I been fortunate in having both of them together. The debt I owe them can never be paid.

Margaret became 'Flim' many years ago on Tiree. We had a car inner tyre tube which we secured to the shore with a stout rope. The first campers found its buoyancy irresistible. They christened it 'Flimsy' and we took it to Balephuil where the great Atlantic rollers come in one behind the other as far as the eye can see, as far as the horizon and the lighthouse on the Skerryvore.

By some negligence on my part the inner tube was left behind and there was mourning on Johnny Kennedy's twenty seater bus when the loss was discovered. On an impulse someone turned to Margaret and said, 'We can't do without Flimsy. We'll christen you Flimsy instead.' The nickname stayed in the diminutive form of Flim and because of her popularity so named are innumerable dogs and budgerigars.

To the children Hazel has always been 'Mrs Belsey' or 'Mrs B' and they speak her name with the same affection as they say 'Flim' or 'Skipper.' In song they christened her 'Greedy Phoebe' because she enjoys the food they cook and she has often been called 'Oliver' because she always asks for more. The mature and sensitive among them have referred to her as 'Julie Andrews' because she loves to wander on the mountain slopes searching for wild flowers to grow in her peat garden and because children cluster round her like bees round a honey pot.

The children and the islanders have given us great happiness. I would not have wished to own it alone. What is done is better when it is done together. There were camps before the Hebridean ones, camps in the Yorkshire Dales where we learned the necessary skills to dare to wander so far away but island fever attacked us many years ago and will not leave us alone.

In the early days my colleagues remarked somewhat sarcastically, 'You're not going to the Hebrides again?' or 'You're going to Arran? Can't you find a different kind of place?'

'You're not taking children on holiday again, are you?' said a fellow teacher. 'I don't know how you can! Don't you want a holiday? I'm glad to get rid of them at four o'clock!'

When we first started going to Harris the response was initially enthusiastic. 'Paris!' Their pleasure was complete. 'Thank goodness you're making a change.'

'Not Paris. Harris,' I explained patiently.

'Harris?' they asked, 'Where's that? Not the Hebrides again?' They do not understand, as we have learned to, just how necessary it is for children to return, to repeat experiences and to become intimate with a beloved place.

Now, twenty years later, people take it for granted. Parents ring in December asking for camp dates. 'Harris this year?' my friends enquire affably. 'Still going to the islands?' They accept but they do not understand. How can they?

We try to explain. The lovely isolated strands and the soft flower studded machair are so clear in our memory we have only to close our eyes and there are the pure white beaches, and the incredibly clear sea, the blue, blue mountains and the myriads of flowers. We have only to close our ears to the traffic and we hear again the wind in the canvas and the din of the surf. We hear quite clearly the sound of the Gaelic, the cry of the sea birds and the monotonous, never ending note of the corn-crake in Dolly MacLeod's corn. It needs but little of our imagination to evoke the scent of peat and woodsmoke and the clean salty smell of the spray. You have to have seen and heard and breathed in deeply to know and only those who know can understand.

Few, if any, have taken children year after year to these islands in the west.

Essentially the land is ours. Should anyone ask the way we have advice ready to give. Before anyone presumes to take other people's children to shores so far from the beaten track, security must be earned. It is important to have walked the narrow roads, climbed the hills and camped on the shores. The respect of the crofters must be earned and their ways understood because so much depends on them. It may be impossible to have learned their native Gaelic but one must understand the twist of their English which is, after all, only their second language. One must become, in the words of our late friend Mary Mackay of Northton, 'a friend of the people' and be no longer a stranger or a tourist.

Margaret and I wandered among the islands for many years before we dare venture so far with children. We stayed in crofters' homes. We remember particularly our stay with Margaret Lamont. She took us to the only island wedding we have been fortunate to attend. We camped on lonely shores and made contact in the simplest possible way by asking for our water carrier to be filled. We found hospitable people with a sense of humour unequalled in any other community we know. We found isolated beaches of unsurpassed beauty; a cleaness, a happiness and an emptiness never experienced before. We became obsessed with the idea of taking children there and we have been doing so ever since.

It is impossible to measure the influence these summer sojourns have had on the individual boys and girls we have taken. We are content to know that they never pass us in the street without mention of their happy days. They come to visit us in great numbers, bring their husbands, wives and children who have already been promised that they can go to camp with Skipper and Flim when they are ten. Many return to the islands themselves. Several have given voluntary service overseas.

Linda went to Malawi. We have had so many Lindas. This one came to see us on her return. 'It helped a lot having been to camp,' she said.

'In what way?' we wanted to know.

'Tolerance, I think,' she said. 'I could wait patiently all day, in the hot sun, for a bus which should have come in the morning. It was hot and smelly when it came and crowded with people and animals but I could clamber on happily and sit on a crowded seat and enjoy the rough journey. I'm sure I learned that in camp.'

Most of our girls and boys have chosen vocational careers, many are teachers, nurses and social workers, others are good wives and mothers. Dorothy has worked with blind babies and Monica with the mentally handicapped.

Over the years skills have been passed down from one generation of campers to another and experience has been collected and stored and improved upon. Good children have been trained by good teenagers. Well balanced youngsters have brought like friends until the strain of our community is becoming pure. The art of living together in tolerance and gaiety is being well learned and Margaret and Hazel and I feel that the harvest, though incomplete, is good.

2

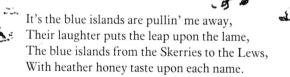

It's the blue islands are pullin' me away,
Their laughter puts the leap upon the lame,
The blue islands from the Skerries to the Lews,
With heather honey taste upon each name.

Chapter Two

WHAT STRANGE magnetism there is in islands which compels our return year after year after year! No wind however strong and tormenting, no rain however horizontal and biting, no blistering heatwave affects our unshakable love of the Hebrides. Extreme conditions only increase our respect for the land and the people and their Creator and fill us with wonder at Nature's extravagance.

There is such variety. No island is like another, none imitates its neighbour. Each could have been fashioned by a different creative hand, each could be the masterpiece of a different god of the open air. No two are the same, neither is one part of an island similar to another. Separated by only a few miles the east coast is different from the west in colour and mood and character and when one crosses the wastes and mountains and peat bogs of the interior one never expects the glory which awaits one on the shore. Even the twin islands of Coll and Tiree, isolated from the rest of the Hebrides by miles of ocean, bear no resemblance to each other and support two differing communities.

There is something intoxicating in the smell of peat drifting from the thatched and slated cottages, something heady in a wind which blows straight from a clean sea to which we are addicted. There is something in the feel of marram grass and flowers under our bare feet which is rare and as necessary to us as our homes in Yorkshire and the work we love.

To trail our feet in the shallow water of the evening tide, hearing only the sound of the oyster catchers and the surf breaking on the shore, seeing the sunlight on the water and the seals at play give nourishment to our souls. It relaxes our minds as nothing else can and brings us nearer to an understanding of the infinite and the peace that can be ours if we can only give it room.

We have a need, too, to climb high on the hill and look far into the distance, to know the height and depth and listen to the silence; to feel healthy and strong and free and then to bend in wonder over the gentian and the wild orchis, the heartsease and the tormentil which are so small yet grow so bravely on the mountain. We have found the delicate violet growing high on Temple Hill and seen primroses grow so dangerously near the Barra sea. Each year we need to see the sun go down in scarlet splendour, flooding the sea with gold and red, to watch the moon rise over the rocky horizon and to see her reflection among the water lilies that bejewel the fresh water lochans.

And there are abstract things just as essential to us and which we find in such abundance in the Hebrides. We need to work and share together. We find it necessary to test our endurance and exhaust ourselves. Only when we are really tired do we appreciate bed; only when hungry do we know what enjoyment of food really is and only when we are dirty do we bathe and feel really clean. All experiences are sharper, more valuable, because they are uncluttered by the ordinary things which make up our daily Mainland lives, things which we know and love but which obscure our perception and dull our response. Home is dearer to us because we have been away, warmth is felt more gratefully because we have been cold and little things become more meaningful and precious.

Laughter, too, is a rare commodity which breeds on the islands as prolifically as the rabbits on the sand dunes and the midges in hot weather. It is a medicine and a tonic which can be recommended but not prescribed and we cannot live without it. We are not solemn, here in Yorkshire, but we have work to do and a role to fulfil, but it seems to me, always, that our fortnight in the Hebrides will be remembered most for the spontaneous, clean laughter which is always bubbling over, releasing tension and breeding courage and loyalty and security.

But if there is magnetism in the islands to pull us back year after year, there is an even greater and stronger magnet in the character of the people who live there and who greet us every year with, 'Ceud mile failte,' a hundred thousand welcomes.

'Welcome to the country and welcome to the house,' they say when we arrive and, 'We'll be seeing you next year, if we're spared,' they say when we go.

For a fortnight every year they accept our presence on the machair as they accept seed time and harvest, as part of the year's activities to be enjoyed and participated in. We admit sincerely that without them our stay would be as tasteless as porridge without salt or apple pie without cream.

This is a busy, fast and interesting world in which we live but it is sometimes dishonest, often sordid and vulgar. Our children must often feel a little insecure and bewildered however well adjusted they are and however meaningful their family relationships. They know that at night doors must be bolted in case someone comes to steal. They know that unlocked cars are often taken and that shopkeepers must employ detectives because some people cannot resist the temptation to take, what is on display, without payment.

It is quite a new experience for many children to know that the only thieves we have in camp are the cows which steal our tea towels from off the fence and the potatoes we have laboriously scrubbed and carelessly left in a pail, or the crofter's cat who knows how to get into our store tent skip. It is nice to know a place where we can leave camp all day and know that when we return we will find our valuables exactly where we left them and that nothing has been disturbed or taken. There are not many places on the coast where one can feel so sure.

There is a warm feeling of happiness, too, in the knowledge that the islanders trust us implicitly. To draw the countless gallons of water we need each day children must enter a crofter's house, often when it is unattended. They are placed in situations which require consideration for other people's property, absolute honesty and courtesy and they respond spontaneously. Critics of modern children will not believe this but it is so.

It is an annual wonder to me that the crofters welcome the children so sincerely and are so patient with them in such great numbers. They put up with their presence on the fank wall, their fumbling fingers when they help with the marking and their clumsy handling of great armsful of wool. It amazes me that they will also allow them to try their hands at the shearing, the milking and the stacking and thatching of the peats.

Our friends do not mind how many children follow us into their homes like so many pet lambs or shadows that go in and out with us. They do not grumble when bare feet walk sand into the house or unsteady hands spill water on the doorstep. They are quite unperturbed when we ask them to dry beds which have been wet by rain during the night and they happily welcome children round their warm stove when hair must be dried before bedtime.

For many years on Tiree three families fed our whole party on arrival. We were not allowed to pass the three houses at Salum without first being fed. Fifteen in each house demolished a stack of sandwiches, mountains of scones and pancakes and innumerable cups of tea.

This was a typical island welcome. The hour and a half it took for our skips to be unloaded from the boat and brought to Happy Valley, named by the islanders in our honour, was never tedious for there is no more entertaining hearth than a Hebridean one.

No matter where we have wandered, whether it has been Cornaigbeg or Ruaig, Northton or Scalpay, Stornoway or Tarbert, Salum or Luskentyre or Machrie, Strond or Tangasdale, Northbay or Rheinigidale our children have been welcome, have sat crosslegged on the floor and got up full. Few have taken it for granted. Nearly all have been aware of the extraordinary generosity of their hosts.

It is no small thing to entertain so many children in a house. We can appreciate this from personal experience. Hazel has Brownies in her house and garden every week and we have school children, Guides and other people's sons and daughters almost perpetually in our farm house and buildings.

At Games and Regattas our children have been welcomed and allowed to take part. The juniors have raced with island children and jumped with them. Our heavyweights have competed in the Tug O'war and our Sea Rangers have been crew for an island skipper. Our Yorkshire boys and girls have walked the Harris footpaths with islanders to raise money for the Hall in Tarbert and our seniors have served tea at the Sheepdog Trials.

Our children are not so skilled or so considerate that they do not get underfoot, nor so competent that they do not make mistakes but the island people are infinitely tolerant. They carefully explain how to spin and weave, feed the cows and calves and lambs and how to lift the potatoes. In the early days children were annually allowed to tidy Calum's shop and help serve behind the counter. And what's more, the tolerance of the islanders is seasoned with a delightful sense of humour which leaves no one shy.

At barn dances and céilidhs we have often outnubered the adults. We have danced badly and clumsily and stepped on many toes. We have risen to join in in embarrassingly large numbers and attempted steps we have not understood causing near chaos and catastrophe but no one has grumbled and a spirit of good humour has prevailed.

We have danced to the pipes in Calum's barn until two in the morning and to the accordian on the machair so energetically that the musician has been loathe to go home and has continued playing on the dunes until long after we were abed.

Just a few days ago we were in Stornoway enjoying a Lewis céilidh on the eve of our homecoming. People do not appreciate the land or the people of their home country. 'What makes you come back year after year?' Hazel was asked.

'Because it's so ideal,' she answered.

Ideal? Yes. Ideal for children, ideal for camping and swimming, for appreciating beauty and for learning to give generously and receive graciously; ideal for fun and laughter and singing; for forming relationships and mixing with tolerant grown-up people. We owe the islanders an immeasurable debt of gratitude. Calum called us the 'Annual Invasion' and indeed we must seem so. They have been so few to do so much for so many sassenachs.

3

My heart grows sick for thee,
Here in the Lowlands,
I will return to you
Hills of the North.

Blue lake and rocky shore,
I will return once more.
Boom didi hidi, Boom didi hidi,
Boom didi hidi, Boom.

Chapter Three

ONE FORTNIGHT a year in the Hebrides must inevitably be preceded by many weeks of preparation and the collection of our equipment was an experience we would not have liked to miss. This year, for the fifty campers, twelve pieces left our local station in advance of the main party. These consisted of six wicker skips holding tents, kitchen equipment and tinned food, a couple of boxes and four bundles of poles. The total weight was, perhaps, one ton.

Each year we improve our gear, add to it, lighten it and discard items we find we can do just as well without. We have unearthed the best sources and have become well known by General Dealers and Army Surplus merchants. Buried in their clutter are valuable cooking utensils and kitchen ware and they have poles, boxes and grids piled outside. All our rectangular, stainless steel billies, with a four gallon capacity, are ex-army and our prototype oven was found on a scrap heap outside a converted chapel.

Most of our equipment was collected in the days before we owned our own transport and we have suffered jeers and ribald remarks as we struggled home on the service bus with zinc baths, tin boxes, grids for the fire and sixfoot poles. It is hardly surprising that we are well known by all the bus conductors and it amazes me that they give such willing assistance and continue to greet us in a friendly way.

One of our best friends, in the pre-landrover days, was Mr Ainley, the owner of a small ex-army American jeep. He had recently undergone a serious operation and being our chauffeur and haulage contractor was good for his morale and of invaluable service to us. Whenever we unearthed something too big for the bus we merely phoned him and he seemed to think it a pleasure.

'Right you are, Captain,' he would say and I knew his smile would be from ear to ear. We consider him one of our founder members.

I may not be well known in the best fashion houses or exclusive restaurants but every junk dealer in town has a friendly smile for me and greets me with, 'I've just the thing fer yer. What d'yer think about that then?'

I am equally well known in the local market. Arthur sells me tent material and blue poplin. In the early days we made all our camp shirts. I have had many embarrassing moments. One amusing one was at Arthur's stall. A thin, middleaged woman was holding the only piece of blue poplin Arthur had that day and I hovered at her elbow ready to take it should she decide not to buy.

'Wod it do fer mi 'usband's pyjamas?' she asked Arthur.

'Nay. It's a bit dark,' he answered. ''Appen yer could breeten it up wi' a bit o' red o' yoller.'

'What d'yer think?' she suddenly asked me. 'Ah've allus ter mak 'is pyjamas. Oh 'e's that wide rahnd middle.' She shook her head in exasperation and then laughed, 'An' then 'e weern't weer trahsers!'

Suddenly shocked by what she had said she put down the fent and hobbled away. The blue camp shirts lasted years and the odd ones still turn up in Rummage Sales.

I do not know what we would have done without Gerry. Large and kindly he sells toilet requisites and plastic bowls and pails. He calls me 'Love' and 'Darling' and 'Beautiful.' These are endearments a spinster seldom receives and, though he showers them liberally on all his customers, a visit to him definitely boosts morale.

From him I bought over a hundred beautifully stacking, plastic plates for just one shilling each. They are light and indestructable. They will last a hundred years or more, I would fight to retain possession and I would not sell them at any price. I took every one he had and he has never had any more. If he had I would buy them for all my friends who take camps and holidays.

We never cease to marvel at the kindness and courtesy of rough working men whenever children are mentioned.

'What d'yer want that fer, Missus?' I am asked a little incredulously.

'Well,' I try to explain. 'I'm taking a lot of children to camp in the Hebrides and this is just what I want.' Immediately nothing is too much trouble.

The local hospital was being pulled down and Margaret and I went to see what we could find. Our formica topped table is a half-crown cupboard door and we found an aluminium steamer on a rubbish tip. It cost us nothing but the price I paid for a new lid. I had it specially made in the dirty workshop of a panal beater. No job seems too petty or too fiddling for the kindly man with the dirty overalls and hands. I took him my old oven a few months ago. It had rusted away with many years of travelling back and forth and, with the intense heat of countless peat and log fires, the door had become unhinged.

'Could you make me another oven, just like this?' I asked, embarrassingly aware that it was a tedious and probably profitless job for a busy man to do.

He wiped his hands on a piece of rag and together we lifted the large, rusty tin out of the landrover. 'Did yer say it wor an oven?' he enquired quite without sarcasm.

I explained. 'I think the old one's a bit past mending.' I added hopefully.

'Aw, aye,' the good man agreed. 'Ah'll see what Ah can do.'

If close association with the Hebridean people has taught us anything it has taught us not to bargain. We never discuss money with islanders at all. It would not only be a waste of time but both parties would find it acutely embarrassing. Mutual trust is important and we value it immensely.

Very few islanders will even name a price. We are used to the inevitable, 'Och, and I will chust leave that to you, Chean.' We have had to learn how to offer a suitable sum which we can afford and which they believe to be generous and in the same way exactly we do not quibble about our second hand equipment. Our relationships are good. I do not think we have ever been overcharged.

From bus drivers, porters and station masters; from stewards on trains and boats, haulage contractors, waitresses, and taxi men; crofters, school teachers and janitors and indeed almost everyone we encounter we experience only courtesy. Only when we have to pass through Glasgow and we encounter drunkenness do we ever meet with unpleasantness. Even that can be funny sometimes.

Brenda had a very large, solid kit bag which she left beside a seat in Central Station whilst she went to the toilet. When she returned there was a drunken man on the seat, leaning heavily on her kit bag, sound asleep. No amount of shaking would wake him and when we gently pulled away the improvised pillow, in order to catch the train, he slid unconciously to the floor. We were sorry for the old man but there was nothing we could do for him and the episode had not been without humour. Baby Bear could not have looked more surprised on finding Goldilocks in his bed than Brenda had looked on finding the man asleep on her kit bag.

There was an encounter with a very intoxicated male shovenist I will not forget in a long while. The distance between Central Station and Queen Street Station, from which the north bound trains depart, always poses a portage problem. Hazel thought to solve this, one year, by suggesting we ask permission to use one of the passenger luggage trolleys to transport two small but heavy skips and a few kit bags. As one trolley was labelled 'Queen's Street' we were allowed to return it to its home station, killing two birds with one stone and doing both ourselves and British Rail a good turn.

The task suddenly seemed easy and we wheeled our load jauntily into Union Street. Immediately a very drunken Glasgwegian insisted on taking over. He was clumsy and unsteady and the skips and kit bags rolled into the gutter.

'Never mind,' I pacified him. 'Let me do it. I can manage.' But the man was adamant. He was going to push that trolley and what was more he was going to push that trolley down the middle of Glasgow's main thoroughfare.

'Oh no you're not,' I told him. 'We're keeping on the pavement and we're not spilling skips into the gutter. There are breakable things inside!' I looked round me. The others were keeping a safe distance away and shoppers were watching with mixed amusement and concern.

He began to curse me efficiently. No woman with an English accent and a schoolmarm air of authority was going to tell him what to do! No way could I rid myself of him. I used every ounce of my strength to keep him on the pavement and the skips on the trolley. His underfed dog trailed him miserably and when he wasn't cursing it he was blackening my character as it has never been blackened before. For a man of slurred speech he was surprisingly articulate. I was a fool and an idiot and undoubtedly a leader in the Woman's Lib Movement. The taming of the shrew could not compete with the treatment I deserved. Then came his crowning insult. 'Ye shshshould 'a' been i' yon filum wi' Humphrey Bogart inshtead o' Catherine Hepburn!'

Finally he gave up, muttering he wouldn't help such a hag. Another old man was lying dead drunk on the steps of an imposing building. 'Quick, Skipper,' laughed our Catherine, 'Before that one wakes up!'

But most encounters leave us happy about the human race. We are accutely aware that when we are travelling on foot we are a fifty strong caravan of heavily laden children, bowed under rucksacks and prodding each other with kit bags. We would understand if people grumbled. They seldom do.

Neither did the taxi man we hired to take as much kit across Glasgow as we could fit into his cab. When Pauline and I finally crawled in on top of it all we were bent like pot holers negotiating a crawl. I was unprepared for Pauline's smile of obvious pleasure and her sigh of satisfaction.

'Skipper,' she said with a small catch in her breathing, 'I've never been in a taxi before.'

Equally forebearing are the men who handle our skips; those who struggle with them from the farm garage where they are packed, those who put them on trains and boats and the crofters who lift them onto the machair when they reach their final destination. They all weigh over two hundredweight.

They leave for the island nearly three weeks in advance of the party and providing we do not exceed the 50 lbs or so per child and 100 lbs per adult they go free of charge. It is always a relief to tie on the labels and wave them on their way.

By the time that all the food has been bought from the cash-and-carry warehouse, all the equipment belonging to the kitchen washed to shining cleanliness, every tent checked and pole counted, Margaret and I are ready to throw in the sponge, write out our resignations and set off alone with a little white tent. There is no freedom so complete as that found wandering among the islands free of responsibility and uninhibited by time. At this moment we long desperately for Jura and Colonsay, for Coll and Islay where we have never had children and of which our memories are wholly carefree.

But just in time Hazel arrives like a tonic to whisk the assembled equipment into the skips with a skill and speed which can only be achieved with years of practice. She lends her weight and together we sit on the skips to close the lids. Until a nursing career claimed her daughter and the army took her son, they came with her and their excitement in the coming adventure would invigorate us when our enthusiasm was at its lowest ebb.

Preparation is important even after many years. Routine and practice make things fractionally easier but essentially the work remains. Only our relationship with the children, entertaining them and solving their problems becomes less difficult year by year.

We have a Hebridean friend, Dolly MacLeod, who understands this perfectly. He and his wife have brought up a family of fourteen in a small, white house on a crofter's income. Its members are close and affectionate, bonny and full of fun. I was returning to camp behind my family of fifty after a Sunday afternoon's Gaelic Service in the small schoolroom at Luskentyre.

Our island friend was walking beside me. It was his deep and lovely voice which had led the Gaelic singing which falls so strangely on our English ears.

'The children were well behaved, Chean,' my friend remarked.

'It is not easy for them,' I said, thinking of the long service, much of it in a strange language and the number of children exceeding that of the adults by four to one. 'Somehow,' I continued, 'their behaviour seems to get easier every year. We seldom have any trouble at all.'

'Well now, Chean, I think I can tell you why,' said my wise friend. 'I have had fourteen of a family and we spent a good deal of time on the first born son and after that the others chust learned by example.'

He was right. Margaret and Hazel and I spent many hours on the first campers so that their example is now the only text book we need. If unbroken tradition made things easy I admit it took time, that valuable commodity of which God made plenty, so the islanders say. We buried many mistakes in the sand, so to speak, and tried again.

Because of the necessity to keep down weight we have to omit many pieces of equipment we might find useful in a Mainland camp. The sand on which we camp in the Hebrides makes things easier. It absorbs water like blotting paper and remains constantly firm and dry.

Therefore we can dispense with wash cubicles. There is no reason why a tidy tent, pitched on sand, cannot be used as a bathroom now and again. Continual swimming in so clear a sea ensures we all have a daily shower and hands and faces can be washed with hot water and soap outside.

Neither do we take a first aid tent. Psychologically we believe that a sick tent is bad. If children do not feel well we think it is wrong to isolate them and if they are ill we want them in our tent during the night where we can attend to them without battling through wind and rain. We find headaches and tummyaches disappear with a good night's rest within the security of our tent.

'You'll be all right,' we say confidently as we tuck them up between us. They always have been so far.

'I feel mighty sick,' groaned Kathy, one of our Canadian girls after a hectic day on the shore and a late night singing.

'Bring your sleeping bag into our tent,' we said. 'You'll be fine!'

She was. Next morning there was nothing in the plastic bowl we had strategically placed just outside the tent but one inch of rain water. Unfortunately, on wakening, Kathy stretched out comfortably and managed to upset every drop of that water and channel it directly into her sleeping bag. It was some yell she let out and there was a rude awakening for us and a glorious scuffle in the tent.

It is necessary to keep the weight of our tentage and cooking equipment low enough to enable us to take all the catering size tins of food necessary to feed well yet keep the cost low enough for even the least affluent family. Summer Camp for our children is not a once in a lifetime experience but an annual event. The cost per person has risen from £8 to £23 over the twenty years. With £8 in the 1950s we were able to buy breakfast on board and book a berth for each individual. Now with £23 we make all our own meals and put two in every berth and two on the cabin floor. This is the price we pay for inflation. Still there are few people who get a fortnight's holiday for so small an amount.

Keeping down the weight has occupied our thoughts for many prepacking hours and we have reduced our necessities to a mimimum. Gadget poles are counted before we go and we take few spare pegs and replacement ridges. Past storms have emphasised the danger of going completely without. The weather in the Hebrides can be utterly beautiful or magnificently violent.

Last year we were left in no doubt at all that our fifteen year old Icelandic ridge tents were done. They took a severe beating and when canvas is rotten it will not patch. We spent the winter months in a massive money making exercise and bought eight more Icelandics. We had Coffee Evenings and Sales of Work, we sold Christmas Cards and wrapping paper in an all-out effort to be prepared against torrential rains and gale force winds.

I vividly remember the delivery of one new tent and am hardly likely to forget. I was returning from school, in mid-January, after a heavy fall of snow had isolated the farmhouse and prevented all wheeled traffic from getting any nearer than the farm gate, a quarter of a mile away.

It had been a day of wellingtons, wet anoraks and snow crazed children and I was in no mood to think about the joys of camping. I was walking home, carrying a full rucksack, extra supplies of food for a snowbound weekend and a pair of new, heavy duty wellingtons.

It was almost dark when I reached the farm gate and saw a blackness against the snow. On investigation I found it to be my latest new tent costing £97, left at the mercy of the winter storm. Finding the road blocked the carrier had abandoned it, leaving it to sink deeply into the snow. I was furious.

There was no alternative but to hump the wooden poles across the top of my rucksack and struggle the last quarter of a mile home through the deep, virgin snow. I was incensed with the thoughtlessness of the irresponsible carrier. Sweating with exertion and anger I retraced my steps up the steep gradient back to the gate for the heavy, wet, canvas tent. I floundered in the drifts convinced of the insanity of camping.

As is the way of things not one drop of rain fell this year. The sun rose from behind Ben Luskentyre and climbed into a cloudless sky and it dropped, each evening, in scarlet majesty behind Taransay. Camp shirts and shorts were scarcely soiled for swimming costumes were donned after the flag was unfurled and not replaced until campfire. The only reason we needed tents was to find some escape from the midges when we finally left the shore in the late evening.

There is a lovely feeling of respite after Margaret, Hazel and I have sealed up the skips, tied on the labels and waved them 'Goodbye' on their long journey. We await, with some anxiety, the card saying that they have arrived safely. What we would do if they did not, does not bear thinking about.

There is only one more job to do and that is to fill the freezer with fruit pies and sausage rolls for the journey. There is, at this time of the year, an abundance of food in the farmhouse garden. Our gatherings of tomatoes, cucumber, and lettuce, windfall apples, blackberries and rhubarb, on the eve of our journey, makes our kitchen look like a Harvest Festival.

In more than forty homes excitement is growing. I am normally patient but this is one time of the busy year when I sincerely wish that we had no phone and that my name were not Skipper. It rings perpetually and I know, as I lift it, that I'll hear the inevitable, 'Is that Skipper?'

'Skipper, what time do we meet?'

'Which day do we come home, Skip?'

'Skipper, do we need a packed meal?'

'What's our camp address, Skipper?'

'What'll I do, Skip, I can't get my sleeping bag in?'

'See yer, Skipper!'

You would think that they'd never been told, never had the written instructions, never been before. Ah well, no one can have perfect children.

4

We're all going on a summer holiday
No more working for a week or two,
Fun and laughter on our summer holiday
No more worries for me or you,
     For a week or two.

We're going where the sun shines brightly,
We're going where the sea is blue.
We've seen it on the movies,
Now let's see if it's true.

Everybody has a summer holiday,
Doin' what they always wanted to,
So we're going on a summer holiday
To make our dreams come true,
     For me and you.

Chapter Four

WHICH EVER way you look at the timetable it takes two days to get a party of children to an island in time to pitch camp and settle in. We've tried every possible way, except air which is out of the question when equipment can go free in advance on the purchase of a rail and boat ticket.

First comes the long journey north. This is now extremely comfortable and the new open coaches with tables between every four seats were, I'm sure, especially designed for parties of travelling children. We find it important to put as many rucksacks and kit bags into the luggage van as we possibly can. We usually put in more than we should in our enthusiasm to be rid of clutter. Always do we find somebody's mug and spoon have been buried, always do I have to lend someone money because a purse is in a pocket under the pile and always there is someone whose book or cards or drawing materials are useless because they are in the luggage van, somewhere under the mountain.

We manage to organise ourselves least well in the local station with fathers, mothers and uncles to help. It is a classic case of too many cooks.

There is a moment of suspense when numbers are counted. Occasionally we have an anxious ten minutes waiting for the last arrivals but no one has yet missed the train altogether. There was an occasion when we nearly missed it ourselves. Mr Ainley was our chauffeur in the small, ex-army jeep days. It was terribly hot and the engine was very over heated. We piled our gear into the back and clambered in.

'I'm worried,' said our friend. 'I've had a struggle to get here. The engine keeps seizing up. How much time have we got?'

Unlike the islanders we never have plenty but we always plan to meet in the station with half an hour to spare for emergencies.

'Very little,' I groaned. 'We'll cross our fingers.'

It was not enough. The funny, faithful, little vehicle coughed and spluttered towards the hill in the farm road. It reached the bend with difficulty. It was trying very hard but it was too old and too hot. Not a hundred yards from the farm house it came to an ignominious stop.

'I'm afraid it's not going to do it,' sighed Mr Ainley. 'The sun's too hot on the bonnet. She won't cool down in time.'

It was like one of those funny films, 'Genivieve' perhaps. There was no time to call a taxi or send for a friend. In desperation my father ran to start up the tractor and hitch on the trailer. The jeep was blocking the road and we had to make a detour up the field. The rucksacks and boxes of food for the journey threatened to bounce off the trailer all the time and in trying to control them we were in danger of falling off too.

Some miracle decreed that there was a bus from the village to the town at the precise moment we and the tractor arrived and, by the luck of the gods, we got to the station in time. That was the year our entry into Glasgow was delayed while ice was put on points swollen by the heat wave.

Susan was equally lucky one year. Her mother went to work as usual on the morning of our departure.

'Aren't you going to wave Susan off?' a workman asked.

'She doesn't go until ten tonight,' said Susan's mother.

'It's ten this morning,' her friend was certain.

In a panic Susan's mother left work and ran all the way home. Susan was still in bed, her bags only half packed. They re-checked the written itinerary. Ten o'clock in the morning it was. How they ever made it they will never know. The fact remains that, up to now, no one has ever missed the train.

Someone caught it who should have remained on the platform. Valerie had an anxious mother who insisted on arranging things for her on the luggage rack. She misjudged the time and was still on the train when it began to pull out of the station with every child waving from the windows. She had to remain with us for the next ten miles to Skipton and we had to give the poor woman her fare home. Valerie was mortified and ashamed and ignored her mother most of the way.

There is definitely no need to feed children before Glasgow. Their bags have a store of food comparable to the widow's jar of meal. Crisps, sweets and fruit, cans of orange and coke, sandwiches and cheese biscuits are continually eaten. Comics and magazines and paperbacks are read from cover to cover and passed round from child to child. Our children are always well prepared for the journey. We were amused one year to be approached by a flabby young man, in his early twenties, who hovered near the carriage door and finally found the courage to come in and ask if he could borrow a few comics to while away the time. Our children were only too willing to oblige him. Apparently they had fathers and uncles who liked reading comics too!

Any hopes that the journeys we were to make would have any real educational value were dashed in the very early years. Only Janet took any geographical interest in the route. She, alone, made a list of the stations en route and followed the journey on the map. Everyone else has counted horses or bridges or advertisements for paint. They all know when to look for deer and want prior warning so that they do not miss the Pass of Brander or the Monassie Gorge and they want to be at the window to wave madly to Cathy and John when we pass their home at Spean Bridge. But children are not sightseers. I am convinced that children travelling in parties are primarily interested in social relationships and not in places. Parents pay great sums of money for their children to travel abroad and when they return they tell of the giggle they had in the bedroom, of the hat lost out of the window, the shoe that fell on the line beneath the stationary train and the toilet door that stuck.

So we have learned to fill our travelling hours with social activity and what is more comforting to children, travelling at great speed away from home, than food. By Glasgow they have exhausted their own supplies. There is a very convenient self-service cafeteria close to the station. It used to be possible to get fish and chips and tea and bread and butter for half a crown. In those days we paid for the meal out of the kitty before taking everyone into the News Theatre for one shilling. The service was good and quick and our annual visit was remembered by the staff. Now meals are so expensive we can only afford a snack, a bowl of soup or a carton of yogurt and we invariably wait until we get into the next train for a proper meal. One advantage of a snack at the cafeteria is that there is a very nice ladies' room where conscientious madams can freshen up and squirt perfume at each other.

Whilst we eat it is essential to leave our kit in railway cages in the station. We need three and the children are excellent at finding the necessary number and pushing them to the luggage van. They know how to work the brakes and steer so that other passengers are not in peril and they know how to pile on the gear so that nothing falls out.

One year Beverley's kit bag must have bounced out of the cage in Central Station and the loss was not discovered until we were boarding the train for Oban in Queen's Street Station. She was immediately in tears. I comforted her with instant action. The train was almost due but we had just time to run and report the loss.

'I wouldn't care,' she sobbed, as we ran madly for the left luggage office to fill in the necessary form, 'but it has my new penknife in!'

Children's priorities are quite unpredictable. Due to an extremely kind ticket collector on the Oban train, who promised to hunt for the bag personally, it and Beverley were reunited within twenty four hours.

It is depressing to know that someone must always stay with the equipment, whilst others eat, or something will be stolen but faith in human honesty is restored when we reach the Highlands and Islands. An incident this year is only one of many.

We were on our way by bus to the beginning of the green track to Rheinigidale. We stopped at the Post Office in Tarbert to send some letters home. As our bus pulled away from the village the driver realised we were being followed by a car whose driver obviously wanted a word. He pulled into a passing place and allowed the car to draw in behind. Usually, when this happens, there will be a long conversation in Gaelic and some goods, or equipment, or a basket of fish will be passed through the window. On this occasion, however, I was the person the man wished to see.

'Och, I've been looking for you for days,' he said. 'I'm from the boat, MacBraynes. I've a wee paper bag here with sweeties. It was picked up on the boat the day you came. There are a few pieces of silver in the bag too. Will you see do they belong to one of the children?'

Some of the girls had been eating bon bons but none could remember having put any money in the bag so no one would claim it. A few sweets and coins today are almost worthless but the MacBrayne man was prepared to search for the owner lest it be a child.

Our children are not always honest. One morning towards the end of camp an island friend brought a message to say a parent had phoned believing that his child had run short of money and, as time was short, would Skipper lend a pound. 'Of course I will,' I said. 'Who rang?'

'Well, I'm not sure,' said Rachel with endearing island vagueness. 'I wasn't hearing him very well.'

25

When I asked the children who it would be every hand went up.

Scarcely have we settled ourselves comfortably on the north bound train than the chore of providing a proper meal begins. Preparing it and serving it down the long reserved compartment, eating it and collecting the dirty dishes, washing them in the confined space of the toilet wash basin and then re-packing the picnic skips, occupies everyone for a long time and considerably shortens the journey.

It provides amusement for us and for passengers making their way to the restaurant car and ticket collectors who wait patiently while I lick my fingers, wipe them on a tea towel and dive into my bag for the flimsy bit of paper which represents fifty tickets. Never once have we encountered any annoyance. But then, we are clever with practice and we leave no litter or crumbs and if we spill orange juice we mop it up.

Most remarkable of all is the tolerance of the steward announcing that meals are ready in the dining car or trying to sell his coffee and ham sandwiches. It would be reasonable to expect some annoyance from him when faced with competition of such magnitude. But no, he obviously thinks we belong to the same catering trade union and are therefore comrades. He even provides us with ice cubes on a hot day and never refuses to fill our water carrier.

He knows, of course that when our big family has been fed the adults in our party will need his tea or coffee. Then he will entertain them over his coffee bar with stories of his army catering days and illustrate his narrative, about water pollution and camping in the raw, on a piece of kitchen paper, and finally give them extra sugar lumps.

Dear Gerry. I bless him every time we use his plates. Whatever the food it looks all the more appetising when served on clean, neat plates. Six of them fit perfectly on the plastic trays I bought for 10p each in the disused chapel which is now an Army Surplus Store. They were buried deep under a pile of clutter and covered with dust.

'I'm looking for trays, Joe' I said.

'Ah've nowt,' said Joe, 'Nowt at all.'

I continued to rummage. I am a persistant woman and I have learned that you can usually get what you want if you try hard enough and look under the surface.

'What are these?' I said triumphantly.

'Well, Ah'm blessed,' said Joe. 'They must 'ave been there donkey's years.'

We serve every meal on a plate. Corned beef or sausage rolls, tomatoes, cucumber, cheese, beetroot, egg, piles of crisp lettuce and plenty of bread and butter; crackers and Ryvita spread with jam or pilchards or crowdie. We even serve portions of chips hurriedly bought, on the spur of the moment, when we spot a nice fish and chip shop near the station.

'Can I have fifty portions of chips?' we ask and watch the reaction with interest. We are not immediately understood so we patiently repeat the order.

'Fifty? Och, I was sure I was mishearing you.' The amused waitress turns to a colleague. 'Och,' she gasps, 'there's a lady here wanting fifty portions of chips!' They laugh nervously but cope with everything but the bill. After they have supplied the enormous order the enormous sum is quite beyond them. Fortunately we know our fifty multiplication table very well indeed.

For second course there is fruit and cream or apple pie and evaporated milk. Stewed fruit is put through a funnel into a plastic gallon container and can be squeezed out onto plates like toothpaste. We fill several such water carriers with apples, blackberries and rhubarb and one with custard. The plastic age is ideal for campers and travellers.

If this is not enough there are cakes and scones and pancakes until even the most insatiable appetites are satisfield. The restaurant car could not provide more and serving on plates eliminates mess. What's more everyone is involved in some way even if it is only by being part of the human conveyor belt so everyone is having fun and entertainment.

An old lady was struggling to the dining car and when she reached our compartment sat down heavily against our 'kitchen' table where the orderlies were busy dishing up.

'This isn't the dining car is it?' she asked hopefully.

'Sorry,' said the bread butterers.

'Oh dear,' said the old lady. 'Is it far?'

'It is rather,' said someone kindly. 'It's about three carriages away.'

'Oh well, I'll not bother. Me legs would never make it,' she decided.

'Would you like some of ours instead,' someone offered. 'Is it all right if we feed this old lady, Skip?'

The question is a mere formality. They are always bringing strangers to the table. They always know what the answer will be. As I turned to nod my head the old dear already had her plate. The children talk to anyone. They immediately attract foreigners, fellow campers and hikers, young ladies with babies and old ladies with dogs. Before they have travelled far they know the guard, the ticket collector and the steward and have told all the people in the next compartment where we are going or where we've been. They are seldom any the wiser for the names of islands make little sense to ordinary passengers.

'Are you coming or going?' one of our many Margarets was asked one year when seven of us were returning from a trek on many islands.

'We're going home,' she said.

'Where've yer been?' asked the man. He had a Yorkshire accent similar to our own.

'We've been to Seil and Tiree and Barra,' she said, 'and South Uist. Then we've been on Eigg and Rhum and up to Loch Coruisk in the Cuillin, on Skye. We've just come today from Fort William.'

At last the man heard a word he knew. 'Fort William!' he said. 'By gum but they say it's wild up there!'

Mostly, if we can, we like to travel by day. Twenty years ago I did not mind so much. Children sleep well anywhere but I can only sleep well if I am lying down. A hard floor poses no problem, the proverbial clothes line would do, but sitting up I sleep badly so we avoid night travel if possible and arrange overnight accommodation.

I remember one night journey when Hazel and I were dozing in the last seat of the reserved compartment. We became aware that a West Indian ticket collector was bearing down on us, his jet black face intent upon his job. Startled into action I confusedly began to rummage in my too full bag for our ticket. Succeeding at last I held up the flimsy bit of paper only to realise that the good man was roaring with uncontrollable laughter, his persil white teeth shining like a row of pearls in his sooty face.

The laughter was infectious and we were soon laughing with him though we had no idea whatsoever what it was all about. We even looked at each other to find some cause for merriment. The children wakened and stared at us and then, because they could not help it either, they began laughing too. And the more we laughed the more the West Indian shook.

'What are we laughing at?' said one sensible member of the party.

'Oh dear, oh dear,' laughed the jovial man.' I no ticket collector. I count people on the train. You last compartment and you make me forget number. Now I start all over again.'

'Oh, I'm sorry,' I apologised. 'Was it my fault?'

'Oh well,' said the good man. 'I enjoyed laughing.'

Filling water carriers en route seldom poses a problem. There is always a tap on the platform. It usually has a long length of hose attached to it but that does not matter for the nozzle is the right size for the neck of the plastic carrier. The water comes with rewarding force and the carrier is full in no time. Ticket collectors, in their station boxes, are used to me nipping out, carrier in each hand, to find the tap. Only once was there catastrophe.

We were returning from Oban in the days when the train travelled through Glen Ogle and via Loch Earnhead and Stirling. It was a thirsty, hot day and everyone was gasping for water. We had plenty of squash but nothing with which to dilute it. I cannot even remember with certainty at which station I leaned out of the train and asked the guard if I had time to fill a water carrier. It was the kind one can fold up and pack in a rucksack pocket.

The guard was an accommodating kind of person.

'Och aye,' he said. 'There's plenty of time.'

I do believe a Highlander would say that if a bomb were about to explode. I dashed into the snack bar, leaping the patient queue to thrust my bucket over the counter. No one complained. Not even the pretty little waitress. She handed it back and I hurried out onto the platform. I could not believe my eyes when I saw the train pulling out of the station with all my children hanging out of two dozen windows.

But like time and tide the train would wait for no man. I stood on the platform in my shirt sleeves, clutching my purse in one hand and a bucket full of water in the other. I turned dejectedly and began emptying the water down the drain. I no longer had any need of it. There was nothing else I could do.

By sheer goodfortune, considering how few trains use these Highland lines, a train from the north followed the Oban one not twenty minutes later. The look on a ticket collector's face when you present him with a ticket and a large number of children is nothing to compare with the look on his face when you present him with a ticket for forty and no children. I'm sure he thought I was pulling a fast one of some kind. He handed me back my ticket but he was eyeing me queerly all the way down the compartment.

I was able to rejoin my family in Glasgow 'I had to hold Barbara away from the communication cord,' laughed my sister, 'and I had an awful do with the ticket collector.' Now no one leaves the train unless we know the departure time.

Delays are something we accept philosophically as something we can do nothing about. We were told in York Station, shortly after midnight, that our London to Fort William train was three hours late. There was no fuss. We went into the buffet which remained open very late in those days, and dawdled over a hot drink.

'There's a man talking to Mrs Belsey,' I was informed. He had obviously had a little too much to drink and was feeling very benevolent. When he heard the train was late he felt sorry for the children, wanted to buy them all sweets and could not be persuaded otherwise. Unfortunately he could not count and Hazel had to supplement his purchase so that there was enough to go round.

He need not have worried. On enquiring I found that an extra coach was being put on at York specially for us. It was sitting, happily waiting in a siding and we were able to get in and fall fast asleep. Few even wakened when we were eventually coupled onto the northbound train. Good old British Rail! We have nothing but good to say of them.

On the first overnight journey, before we learned more wisdom, we suggested that sleeping bags should be unrolled and some laid flat on the compartment floor so that all could sleep. The chaos was unbelievable. Giggling chased away sleep permanently. Since then we have learned the art of sleeping and all fifty of us can lie down in a school hall or boat lounge or in crowded cabins on board and, accepting a rule of no talking at all, fall asleep immediately and remain so till morning.

It was not always so. I remember a night in the Scottish Guide Headquarters in Glasgow when we got not one wink of sleep. It takes time to breed a feeling of complete security whatever the surroundings. Only when children feel safe can they relax enough to fall asleep together.

We have slept in the church hall in Tobermory, in barns on Tiree and Arran, in schools at Ruaig, Tarbert and Mallaig, in the Army Headquarters in Portree, in lounges on the 'Hebrides' the 'Claymore' and the 'Clansman,' in berths on 'Suilven' the 'Claymore' and the 'Hebrides;' we have slept in the single school room at Luskentyre and scattered all over Rachel MacLeod's and Marian MacLean's houses, in a bus at Crossapol and under one big tarpaulin at Salum and we have slept at once and all night through.

It is an art and a blessing for tired children are fractious and those who sleep well wake amenable and busy. It is a happy state which cannot be achieved immediately but which is acquired over years of stability, tradition and consideration for each other.

Only once was the rule of 'not talking' grossly abused. Some kind visitors to Salum House thought it most irregular that a lady should have to sleep on the floor of Calum's barn. As the boat was to leave Scarinish at 6 am there was no alternative but to strike camp the previous evening and sleep in the barn. To compromise they intercepted our late arrival and handed me a very luxurious lilo. I find it acutely embarrassing to enjoy comfort when others have to make do with hard concrete but it would have been churlish to refuse so kind an offer.

Getting such a large family to bed is orderly chaos. It is wisest to say, 'Hot chocolate and biscuits IN BED,' as this ensures that ever hungry children aim at getting in sleeping bags as quickly as possible. Also eating and drinking do bring a relative silence which is more easy to develop when torches have to be extinguished and absolute silence insisted upon.

We managed reasonably well, that night in Calum's barn, though with less ease than we do now after many years of practice. There was quietness but it was not yet accompanied by the deep breathing which denotes sleep. It was still very vulnerable.

'Share this lilo with me,' I had said to Toots and Ann, Judy and Janet. 'It'll make a good pillow!'

Sleep was stealing over us and I could feel myself relax and begin to drift into oblivion too. Then suddenly the silence was broken. There was the loudest ppppppps sssssss that any lilo could possibly make. I started to shake and Margaret, who has the same sense of humour, started to shake too. There was a giggle and a scuffle and a torch flashed. No one could find the stopper for the noisy bed. Sleeping bags sat up. Everyone was laughing. It was just as if we were at the circus and there was clowning in the ring. It was a miracle that we ever slept that night.

Air beds, I believe, are a mixed blessing. Only a few have ever been used for the machair. That flower carpeted sandy strip which borders the western sea board of the Hebrides, is as comfy as an interior sprung mattress. Air beds make the most out-landish noise when being inflated and are certainly not to be relied upon.

'I think my bed died a natural death last night.' said Susan, viewing the deflated object with despair. It had far more plasters than a nasty accident case.

Nowadays we prefer not to use the boat lounge although MacBraynes have been extremely helpful and allowed us sole use of diverting other overnight passengers into the bar lounge. Our sleeping bags have been unrolled and comfort found. However it is not long lasting enough. Boats invariably sail in the early hours and suddenly sleep is snatched from us, passengers begin to come aboard and we have to get up in a hurry. It was through sleeping in boat lounges that we learned the art of dressing inside a sleeping bag and how to do the necessary contortions to fasten hooks and eyes and aim legs into invisible holes.

In any hurry things get misplaced and on one occasion the purser approached me with a smile and dangled before me a very small pair of navy blue knickers. 'Do these belong to you?' he asked.

It makes a change. I am usually asked, 'Skipper, have you a jumper that two of us can get into?'

'Whatever for?'

'We want to go to the Fancy Dress as Double Knitting!' pipe Helen and Michelle with a grin.

Such a request is not very complimentary for I am not a large lady by any means.

Every child enjoys a boat and we have sailed hundreds of hours with as many children. They have investigated every nook and cranny and made many friends. Automatically I shake hands with the stewards and the purser. They all know me.

'Is your sister not here?' they always ask. One of them adds. 'How are all her animals?'

One particular steward used to greet us affectionately every year. One summer we were unfortunate in our choice of date for the outward journey. It was the Highland Games, on one of the Islands, and because of this the boat had to do an extra sail out to collect merrymakers and we were unable to board her until the early hours. We had waited very patiently in the waiting room on the pier and we were all more than ready to crawl into our bunks and get some sleep.

Hazel and I went down to the steward to claim our cabins and found the man very confused having obviously celebrated with the spectators coming from the Games. In our experience Highlanders and Islanders are not the heavy drinkers that rumour suggests. Our friends only drink at weddings and cattle shows, Games and occasionally at dances. On all the other three hundred and sixty days they are quite sober. Many of our friends do not drink at all. Therefore it is with tolerance we will accept them on their few hey-days and holidays. This man had given us many a late cup of coffee and had patiently refilled the children's toast rack in the days when we could afford breakfast on board. Children, then, ate half price. Sadly those days have gone for ever.

We did not condemn the confused state of our friend and patiently tried to help him sort out the problem of our berths. There were other passengers standing by and several already appeared to be in the wrong berths so there was confusion every-where. We struggled with him but were getting nowhere and our tired children were hugging their unopened kit bags wearily. Suddenly the good man had a brilliant idea.

'I'll tell you what we'll do,' he beamed happily. 'We'll short it all out in the mm mmorning!'

Fortunately the other passengers were also amused and willing to come to a mutual arrangement with us. We were all able to get to bed and leave the poor man to sleep off his overdose.

There was a younger steward on the 'Claymore' that year we suffered a very rough crossing of the Minch between Tiree and Barra. I had ordered afternoon tea for everyone to be eaten between Castlebay and Loch Boisdale. The great seas lifted the boat so high, dropped her so low and then rocked her so sickenly from side to side that mostly everyone lost lunch overboard.

Our sick bay on any boat seldom has many occupants for friends and activity exclude nausia. Usually there are no more than two pale faced children to cuddle in the fresh air on deck. On this journey almost everywhere one turned there were members of the family leaning over the rails. We were constantly wiping sickly faces and forcing miserable creatures into extra woolies.

There was another party of children on the boat that year, a group of Boy Scouts led by some friendly Catholic monks. They were heading for Eoligarry, on Barra, and the two groups of children chatted aimiably over the rails and chased each other

31

round the deck until the heaving of the boat left them all in the same undignified position.

Joan, one of our seniors, seemed to have a magnetism for small boys. Whenever we were on Tiree, small island boys found their way onto her knee. It was no surprise to see her holding two Scout heads over the rail and then begin to mop them up with kitchen roll. She caught our amused eye and shrugged her shoulders as if to say, 'I don't know how this happened! As if we haven't enough!' Nor was it a surprise to us when Joan became a nurse. Later she married and none of us expected her first baby to be an angelic little girl. That fact surprised us far more than the arrival of twin boys a year later.

Julia and Joan, Margaret and I struggled with Nightingale determination to keep the ward in control but the whole charade was a bit of a fiasco. We tried manfully to see the funny side.

'Watch out when Paul's sick,' laughed Sue. 'It flies horizontally!'

Ten year old Jill was sitting immobile on the deck, her face an eggshell green and almost transparent. 'Whatever would your mother say if she could see you now, Jilly?' I said.

Suddenly Jilly untipped all over the deck and I groaned my dismay. As quickly as if it had been her profession, Julia moved in cheerfully. 'Oh dear,' she said. 'Up you get Jilly and let's mop you up!' Thank heaven for Julias!

The young steward tapped my shoulder. 'What will I be doing about your order for afternoon tea?' he enquired. 'I'm sure they'll not be wanting anything at all. Will I chust be cancelling the order?'

What an understanding fellow he was!

'Please do,' I was very grateful to him. I am not normally a mercenary person but I confess that it did cross my mind that it's an ill wind that blows no one any good. The rough crossing was going to save a considerable amount of money which, no doubt, would come in very useful later in the camp.

Half a dozen well seasoned travellers howled me down when I announced that the meal had been cancelled.

'Aw Skipper, we're starving,' begged Heather.

I hastened to compromise. 'I don't mean no one can have tea,' I reassured her. 'Anyone feeling well can go down. It's just that tea for forty is cancelled.'

Barra was filling the western horizon and sailing into the shelter of the island we found calmer water. The boat stopped its eternal pitching as the helmsman steered her past the castle in the bay where the MacNeil, when he had dined, gave permission for the rest of the world to do so. There was the usual activity on the pier, the securing of the gangway for disembarking passengers and the winching off of cars.

When the boat finally pulled away from Barra and began her evening sail along the eastern coast of the Long Island, I told those who wished to eat that they could go down into the saloon and everybody went. Every man Jack of them.

The steward winked at me. 'Och, and I neffer would have believed it!' he said.

I made a cheque out for over thirteen pounds and my only consolation was that not one of them lost a penny of it. As we sailed gently past Eriskay, in the wake of Bonnie

Prince Charlie, the memory of their mal-de-mer sank to the bottom of the sea and was forgotten. The thing they most remember about that journey, when it ended in Loch Boisdale, is that we had to step out of a great hole in the side of the 'Claymore', into the arms of our sailor friends and be lowered into a small boat. That year the Loch Boisdale pier was under reconstruction. To the great amusement of the gang the sailors pretended they were going to drop me into the sea. The only gale they remember is the gale of laughter which followed my undignified entry into the boat.

There is a more recent gale we will always remember. My sister and I have landed on twenty-four of the Hebridean islands and, between us, Hazel, Margaret and I have landed on sixteen with over two hundred and fifty children but, for me, the outward sail to Tiree in a force eight gale, really took the biscuit. It unexpectedly followed an idyllic day on Iona, a calm day of turquoise sea, airforce blue mountains and azure sky.

Our party of fifty five mostly lined the rails of the 'Columba' as she plunged purposefully wide of Arinagour, on Coll, without attempting to land any passengers or freight. Our reason for being at the rail was dignified. The sail had only just become stormy and our journey was nearly over. A large group of boys and girls clustered on deck singing lustily into the wind. Several seniors helped me dish up food on the heaving deck. A few, only, clung to the rails, comforted by sympathetic friends, wishing they were dead and caring not one atom whether the ship went down or not.

The Sound of Gunna was passed and Tiree floated heavy and low in the white water of a rapidly swelling sea. Even her colour washed houses, which stand so bravely silhouted against the skyline, kept disappearing as the 'Columba' sank in the deep valleys of the sea.

We turned towards the island and headed for Scarinish pier but to cross the rougher water, when the bar of Gott Bay was reached, was to enter, for a few moments, a veritable Corryvrekan. There was an ominous grinding and creaking of straining timbers beneath us and the bows swung south again as the attempt to enter the bay and approach the pier was abandoned.

'We're passing the pier. Hey, we're passing the pier!' It was unbelievable. I was immediately surrounded.

'What's happening, Skipper?'

'Heck, we're not going to land!'

'Are'nt we gonna land, Skipper?'

'Why don't we go in?'

'Skipper?'

Skipper . . . Skipper . . . Skipper . . .

Why am I supposed to know everything? Why haven't those who have been with me innumerable times learned that I am fallible, that there are some things I just do not know, especially those nautical.

An announcement on the loud speaker informed us that, owing to adverse weather conditions, we were unable to land on Tiree but that we would stand off the island for a while and hope for a lull in the fury of the gale or a shifting of the wind into a more favourable quarter. The captain was persistent and tried again and again to cross the bar. After the third abortive attempt, a tortuous one for the growing line of sufferers, we resigned ourselves to the near certainty of having to return to the Mainland and hole up in some sheltered harbour until the gale was spent.

'We'll never pitch in this anyway,' said someone philosophically.

'Oh yes we will,' I assured them. 'If we can just get on that island we will jolly well pitch all right. You'll see!'

'He's trying again,' said a lookout two hours after the first attempt. 'He's having another go!'

Twelve year old David was leaning miserably over the rail. Judith warmed him with her closeness. His sister Marie hovered close by. Ann curled up white and helpless among the blankets we had laid on the ropes below the companionway. Linda held a child on either arm. She was shocked by her own poor performance, the unexpected churning of her inside. Clustered round the picnic skips were the pale-faces of our tribe.

A plastic container of concentrated orange juice fell over oozing its sticky liquid all over the deck. Crawling on hands and knees I used a clean tea towel to mop up the yellow mess.

'Aw don't, Skipper,' groaned the squeamish, turning greener. 'How can you?'

The whirlpool was beneath us for the fourth time and our cargo shifted, the picnic skips sliding heavily down the 40° slope of the deck. But the steersman's hand was steady on the wheel and the bows headed relentlessly for the pier.

There was a sea journey to Tiree which will be remembered because the electricity supply failed. We were standing off Coll to allow for the disembarkation of passengers into a small boat, when all the lights went out. There is now a strong pier at Arinagour and boats can sail right up to it. There is no need any longer for the small boat and its redundancy has taken away some of the novelty of the sail.

With the failure of the electricity supply, engines stopped. With no power and no sail we looked like being there all day. Hazel and I sat in the half light, on the laundry basket, in the now empty space recently filled with Coll luggage and buttered slice after slice of bread.

There is no activity we enjoy more than preparing food for our family, closely surrounded by the most helpful members of it. There seem, at first glance, too many hands but there is system not chaos. Janet butters, Grace spreads, Sylvia shares out the tomatoes, Marion the eggs, Jenny the cake and Brenda the fruit. Janice pours out the squash and Wendy walks round with the litter bin. The close proximity of so many caterers over us, pressing past us and treading on our toes never tries our patience. It is one of the joys of our journeying.

I remember that this meal was interupted by Nellie calling down the companionway, 'Quick, you lot. There's sharks up here!' And so there were. A dozen or so basking sharks were swimming curiously very near to the boat, their dorsal fins vertical above the waves.

'Remember Arran,' somebody said, 'when there were fifty in Machrie Bay?'

Boats are not just sea going vehicles that take us from Oban to Mull, Tiree,

Barra and the Uists; from Mallaig to Skye and from Uig to Tarbert on Harris; from Ardossan to Brodick and from Ullapool to Stornoway. They have a hundred and one more uses than that. They provide warmth and comfort after a cold, early morning start and their televisions bring us the latest news. 'The Queen is having another baby,' we learned from one, 'Robert Kennedy has been assasinated' and, on one, we saw a successful 'splash down' from space.

The ladies' room was specially designed for us. We invariably make a beeline straight to the boudoir to wash our dirty tea towels. The radiator there is red hot and before we disembark our kitchen linen is always clean and dry. Gaily we wash up our fifty plates and refill our water carriers. We scrub our hands, clean our nails, tidy our hair and titivate our faces. If we have accidentally spilt water we ask the stewardess for a mop and repair the damage. If she is the daughter of a friend on Barra we chat happily about our mutual friends and well known places. We ask her if there is any chance of a quick shower, send our love to her mother and hope we will see her on the journey home.

On board the children investigate the intricacies of getting into a life jacket, learn how to polish the brass, how to climb the companionway steps three at a time and how to fly the flag from the stern. They have scrubbed the decks, laid the tables for meals, fed the seagulls, used the gentlemen's toilet by mistake and entered the captain's cabin to wake a sleeping occupant they were sure was a member of our party.

Many have been baptized by seagulls but none more revoltingly than I. The episode is unforgettable. I was talking to a tall gentleman which necessitated tilting my head at an angle. A seagull passed overhead and I caught the unwanted refuse in my mouth. No matter how disgusting the incident the children find it hilarious. They could hardly control themselves the morning they saw the elegant, old lady walk up Mallaig pier safely hidden under an umbrella though no rain was falling and the early morning sun shone but weakly.

'What's she got that up for?' asked the boys. Then when the penny dropped, 'Blimey, she's scared o' t' seagulls!'

There was great amusement in the cafeteria one day, returning from Tarbert to Uig. Children are observant and a group who were treating themselves to coffee and crisps saw an elderly man being guided into the saloon by a well meaning friend obviously intent on sobering him up before Uig was reached.

'He's drunk!' said Jackie.

'He's goin' to fall,' said Alyson, 'Whoops, he nearly went.'

'Don't stare,' Julie reminded them ineffectively.

The younger man wedged his friend in one of the armchairs and pushed him securely up to the table before going to the food counter.

'He's falling asleep,' giggled Janice. 'He's dead drunk.'

His returning friend roughly awakened him and placed the hot drink and food beside him. He pulled out his own chair and sat down clumsily, obviously embarrassed and not daring to look at his fellow passengers.

'He's taken his teeth out,' Susan suddenly gasped in disbelief. All the children turned to look. Unbeknown to his friend the drunken man had indeed taken out his teeth and laid them on the table behind his saucer. His arms were spreadeagled on the formica, all his movements were without co-ordination.

Now there is nothing so funny to children as false teeth and they were fast losing what little self control they had left.

'Stop staring,' begged Julie, 'and give up giggling.'

'We can't help it,' said someone. 'Golly, he's gonna swipe them off the table any minute.'

They were all silent and watchful, waiting for the moment when the teeth would reach the end of their runway and begin their flight. Julie was on the verge of collapse. Her back was to the old man and she was getting her information from the children's faces. She found the slow, deliberate crunching of crisps and the neglected cups of coffee amusing. Every now and then breathing would stop, then giggling would begin again followed by more silence and suspense. Eyes were popping and blind fingers were unable to find the crisp bags.

Then, quite suddenly, all eyes were averted as if they, too, were embarrassed to witness the final fate of the dentures.

'They've gone,' whispered Jackie, her hand over her astonished mouth.

'They're on the floor,' giggled Susan. 'What'll we do?' All were concerned.

'I'll pick them up,' volunteerd Jackie. The rest giggled nervously.

Jackie tip toed to the neighbouring table, bent down and gingerly picked them up and put them on the table. 'Your teeth,' she whispered hoarsely, as if she had been saying, 'Your serviette, sir,' or 'Your newspaper.'

Neither men appeared to have noticed. Wide eyed she hurried back to her seat, only the dentures smiling up at her.

'Come on, let's go,' said Julie.

'N n n no,' giggled everyone. 'Let's stay and see what happens.'

Eventually the younger man succeeded in getting his friend out of the chair and they wove an irregular path to the door.

'He's left his teeth,' spluttered Alyson. Everyone of the Yorkshire kids was in an agony of suppressed laughter.

Jackie jumped up and called after the two men, 'You've forgotten your teeth!' but they were quite deaf. Her courage was spent. She was quite incapable of running after them. Her friends were sagging helplessly in their chairs in various attitudes of very painful merriment.

'What 'ave I to do?' pleaded the heroine.

'Oh, I've gotta pain,' groaned Alyson.

Jackie fumbled in her pocket and produced an envelope. A most resourceful child! She pushed the smiling dentures into it with a spoon. They looked less indecent. She rejoined her contorted friends and almost at once the younger man returned. I would love to know how he accounted for the old man's teeth being in an envelope.

An amazing child, this Jackie, very gullible and easily taken in. On one occasion my parents and brother were travelling on the same boat as we were on their way to stay with Katie and Angus in their lovely cottage on the Luskentyre shore. Our observant children had spotted television Blue Peter personality, Valerie Singleton, in the lounge of the 'Hebrides,' shortly after we left Skye. Eager to tell the world Jackie ran on deck and, seeing my mother comfortably relaxing in the sun, asked her, 'Have you seen Valerie Singleton, Mrs Brown?'

Now when there are nearly fifty children of ours on board, an old lady may be forgiven for not knowing all their names. She thought Jackie was looking for a lost friend and suggested, 'I think she's in the dining saloon with Skipper.'

In a frenzy of excitement Jackie tore down into the cafeteria. If Valerie Singleton were hobnobbing with Skipper, over a cup of coffee, she was going to be there. Her flushed face became drained with desappointment when she spotted us alone, oblivious even of the fact that we had a celebrity on board. The temptation to pull Jackie's leg was too good to miss.

'Didn't tell you before,' I confided, 'but the Blue Peter team are coming with us on a special assignment. To camp and all that!'

She was completely taken in and believed every ridiculous thing we told her. We whiled away an otherwise uneventful sail by fabricating all sorts of exciting nonsense before she finally said, 'You're codding.'

Several months later the TV programme was shown and fifty campers were glued to their sets searching for a sign of at least one Yorkshire child. We knew they were on board but we searched in vain. It could have been a different boat at a different time except for one thing. The bus which had brought us from Armadale could be seen quite clearly on Uig pier. It alone proved that we were there.

Our journey is not complete without a long bus ride. We are known between Brodick and Machrie, Tobermory and Fionnphort, Armadale and Uig, Tarbert and Stornoway and between Ullapool and Inverness. We are known for the embarrassing number of our rucksacks and kit bags which fill the boot, the luggage racks, the back seat and the aisle; for the innumerable children who sit three on a seat, sing lustily most of the way and eat huge quantities of food.

For their patience and their tolerance the bus drivers of the Highlands and Islands have no equal. They deserve a mention in the New Year Honours' List and a certain entry through Saint Peter's Gate. They uncomplainingly climb over our picnic skips into the driver's seat and never murmur when we begin to fill fifty-one plates. They find us suitable streams for washing up or take us into their depot where there is hot water and somewhere for us to wash and brush up. They wait'patiently for the last person to arrive, stop anywhere en route for a sick child, drive right onto the pier to reduce the distance we have to carry our kit and are altogether the nicest men in the world. It cannot be that the news that we leave no litter at all has reached each one of them. They are, I'm sure, just a very nice breed of men who behave courteously to everyone.

One very hot summer we began our holiday on Mull, staying in the church hall overnight in Tobermory. We hired a bus to take us to Fionnphort and sailed to Iona. Mull is a very beautiful island and we love its mountains and its white waterfalls cascading down the precipices into the deep sea lochs. But during that summer the streams were dry and the waterfalls silent.

It was very hot in the coach and suddenly, without any warning, Robin was sick. He had instinctively risen into the aisle but he could not reach the front and unfortunately emptied his tummy all over Liz and the bus seat.

'Find a stream and stop as soon as you can,' I begged the kind driver. At any other time on Mull a stream would have been found almost immediately but that year there was drought with a vengence in the Hebrides. We were all glued to the window looking for water and dear, patient Liz never complained at all. We mopped her up, as best we could, with a kitchen towel and stripped her of her soiled clothes.

The water when we found it, was a poor little puddle, muddy and full of weed but Liz was in a mess and we could not wait until we came to the sea once more. Everyone piled out of the bus grateful for a little, hot fresh air. Willing hands searched for soap and towel and a collection of talcum powders with which Boots would have been hard pressed to compete. With a mug we poured the cleanest water we could find over the unfortunate child. Her face and hair and chest we lathered with soap and we towelled and powdered her dry. It was the best entertainment we had had for ages. Even Liz enjoyed it!

Everyone wanted to lend her shorts and shirt and give her chocolate rewards. They sang, 'For she's a jolly good fellow, and so say all of us' and the seat was given V.I.P. treatment too.

All the while poor Robin sat nursing his humiliation and his empty tummy but the interval by the roadside gave him the fresh air he needed and when he got back into the coach, one hundred per cent sure that we didn't blame him for the accident, his nausia had passed and he did not disgrace himself again.

The sail across to Iona is over a sound clearer than any other in the British Isles and was utterly peaceful. The atmosphere must have impregnated every child to such a degree that everything they did, or said, that day was tolerant and friendly. Margaret and I and Phyllis Blamires who was with us that hot summer could feel the perfect happiness which hung over the island and blessed our children and we relaxed so completely that we did something we seldom do when in charge of children. We slept. Not dozed fitfully, we really slept, all afternoon, curled up on the white beach of that beautiful, holy island, warmed by sunshine and lulled by the turquoise waves.

When we were waiting on the pier for the little boat to take us back to Mull, a lady came up to us. 'I've been watching the children all afternoon,' she said. 'They've all blue blouses and shorts. Do they belong to a school party?'

'No,' I said, 'the girls are Guides. The boys are children from my school, or brothers of the girls, or children of my friends. Some come year after year. We like having them.'

'Well,' she said, 'I'd like you to know they are the most well behaved children I've ever met. You must have been proud of their behaviour on the beach this afternoon.'

We were embarrassed but in all fairness I had to reply, 'As a matter of fact we have no idea, at all, of their behaviour this afternoon. I'm ashamed to admit we fell asleep on the hot sand.'

'Good gracious me,' she said. 'You mean to tell me they weren't even being supervised!'

We have never forgotten the incident. It still gives us a warm glow of pleasure.

It is possible to deal in a recognised way with Mainland Bus Companies, to order in advance and to have a price quoted. It is virtually impossible to do so with proprietors of island buses. They have ways of their own but they number among the best friends we have.

I wrote to one, a respected gentleman whom we have known and loved for many years. I told him of the dates of our camp and the exact time and place of our arrival by boat and said we would need him to meet us with his bus. I received no reply and when all my other arrangements were made I again wrote to say his was the only piece of the jigsaw missing and that I sincerely hoped he would be able to collect us on arrival.

Again I had no reply but as I was going to the island for the Spring Bank holiday I decided to leave the matter until I could see him personally. His welcome was warm. No welcome is warmer than an island one.

'Well, well, Chean, it's yourself and Margaret too,' he exclaimed with real pleasure. 'And how are you? And the wee girls?' He knows us all. His wife put on the kettle and we settled down for one of the most pleasant and entertaining visits we ever make.

It was a long time before I mentioned the bus. When I did it was obvious he had not noted the date properly. My island friend did not appear to have an engagement diary to record our proposed arrival. In any case there were so many other things to talk about besides business. He was coach driver, school bus and taxi man; he was lorry driver, ambulance man and provider of the fire engine and he knew his job better than I did. What's more he was utterly reliable and I hated to press the point.

At last he said with finality, 'I'll tell you what we'll do, Chean. Chust call me on the telephone when you arrive and I'll chust send the bus right away.' Only those who know the islanders as well as we do dare take a party of nearly fifty children to a beautiful, but remote island, five hundred miles away from home, with an arrangement as flimsy as that. We know that everyone on the island will know, when the time comes, that we are coming and we trusted him implicitly.

Island bus drivers may not think it is necessary to give written confirmation that they will be of service but neither do they expect us to book in advance and be punctual. If we are a little late, time means nothing to them. They do not expect us to know the exact day we will want to go to Balephuil or Stornoway, to Crossapol or to Rodel. They understand perfectly that we will need a fine day for most of the excursions we want to make.

One morning the early sun will peep in through my tent door promising a lovely day and I will poke my head outside and see blue sky and fluffy white clouds. 'This is a day for Balephuil,' I will say to myself knowing that all I have to do is phone for the bus. The island is immaterial; all island bus drivers are the same. Until recently it was not even necessary to know the phone number. The operator, herself, was a human directory.

'I want to speak to the garage at Crossapol,' or Northton, or Tarbert it made no difference. Often I needed only to say, 'Can you put Nancy Kennedy on the phone for me?' or 'Put me through to John Morrison, will you?' Within seconds I was speaking to the right person.

'Hello, Chean, How are you? Yes. I'm sure you can have the bus today. Don't worry now. And how are all the children? Are you enchoying yourselves? Well, I'm sure it is going to be a lovely day right enough. What time will you be wanting the bus now? That will be fine.'

Or alternatively we will waken to a grey, wet day, another in a monotonous succession of similar cold, mist heavy mornings and I will decide we need a change, a rest and some temporary shelter for the day.

'We will go to Stornoway,' I will decide, perfectly confident that we can have the bus. And supposing it is still raining when we have exhausted the shops I only have to speak to the driver and he will take us across to Bravas and south to Arnol and we will visit the Blackhouse Museum there and sit for a while round the peat fire in the centre of the floor and know that Lewis was like that not so very many years ago. Then we will go to the Broch at Carloway and visit the standing stones at Callinish and for a day our bus is a mobile home. It can be very comforting, on a wet day, waiting for a change in the weather.

We went to Balephuil, one year, on a day when the morning was too bright and by early afternoon the rain was falling. We had planned to stay until evening and saunter across the Tràigh à Bheidhe to the shell beaches where the cowries can be found and the green stone hunted for. However, there is no shelter on Tiree except in the hospitable crofts and our numbers are alarming.

'I'll phone for the bus. It'll come straight away,' I said with the authority of one who knows.

'Yes, yes, I'll come over right away,' said my obliging man. 'I was at the hay myself when the rain came.' He did not take long to come, for Tiree is a very small island.

'Will you want to be going straight back to Salum?' he wanted to know.

'It will be raining there, too,' I said. 'Just drive very slowly all round the island and see if it stops.' We were warm and cosy in the bus and we began to sing. When we eventually returned to camp the rain had stopped.

Very recently we went to Rheinigidale, surely one of the most isolated villages in the British Isles, reached only be a green precipitous path or by a small boat.

'Chust give me a ring when you get to the village,' said the driver who dropped us at the beginning of the track a few miles along the Tarbert to Kyles Scalpay road. I did. The only phone, a radio one, was in a small house perched on the rocks above the sea, staring right out across the Minch. The number was Rheinigidale 1.

'It's taken us two and a half hours to get here,' I said. 'Add on another half hour for lunch and some for the extra time it's going to take us to climb the Scriob. Say three and a half hours and we'll be at the road end.'

'That will be fine, och yes,' was the reply. 'Are you enchoying your walk? I'm sure it's a lovely day chust. Don't worry now. I'll be at the track in three and a half

40

hours.'

He was, but unfortunately there was a car parked in the passing place where he had managed to turn the bus in the morning. The Kyles road is hardly suitable for a bus anyway. It took him half an hour to find another turning place. He was quite cheerful.

'Did you enchoy your walk?' he asked. 'I was neffer in Rheinigidale myself at all.'

On the eve of isolation on far islands or on the evening of our return to the Mainland harbour, there is nothing more peaceful than to wander aimlessly along the quay, watching the activity on the fishing boats and the reflection of their lights in the water; to hear the noise of quiet people and unhurried traffic and the never ending screeching of the sea gulls.

We had returned to Oban on a halcyon day when the hills enclosing the Sound of Mull were blue and unreal and the sun warm and caressing on our bare arms and healthy legs. There was a whole evening with nothing to do and the younger ones were delighted when Sarah, Nicky and Mark came to tell us they had found a fair. Pocket money had all been spent so there was a family feeling as many of the young ones crowded round Hazel, equally young at heart, willing to call a round every now and then and to beg for party rates.

The music of the carousels and the calls of the stall holders intoxicated them. From a Hebridean shore to a fairground. They had seen all! The happy camp was over and the lovely island had been left behind in the wake of the 'Columba', 'So peaceful and so little,' wrote Stephen. It was over so, 'Okay, Let's go to the fair.'

The occasion will be remembered because Hazel won a goldfish for Libby and Rachel. A tiny fellow, pale yellow and no more than two inches long. He looked at us, with curiosity, from the limitations and the insecurity of his plastic bag. The incongruity of it! Next morning fifty-six of us rose with the sun and left our overnight accommodation in the Oban Guide Headquarters weighted with the swollen kit of our return. We faced the prospect of changing trains in Glasgow, Edinburgh, York and Leeds laden with kit bags, rucksacks, food skips and presents but prepared to put as number one priority a small goldfish called Oban, swimming happily around in a plastic bag.

I am sorry for people waiting at airports, delayed by strikes and cancellations, hot and bothered, jostled and pushed by the crowd; dissatisfied and disillusioned, annoyed and beligerent, fighting verbal battles with officialdom. No such dischord touches our happy wanderings.

The people we meet have plenty of time. 'When God made Time,' they say, 'He made plenty of it.' When people have time for children their courtesy is without equal.

5

It's the call of sea and shore,
It's the tang of bog and peat,
And the scent of brier and myrtle
That puts magic in our feet;

Chapter Five

WHEN LIFE begins on the shore it is as if there had been no other life at all. The machair is not bare and uninhabited when we reach it, and occupy it, and call it our own. The forests of flowers which carpet it and the multitudes of insects which have their homes there, give it fragrance and character long before the white tents are pitched and the invasion from Yorkshire brings laughter and song and friendliness, a hundred bare feet and a hundred willing hands.

Practice has shortened the time needed for pitching the tents, the hammering in of pegs, the bashing in of poles to make our kit racks and kitchen furniture and the stowing away of our stores. We have a routine. We form a human horseshoe to mark the plan of our village and place pieces of peat where the centre of each tent will be. After that we forget about the children, building their island homes, because there are seldom more than ten who have never been before.

With the seniors, (those grand girls and boys who have been with us so long we miss them dreadfully when they leave college and have no more long holidays, begin nursing, or marry, or begin their chosen vocation away from home), we turn our attention to the kitchen department. Long, long ago we learned that the best way to pitch our dining tent, which we call the D'abri, is in a continuous line with our store. We pitch it so close that the upright pole of one can be tied securely to the upright of the other and so that the inside door of both can be rolled back as one.

Not for us the big marquee with its limited perimeter and its large area of wasted space in the middle. Four icelandic tents, pitched in a continuous line form our D'abri. Rain will not trouble us, mud will not collect and the machair carpet will remain beautiful throughout our stay. Should over eager hands upset the cornflakes, or spill the sugar, a handful of binder twine will sweep the floor and leave it looking hoovered.

Oh, the comfort and warmth of the D'abri! No room in any house is more secure, more luxurious when the butane gas fire is lit and a lamp hangs from the ridge. Bare toes curl up with the heat, arms linked and songs are sung and if rain bounces from the roof, who cares! The hatch from the kitchen to the dining room is a doorway wide and skilful hands open up the packets of biscuits and mix the drinking chocolate. Our D'abri is a home where we are an affectionate and fun loving family where food and choice are plentiful and where entertainment is spontaneous and bubbles up from a perpetual spring. We have no need for radio or television.

Because we have first visited these islands we have found friends among the people and it is inevitable that they invite us into their homes for a strupag (a cup of tea and an individual, generous helping of scones and pancakes). On these occasions we leave the camp and sit for an hour beside a crofter's peat fire. There is no hospitality, anywhere, to exceed that provided by the people of these isolated shores, these silvered, outside edges of the world. Ever hour we spend in their company is too short.

But whilst we have children we are always anxious to return to camp and there is no reward more treasured than to find them all gathered under one roof, happily singing, not needing us at all. It is at such a moment that I love them most. We lift the limp flap of the tent and are welcomed into the magic circle. The moment holds poignancy, something to be captured in our memories and kept for always.

Should a visit to friend's be even later, when the younger children have gone to bed, we can always be sure that the seniors will be still up on our return. They will be playing the guitar and singing sentimental love songs and toasting slice after fattening slice over the gas fire. Long after we are in bed we will hear them still singing and playing. Then the D'abri light will go out and a face will peep round our door.

''Night, Skip.'

''Night, Julie, See you in the morning.'

'Which morning?'

Our camping history is so long we cannot remember a time when we first learned the art of getting into bed, in a limited space. Whilst many of our friends will sigh, in weariness, 'Oh, for my bed,' we have cravings for our sleeping bags. We have never bought one finding it cheaper, by far, to make one's own. The warmth and comfort of one is remembered bliss and always associated with healthy fatigue and well being.

It was therefore a new experience to take to camp, one year, a brand new camping adult to whom tents and lats and sleeping bags were unsolved mysteries and a foreign language.

'I'm absolutely frozen,' said Bessie that first night when, after camp had finally been pitched, we crept into a cold, unlived in tent containing a groundsheet and three unopened rucksacks. There were none of the usual refinements, the kit racks, washing stand and towel rail; no homely conglomeration, no smell of perfume, no half written post cards, no childish offerings of shells or flowers which would, thereafter, make the tent cosy and warm. She could not know that comfort was only tomorrow away.

Hazel and I unrolled the groundsheet and helped her fumbling fingers with the cold rucksack buckles.

'I'll never get warm again!' It was a statement of fact and not criticism. 'I'm BLUE. And I'll never get used to the lats!'

We unrolled her bedding and fluffed out its warmth invitingly. 'I'll never get into THAT!' she said.

I don't think I have ever laughed quite so much since we left college and grew out of giddiness. I filled her hot water bottle and took a last look round the sleeping camp. Experienced campers fall asleep quickly and the first night under canvas each year poses us few problems. They are always tired after the long, two day journey.

With the practised speed of many years of bending and folding ourselves up, of weaving ourselves around each other so that neither is in the way, we unobtrusively slipped into bed to watch the rest of the comedy act. Our merriment was the only hot water bottle we needed.

'Put your undies into bed, Bessie,' I advised. 'They'll be nice and warm in the morning.'

'Ugh! It's the thought of taking them off that's bothering me at the moment,' she groaned. 'Aren't you two cold? I'm perishing.'

I knew what she meant. I have often put a warm hand down into the sleeping bag, felt refridgerated flesh and been horrified to think that the cold hams I was touching were my own. One can sometimes feel quite warm yet one's flesh is frozen numb. Especially one's hind flesh!

'Get into bed quickly,' we prompted|her, 'before the hot water bottle goes cold.'

Finally pyjamad and sweatered, Bessie sat down heavily at the mouth of her sleeping bag and began a belaboured entry. It was like watching a film of the great effort required by a butterfly to emerge from its chrysalis, shown in reverse. She had on a far too thick a woolly and never having pushed herself into a sleeping bag before she found the whole operation exhausting. The effort generated in her a tremendous heat.

Our cold friend suddenly gasped, 'Blimey! I'm boiling.' No visitor to our camps has given us more fun than Bessie did, no newly initiated camper caused more laughter and no one has been more good natured. Needless to say when she became competent, which she very soon did, we were quite sorry to be deprived of our entertainment.

Life on the shore awakens late and there are plenty of valid excuses for this. If we are to have milk for our porridge we must wait until the crofter's daughter has milked the cow and she is not an early riser by Mainland standards. If rain is falling we think it logical to wait for it to stop, believing that if it rains before seven it will clear before eleven. Should the sun rise from behind Ben Luskentyre and begin to climb into a cloudless sky and heat begin to shimmer from the white canvas, then we must lie abed until the midges go. And if the children were very late to bed on the previous night and still sleep soundly then which of us is fool enough to wake them up.

There are many early morning noises but we know them all, Margaret and Hazel and I. From the shore comes the eternal din of the waves crashing on the sand, crushing into fragments the millions of shells which make the silver strand. Seagulls sweep down noisily in their early morning search for every edible crumb. A handful of sheep, struggle under the fence and thunder across the campsite. The crofter's cock and his half dozen wives scratch around the kitchen tent swearing at our tidyness and lack of generosity. The bull parades along the fence on his early visit to the stream which flows in a white torrent of water when it rains and dries up completely after a few days' sunshine. The enormous, black fellow could make match-wood of our fence if he took a dislike to us or objected to our flapping white settlement. Sometimes a whistling and a Gaelic calling on the hill tell us that there is a gathering of sheep from the back of the hill and that tomorrow there will be some interesting activity at the fank.

The sun is high when the first scamper of human feet, beneath their white nightie, dashes over to the latrines and we know that it is time to get up. The peat fire, which never really goes out, must be stirred and fed until the hungry flames leap high. The cooks are called to fill the tea and coffee billies, put on the porridge, whisk the eggs and fry the sausages, butter the bread and jam the rolls.

There is a stir of activity everywhere as beds are aired and rolled. The orderlies lay the sitting ground-sheets, put out the plates and spoons, the cornflakes and sugar. A runner is sent for the milk, the Flag Patrol bend over the hymn books and choose their early morning song of praise. There is a cleaning of teeth on the patch above the water bin, a splashing of water over sleepy faces. Hazel closes the door of our tent and has her morning shower with the new fangled plastic spray Margaret insisted on buying her. And the seniors sleep on. They who stayed awake as long as the noisy corncrake and crawled into bed in the early hours will not wake till the breakfast whistle goes.

Few people can appreciate sand as much as Margaret and I. We spend eight months of the year battling against farm mud which clings so tenaciously to our wellingtons that many is the time it has claimed them completely and we have suddenly stepped out into the mire, barefoot and floundering. Mud walks into our house with every dog and cat and visitor and clings embarrassing thick on our stout shoes and we walk across the fields to the bus into town or merely get out of the Landrover to open the farm gate onto the road.

We learned to camp on Yorkshire's good, brown earth. At Rylstone the mud round the fire was so deep we had to pave the area and make a hearth. We have seen mud so thick at Grassington that one would have believed that the field was undergoing beauty treatment and we have slithered about at Steeton Hall until we have been so muddy that our nationality has been in doubt.

Therefore do we worship sand. Hebridean sand, clean and white and so very easy to dig. And where is there a person who is not crazy about digging sand? Put any human-being on the shore and he digs, either energetically like children, eager to discover Australia, or just lazily drawing his finger through the sand.

'Just look at that!' said nineteen year old Julie watching ten year old Catherine, close to the receding tide, completely absorbed in some digging activity. She was so intent upon her task that she was completely oblivious of the swimmers, the sunbathers and the gymnasts, the scavengers and the artists.

'Isn't that great?' marvels sensitive Julie.

There is no need to ask why Catherine is digging, because she is not digging for a reason. She's digging because that is what you do with sand. You dig. If there happens to be a reason why you dig, that is an added bonus and there are plenty of helpers providing it is not too hot or late evening when the midges are about.

Our children do not know what elsans are. Lats are 'uncivilised loos', deep, deep trenches in the sand. The deeper they go the more exciting it gets.

'The lats are deeper than ever, this year, Mrs Belsey,' calls a bystander. 'Prue's digging an' yer can 'ardly see 'er 'ead!'

And how generous you can be with sand. 'The lats are full again,' reported Penny who was in charge of them that windy summer when the first morning call was always, 'The lats are down again, Skipper!'

Who cares if the lats are full and new ones have to be dug. It doesn't really matter. The soft, white sand comes up as clean and fine as scouring powder and digging gives only the elderly backache.

Blessed, blessed sand! It receives all our dirty water without complaint or refusal, it absorbs every drop we accidentally spill, it can be cleanly cut into the exact shape to receive our oven and it makes the most comfortable of beds. Blessed sand! It could never offend us no matter how much it blows into our water bin or coats our fried sausages on a windy day and when a pile of it is swept up in the bedroom at home, when our rucksacks are emptied, it is ceremoniously kept until next year.

Under the microscope it has colour. Every particle of it is shell. There are the most exquisite shells to be picked up on the western shores of the Hebrides, mauve and pink and yellow, more beautifully painted than any china, more delicate than any eggshell. There are tellins and limpets and cowries by the thousand, razor shells and wentleraps and miniature scallops, cockles and periwinkles and beautiful, purple mussels with mother of pearl linings. Hours can be pleasurably spent collecting them and using them in models and pictures.

To speculate on the number of moluscs needed to create such vast areas of sand would be as futile as to try to count the blades of grass on a prairie, the pine needles of the Scottish forests or the stars in heaven. Although individually the shell fragments have colour, collectively they are white. The mountainous dunes resemble snow slopes and where they plunge into the sea we imagine we have come to the Arctic by mistake.

No children's playground is more perfect for jumping, leaping and rolling and generally abandonning oneself in ecstasy. We adults have lost the art and the acceleration necessary but we are not blind to the dance of children, on shore and dune and we envy them their ability to run up the green slopes and to take off so fearlessly, into space, fly gracefully into the air and land in a cloud of sand many feet below.

Their language is more colourful and dramatic than ours. To them the dunes are, and always have been, the Suicide Jump and Devil's Leap and they have named them well for the height from which they leap is ridiculous and the heap of tangled arms and legs in which they land is often alarming.

'Come on, Skipper, you do it!' they yell and pull me up the slope and, because I am neither old nor decrepit and an active life has kept me agile, I do try. I know what it will feel like to run strongly against the wind to the precipice, to leap into freedom and space and glide weightlessly through the clear air. The high diver must experience it, the skier taking off at the end of a ski jump, the sky divers and those who hang glide. In anticipation of the glorious, invigorating feeling which will be mine, I do try.

But at the moment of blast off my nerve flies away without me and I drop clumsily and heavily over the edge. The children find it even more funny because they anticipated it and they laugh at my failure and their cleverness in knowing what would happen. They do not laugh at Flim. She will still be able to face Devil's Leap when she is eighty. I am ashamed at the timidy of my spirit and the refusal of my steed.

Many of the crofters themselves have never been over the big dunes. 'I was never there at all,' say some of the wives who live beside them. 'Och, I've been on the machair for the cow and on the hill for the crottal but I've never been on the big dunes at all.'

Our children live on the dunes. For fifty weeks of the year the wind sweeps them smooth and moulds them into mountains and precipices and for two weeks of the year each sculpture in sand is disturbed by a thousand footprints. They have taken trays and groundsheets to toboggan down the slopes and poles to help them jump and ski but it was the seniors who filmed themselves dressed in tea towel head dresses and gay blanket robes and who sought out the most blood curdling knives. 'Lawrence of Arabia' looked no more authentic than Joan's amateur movie of a massacre in the desert.

The smooth, hard surface, left by the outgoing tide, becomes a gallery of artistic drawings and an autograph book full of signatures. As soon as camp is pitched, the first breakfast over and the flag unfurled from the long, bamboo fishing rod, the children gallop for the shore. For a fortnight the normally uninhabited beaches will become alive and many feet will churn up the sand and every child will leave a message for the tide;

TIREE IS THE PLACE FOR ME
BUTTERFLIES ARE BEST
HARRIS FOREVER
JENNY WOZ HERE
SKIPPER'S RULE
GLAD THAT I LIVE AM I
I'D LIKE TO TEACH THE WORLD TO SING
STARSKY AND HUTCH.

It is significant that the same instinct to write on a clean surface which exists in vandals and excites them to scrawl obsenities in public lavatories and on street hoardings lives in all of us. It pleases me that I have never once come across vulgarity scratched on the shore. Never once have I had to help the tide to do its work of obliterating the signatures and the caricatures.

There is extravagance in their writings, pomposity and humour, there is creativity and imagination in their drawings but there is nothing to disgust the reader or insult the beauty of nature's canvas.

The amount of flotsam on the beach depends on the severity of the winter and the generosity of the Atlantic in giving up her treasures. Sometimes she scatters her varied debris liberally and bottles can be picked up in plenty, nylon ropes and fishing nets, lobster floats and herring boxes, plastic containers, animal bones, jellyfish and driftwood.

Sometimes the sea snatches away everything she can find leaving the beach so bereft of debris that it is virtually impossible to pick up even the bits of kindling needed to light the peat under the oven and to put new life into the cooking fire when hunger pains demand speed.

The hunt for driftwood must be our first consideration whatever island we choose and each child collects according to his or her personality and we learn a great deal about our children. Some work individually and methodically, picking up little bits and pieces and struggle on alone with a difficult bundle, picking up the fallen pieces and never asking for help. Others work gregariously, jostling and helping each other and having fun all the way. Some chose partners and struggle along with logs more suitable for the building of the Kon Tiki and a few, proud of their own strength, stagger along under tree trunks, bruise their shoulders, boost their ego and wear themselves out completely. Others make so many piles the sum total of which is staggering and they have to admit defeat or ask assistance. Many utilize the containers the sea has thoughtfully left behind, the plastic sacks and herring boxes and large squares of nylon netting. A few splash about in pools looking for sea creatures which fascinate them and forget where their hoard was left. They finally come home with a very small offering indeed.

We find most of our driftwood on the raised, pebbly beaches found in many places in the Western Islands. At the same time we discover the used nests of many seabirds and investigate the rock pools which are the homes of sea urchins and anemones, weird and wonderful creatures we struggle to identify and hermit crabs by the dozen.

Hermie was our most famous hermit crab and he will be remembered as long as children cluster round Hazel, for it is one of her favourite stories. He was found by a group of children who, because they had an empty coffee tin and a wonderland of rocks to explore, decided to make their own marine aquarium and bring it back to camp. Among a score of other creatures was Hermie, an inquisitive hermit crab who had, most certainly, outgrown his residence.

'Look at the silly little thing. He looks like an elephant in a hen house,' said Jenny.

Wind blown heads bent to watch him make his clumsy way across the bottom of the coffee tin.

'He couldn't get right back inside if he wanted to, could he. He's crazy?' said Ali.

'Give him a bigger shell,' said Mrs Belsey, and together they searched among a collection of empty shells at the tent door.

'This one will do,' said Joanna, dropping a much larger periwinkle into the tin.

'Now in you go,' said Mrs Belsey. 'It's a much better house to rent than yours.'

They poured over the tin for some time, deeply interested in the activity therein. No one could replace Hazel and satisfy the children's need for a really interested grownup. I am needed everywhere at once but Hazel can share experiences with them and they love it. A minor distraction caught their attention and gave Hermie the opportunity he needed. When they looked again, seconds later, they found the old yellow periwinkle empty. They searched excitedly for Hermie. One would have thought that if he had been able to understand a language at all it would surely have been the Gaelic and that he would have been nonplussed indeed with the English. But no, he had understood perfectly and there he was, safely and wholly, within the bigger shell. Only his feelers were visible and his protruding front two claws.

Henceforth all hermit crabs are Hermie just as all snails are Fred and all sea urchins are Hamish. Fred was a snail which seemed perfectly happy to live near Jill's tent and when he appeared, which he did at frequent intervals, he was fed on choice vegetables from Calum's garden plot. Fred was very big and he would have provided a juicy meal for any slug eating bird who had been sharp enough to spot him. But there are smaller members of his family and big or small every one is Fred. When her lettuce crunched ominously on that memorable occasion Jill was sure she had eaten Fred.

Hamish was a small, live sea urchin, found by Prue in a rock pool and brought back to camp in a bucket. He was beautiful but he couldn't bear imprisonment and we were too insensitive to know. When he died we felt responsible. I believe he was buried. Certainly no one had the heart to take him home, boil him and take out the flesh to preserve the shell.

The sea is a natural playground for children whether the weather is gloriously warm when they can live in swimming costumes all day or not. They are equally happy messing about the shore when gales are blowing and seas are high providing they are suitably clad in sweaters and cagoules.

Naturally swimming takes up a good deal of our time, especially in hot weather and we have been appreciative of the tremendous responsibility this places on us, particularly in view of our big numbers. It was inevitable that as safe a way of doing this as possible should evolve. It is amazing how simple answers can be. It is not merely essential to have a qualified lifesaver standing by. I believe that it is our first consideration to see that our lifesaver is never needed and to ensure this it is necessary to limit the distance to which swimmers may go.

We do this by means of a boundary line which is kept afloat by white buoys and corks and is anchored at each end with weighted bags. We also keep in contact with the boundary line by running ropes from each end to the shore to be held by an observant non-swimmer. In this way an area of no more than three feet in depth becomes enclosed. If children are not given a limit they get deeper and deeper and cannot hear our calls to return to safety because of the noise of the waves. This experience of the rope is also a parable. In all things it is wise to give children a limit. They can understand limitations when they are given by a caring and not too possessive adult.

The first buoys we used were white, plastic FINA swimming rings which, when inflated, were gay and very buoyant. I bought them from the local garage and they were quite expensive but I was not counting their value in money but in safety. After a few years' use the plugs began to disappear and the plastic to puncture. There were no more rings at the garage and swimming aid ones were even more expensive. I am still surprised at the time it took for us to realise that the white, one gallon, plastic containers, currently in use for squash and washing up liquid, would do equally well and cost nothing at all.

I am even more surprised at the time it took for us to realise that we could fill anchor bags with sand. For years, like idiots, we believed we needed pebbles in order to fill them. This was not very difficult on Tiree where there is a good supply. On

Harris we had to clamber over rocks to find the bay of pebbles whilst, all the time, tons and tons of sand lay at our feet. We still laugh about the ritual of gathering pebbles but our blindness has made us look carefully at many of our fixed ideas and habits.

Sand can easily be emptied out at the water's edge when swimming is over for the day, leaving the line lighter and more manageable. We still have our problems. Carelessness in hanking the wet rope results in a tangle worse than any that could trouble a hank of wool. We have feared for our sanity when trying to sort out the mess caused by too many eager hands on the rope and too many eager feet towing it to the sea.

There have been occasions when the line has not been left far enough above the high water mark, that beautiful trail along the beach where the delicate, whole shells are left stranded when the tide turns. A rise in the wind overnight has been known to throw up the waves viciously enough to snatch the flimsy line and the early swimmers have been thwarted.

One year, during stormy weather, we imagined we had left the line well clear of the tide and well anchored by leaving sand in the bags. It was an east wind during the night. The weight of it blowing on the plastic containers must have been too strong and, little by little, it must have been dragged towards the sea. When we reached the shore, the next morning, we found the line so completely missing that we began to wonder if someone had moved it, a possibility quite ludicrous in the islands where everything we leave is safe.

We found the missing line quite by accident, completely buried in a sandy cove amongst the rocks. One piece only of the rope was showing. We had to dig almost three feet down to free the containers and to untangle the wet rope was impossible.

We do not underestimate the strength and cruelty of the sea and never regard the beaches as safe even though it would be difficult to find safer ones, anywhere in Britain, than those which fringe the Atlantic shores of the Hebrides. To swim outside the line is forbidden and any ball which blows over it must be allowed to cross the ocean alone. No one may follow it. We have seen two balls disappear more quickly than a gas filled baloon rises to the sky. Their rapid departures have brought a stunned silence to the watching swimmers and we have not regretted the lesson and considered the money lost well spent. We watched an orange ball sail from Caoles, on Tiree, to the island of Gunna in a fantastically short space of time. Nowadays no one asks the purpose of the rope and accepts it without argument.

In twenty years we have had only one minor swimming accident but it taught us not to be complacent or think we knew all the answers. The weather on Tiree had been glorious and a number of the youngsters decided they wanted to swim the bay. By this they meant the half of Salum Bay between Calum's house and Bella's small cottage which stands above a pile of rocks and a sandy headland which cut the bay in two.

The challenge was considerable and we try to encourage endurance and determination so we agreed, stipulating only that they should swim parallel to the shore, only yards away from a line of non swimming observers. They were swimming in approximately three feet of water and we believed that nothing could be more safe and that an accident was most improbable.

We were wrong. Most of the swimmers completed the challenge in excellent form. Nellie, at eleven, insisted on swimming on her back and she had a lot of determination. The look on her face said quite clearly, 'I'm not giving up until I get there.'

'Are you okay?' Margaret, who was walking beside her, kept asking.

''Course I am, Flim,' she was always answered.

It was at the completion of the distance, when she had to stand up, that we found Nellie had temporarily lost her balance. 'You'll be okay in a minute,' we reassured her. 'Just take it steady.'

She was very cold so we wrapped her up in a towel and half carried her back to camp. She sat shivering while we dried and dressed her but no matter how we tried we could not get her warm. We pulled a warm sweater over her head and gave her a warm drink. We helped her into her sleeping bag and still she shivered and could not maintain her balance.

We assumed that she must have got too much water in her ears with swimming on her back and that she had kept on swimming long after she should have admitted defeat. She had a great deal of pluck. We had always been aware of this trait in her.

I decided that she must go to a warmer place than we could provide and we sent for Calum to come out in his ricketty old van and take her to the warmth of his kitchen. She sat beside his stove for a couple of hours before she felt warm enough to return to camp. We seriously considered sending for the doctor but she kept insisting that she was all right and was feeling better. She still felt rather wobbly next day.

Exposure and exhaustion can creep up unobserved. The sea is cruel and it is cold inspite of the Gulf Stream which washes the western shores. It is never to be trusted or underestimated for tragedy comes when lessons are learned too late. This experience taught us a valuable lesson and emphasised the fact that we should never be convinced that we are absolutely safe in what we are doing. The unexpected can always happen.

We seldon swim alone. Only very rarely are there other people on the beach beside ourselves but there are water creatures everywhere. Because the sea is so clear everything in it can be seen unless it is microscopic. Crabs of all sizes scuttle away sideways on the sandy sea bed and cause a lot of fun both for the children who run away screaming and for the brave ones who stay and watch and follow the energetic, little shufflers until they disappear into the sand.

In stormy weather jelly fish are numerous and many are left stranded by the tide. There are few brave swimmers when they have jelly fish for company. Sometimes a moving black shape, as big as a small rowing boat but forever changing shape like an amoeba, comes towards us and everyone speculates as to what it must be.

'It's a seal,' someone cries.

'It's a shark!'

'It's a lot of creatures altogether!'

'It's thousands of fish. Look at them! There're millions!'

Seals are attracted to us and often swim about fifty yards away. We have seen more seals on Tiree than on any other island. They bask on the rocks above Upper Vaul and swim frequently in Salum Bay. 'I counted sixteen just lying on the rocks, this morning,' Hazel told us. She had only walked a little distance from camp. Our good friend, Calum MacLean, Calum Salum as he was alway affectionately called, used to play his bagpipes on the shore and seals would swim towards his music.

A great deal of shouting accompanies the aquatic activities of the Yorkshire children. The girls are so much more able to stand the cold than the boys and are usually first in the water. Some run straight in and get wet at once. These are the heroines who take out the line. Others creep in slowly getting wet a little at a time. I have seen unwilling bathers thrown in on so few occasions that I could count them on one hand. It usually occurs when a bevy of ten year olds rushes up to a senior who appears rather reluctant, hovering in the shallow water. Paul has been dragged in but being taller and stronger than they he has coped. Only once have I seen Julie and Linda lift anyone up bodily and carry her into the sea and that showed the measure of their confidence in Mrs Belsey's affection for them and their excellent assessment of her constitution that they dare lift her up, carry her off and lower her ignominiously into the waves.

Margaret and I have been lucky. Normally we have held the lifesaving certificates and the posts of responsibility. We never swim until everyone is safely out and by that time our children's high spirits are somewhat cooled but that does not mean we are never the victims of horseplay. Where there are healthy children there will always be a certain amount of sheer, undiluted daftness and we try to be around at the most likely times to hold the reins before anyone goes too far. Children seldom know when to stop.

The island children are not usually swimmers and mostly they have stood on the sand and watched. Not so Dolly. Dolly lives with her grannie half a mile from the camp and she has recently spent every available minute with us. Seeing the swimmers she could not control the urge to join them. I managed to remove her frock but her vest and knickers were soon saturated. I wondered what her grannie would say.

'Can you swim?' I asked when she strode in to join the others.

'Och, yes,' she said. Then she added honestly, 'But when I move my arums I forget to move my feet and when I move my feet I forget to move my arums!'

She certainly had no fear. We dried her and loaned her fresh underwear and a warm sweater to put over her frock. It amused me to see that she did not take home the wet things but left them until they were dry next day. She was wise as well as brave.

We have never seen a whale but one was washed up on the beach at Luskentyre, some years ago. Very little of it was left by the time we got there in the summer, except a number of vertebrae and a heap of decaying flesh. Joanna, Prue and the boys discovered it one evening at the beginning of camp. They were walking round the bay, just when darkness was falling, on a beautiful, July night.

To wander on the beach at night is a privilege the seniors seem to enjoy. Personally, beautiful though it is and peaceful, bed is always infinitely more attractive to me, at that hour, when I am with children. It draws me like a magnet and sleep weighs heavily on my eyelids. I have great difficulty in keeping awake until their return and the minute they poke their heads round the door with a, 'G'night, Skip. We're back,' I go straight to sleep.

On this evening they had more to say than just, 'G'night.' Hazel and I were already in bed and it was past the hour for us to show enthusiasm or appreciate hefty teenagers crowding into our tent, treading on our feet and falling over our sleeping bags.

'We've found something queer out there,' they reported.

'We think it's a body!'

'It's covered with sand and it feels soft!'

'It's enormous.'

'Oh, get to bed,' we groaned. 'It'll keep till morning. Scoot!'

They were slow to obey. 'We were telling each other ghost stories and scaring each other silly. What do you think it is?'

'I haven't a clue. For goodness sake get to bed.' They went giggling and talkative.

The mystery was solved the next day when the islanders told the boys that it was a whale, or the remains of one, which had been washed up some time ago and which had caused quite a sensation and attracted a lot of visitors.

Apparently, so the boys were told, a whale's tooth could be worth up to ten pounds. After that there was no holding them. As soon as breakfast was over they set off for the great sweep of the bay where it bends majestically to follow the River Laxdale for three miles inland. No place on earth has more beauty. The vast expanse of beach catches the full force of almost every wind and what is washed up on the beach at this point is very soon covered with blown sand.

Treasure hunting boys, greedy for wealth and convinced that they, too, would find teeth if they looked long enough, began to dig up the decaying whale. As they stirred up the sand they also released the vile smell of decaying flesh. This put them off considerably and they changed their minds about the advantages of being affluent and disappeared to find a less smelly occupation.

Towards the end of camp some of the younger children came running for my assistance. 'Come an' help Mrs Belsey, Skipper. She wants a whale bone.'

I groaned. I know Mrs Belsey if she wants something. I have memories of old, rusty iron cauldrons discarded by crofters who have given up dyeing their fleeces beside fast flowing streams. I know all about sea bleached, gnarled and knotted tree roots of indisputable value and beauty but also of incredible weight and size. Seldom a year passes but something weird and bulky has to be packed into the skips for Mrs Belsey.

She is a very determined woman and nearly always gets her way. There was an occasion on which she failed. In an hotel on one of the islands she saw a small, antique table which exactly matched a piece of furniture she had at home and before the end of the holiday she decided she just could not leave the island without first asking the hotel manager if he would sell it.

'Och, I know fine which table you mean,' he said when she phoned, 'but I'm no willing to sell. The only way you could live with that table is to come along here and live with me!' It is the nearest anyone of us has got to a sober proposal!

'Come along, Skipper. Mrs Belsey can't get the bones loose. There's time before dinner!'

Huh!

With difficulty we managed to free one of the huge vertebrae. Several were still joined together with cartilage and sinews and rotting flesh. Hazel had found a piece of nylon rope on the beach and was pulling for all she was worth. She'd plenty of helpers and spectators.

'You're getting it free, Mrs Belsey,' shouted her supporters. 'Blimey, what a pong!'

When we pulled it free we dragged it through the sand hoping to scour off some of the decaying flesh. 'Try pulling it in the sea,' I suggested. 'perhaps the salt will cleanse it.'

But nothing but wind and rain and sun and plenty of time would rid that bone of its odorous smell. Its determined owner said she would tie it to the fence, near the croft and collect it next year.

However, it came home more quickly than we expected. Friends from our home-town camped at Luskentyre shortly afterwards. They found the bone, thought it had been discarded, washed it in toilet soap, covered it in talcum powder and brought it home, still smelling, in the boot of their car. They were very sporting about the whole affair and generously returned it to its rightful owner.

When our fresh water supply is a long way away we carry sea water for washing dishes. It is no use at all for personal cleanliness as no lather will come. During one very hot camp on Tiree I poured a whole bucket of sea water over Alison and Julia. The tide was quite far out and I had carried the bucket very full but when I reached the machair the two of them were frolicking about just like puppies. I couldn't resist the temptation. Most people have longed to do that, just once in their lives. In doing so I satisfied one of my basic needs. They were rolling around in mock battle when the unexpected cold shower came. I found it well worth the chore of having to go back to refill my bucket.

When the weather is really fine swim suits are worn almost perpetually. Joanna Belsey's first camp was a very hot one and she was as much at home in the water as a dolphin and nearly as aquabatic. She had been swimming the last day, before the strike. When the last tents were down and the equipment packed, we had a céilidh and dance in Calum's barn. We had invited nearly all the near islanders and when it finished in the early hours of the morning we slept, most of us, under a big tarpaulin under the stars on the machair. We rose at five to eat tea/toast in Calum's kitchen before going to the pier for the six o'clock boat. We travelled home all day and well into the next night and when we were about ten miles from the end of our journey Jennifer came to me.

'Skipper, I think you should do something about that Joanna Belsey before she goes home. Dr and Mrs Belsey will throw a fit!' It was the year before Hazel's first camp.

I was horrified. 'Good heavens,' I said. 'Whatever has she done wrong?'

'She's got her swimming costume on,' said Jennifer.

As I said before when life begins on the beach it is as if there were no other life at all. Everything belongs to the beach, happens on the beach and ends on the beach. On Tiree we camp only yards from the shore and even our drinking water was carried along it from Calum's kitchen.

It is imperative that the water bin should be full each night before we go to bed. To crawl into our sleeping bags knowing that it is empty is unthinkable. Many is the time that Margaret and I have hurried over to Calum's very late at night. Usually he would be in and wanting to talk and we would be ready to listen for his conversation was always interesting.

On one ocasion he was not in and the house was in darkness. The door was wide open, however, so we went inside. Calum's cow had been in before us and had misbehaved. The soft pats were still warm as they oozed through our bare toes. We had not laughed so much for many a day.

On the shore below the house there are pebbles which are quite difficult to negotiate in bare feet even in the day time. In island darkness they are well nigh impossible especially as they come immediately after leaving the lighted kitchen. Margaret and I have found it dangerous, on several occasions, to be proud of our strength which is not inconsiderable. Possibly he was an experienced man who first said pride preceded a fall. The temptation, if you are big headed, is to fill the buckets too full hoping that in so doing the bin will fill more quickly.

One bitterly cold night I looked into the bin and found it nearly empty. 'Botheration!' I muttered and poked my nose into the door of our sleeping tent. 'I'll have to go to Calum's for water. I don't think there's enough for morning.'

'Do you want any help?' The offer was genuine.

'No, I'll take two buckets. I'll try not to be long.'

The islanders keep very late hours and my friend was no exception. 'Well, Chean,' he said, 'and I was thinking the children had stopped drinking altogether.'

I have a tendency to run when I have stayed too long in genial company. It was late and dark and I tried to run along the pebbly shore with my two very full buckets. I managed the stony bit without incident and grew careless when I came to the sand. Now if you trip with a full bucket of water it spills forward and slightly inwards. If you trip with two buckets the streams from both of them converge to form a lake and should you have the misfortune to fall completely you find yourself suddenly lying fairly and squarely in deep water as I was on that perishingly cold night.

My anorak, my shirt and shorts and every stitch of my underclothes were saturated. The bin remained empty. By the time I had changed and wrung the water of my wet clothes I had lost interest.

Always there is someone on the shore. Someone in blue, picking shells, doing cartwheels, dragging a long trail of seaweed aimlessly or picking up flotsom on the high water mark. Often there is the lone figure just standing in the water gazing out to sea. What thoughts children must have! In the sunset the colour of their legs deepens to chocolate and every ripple in the sea catches fire.

The older, more sensitive ones, those who've been to camp with us many times, invariably come to me sometime during the fortnight. 'Mind if I go off by myself for a bit?' Julie will ask. 'I'll just be on the shore.'

We all have this need, those of us who have been to the islands many times. Viv to wander off and paint for half an hour, Joanna to stand in the waves, Ann to sing to the accompaniment of the surf, Margaret to wander the whole length of the bay trailing her feet in the incoming tide and Hazel to wander off in search of seals or to potter alone on the lower slopes of the mountain, looking for the best flowers to plant in her peat garden.

I, in my busyness, do not envy them. Without them I could not bring children so far away and they do not leave me often or go when my need is great. On the contrary I understand their need. I had my turn in the long peaceful days when I wandered the islands with Margaret, looking for beautiful places to bring children. I have known halcyon days when I did not have to rise and feed fifty but could prepare breakfast for two, in our little white tent on some isolated shore and then eat it with my legs still inside my sleeping bag, comfortably resting against my rucksack.

I have walked alone on a great many shores whilst Margaret has washed up the dishes in a clear stream or at the water's edge and I am satisfied.

Where are the folk like the folk o' the west?
Canty, and couthy, and kindly, the best.

6

Chapter Six

TO THINK of summer camp in terms of just ourselves would be to do an injustice to the nicest people we know. For a fortnight every year we weave ourselves so intricately into the lives of the crofting people that when we leave a part of us stays and something of their generosity and humour comes away with us to make our lives richer and more sensitive.

We have so many friends on so many islands. Some the children have made for us, many are islanders we have known for so long that we cannot remember a time without them. As soon as we get off the boat there are people whom we know and warm handshakes on every side.

It is not surprising that we are now well known on the islands for the arrival of such a large family cannot go unnoticed. Naturally we create interest wherever we go because of our size alone and because of our very healthy appetites. We are known in shops all over the place on account of our very large orders and it is fortunate that most shopkeepers have plenty of time to attend to our strange requests. Together we solve seemingly impossible problems.

We had climbed Ben Luskentyre on a very hot day and I promised the fourteen children who had reached the top that the next time we were in Tarbert I would buy them all an ice cream. Almost every shop in Tarbert stocks everything from food to drapery, from sheep dip to kitchenware and picture postcards. We have known Mrs MacLeod for many years. Hazel bought the wool from her (that Ann knitted into a beautiful Aran sweater) at eleven o'clock at night, just before the boat came in. The brightest colours in our Harris wool rug come from this lady's shop. She must have an iron constitution for she is always there.

I took fourteen climbers into the shop and asked her if she had any ice cream. She was immediately concerned.

'Oh well.' she said, 'and I'm afraid I haven't got that number at all.' She began to search inside the freezer.

'Ice lollies would do,' I suggested.

'Wait now till I look,' she murmured from within the depths of the chest. 'Och, but the weather has been just beautiful and everybody has been buying the ice cream. See there's none left at all except the packs.'

'They would do if you have any wafers and a knife,' I said.

'Wait till I see.' She produced a packet of wafers and a sharp bacon knife. 'I'm sure there will be plenty with four packs.'

Four were more than enough but I could not be ungrateful. We began to slice and wafer the blocks and the ice cream adicts took the messy paper outside and sat on the pavement to lick the cardboard clean.

'Tell some of the others to come,' I whispered to Robert. 'There's far too much here for fourteen.'

The news spread like wildfire. 'Skipper's giving away icecream!'

The shop became crowded and our good lady was delighted. 'There's another pack,' she announced and I opened the fifth and last pack to satisfy the tail end of the queue.

'What have we done to deserve this?' someone asked. The wafer biscuits had run out but the little lady was undaunted.

'Wait till I get some spoons,' she said and every last drop was eaten. 'And how are your parents?' she had time to enquire when we couldn't move for children. 'And your brother? I hope they're in their usual.'

It happens all the time, this sort of thing. A few days later we had a similar experience with another shop keeper we know very well. It was early closing day in Tarbert and nearly six o'clock but she was still open. We were on our way home via Stornoway and we needed fruit and bread for the journey. Our bus driver pulled up at the side of the road and said he was sure we would be able to satisfy our requirements for he could see that her door was still open.

'We're away,' I said sadly. 'Our holiday's over.'

'Och and are you away chust now?' sympathised our friend. 'I'm sure you'll have been enchoying yourselves. The weather has been very warm this year.'

All shopping transactions begin in this pleasant manner. If other people come into the shop they are not in any hurry and are only too pleased to hear the conversation and join in.

At last I asked for apples. 'And how many will you be needing?' The little lady is lame. She pointed to the box and I carried it over to the counter.

'We need fifty two,' I said. She showed no surprise for she is used to the enormity of my requests. On the Mainland I risk being thought to be a nut case when I ask for large quantities but in the Hebrides, if they think me mad they do not let me know.

'Will you count out the number you require?' said the obliging and trusting lady. Several hands dived with mine into the box. There were only fifty.

'Never mind. Two oranges will do fine,' I assured her.

'Don't forget the bread, Skipper,' I always have a memory box at my elbow.

'Can we have some sliced bread?' I asked. She placed a loaf on the table. One loaf feeds only about eight.

'I'll need at least six,' I said.

She was distressed. 'Well, I'm very sorry but I haven't any more sliced at all,' she apologised. 'The boat was very late in and I haven't got my stores up from the pier. I have plenty of the unsliced.'

We had packed our bread knife in the skips for home and had only penknives and table knives which are quite impossible with soft bread. We knew this from experience. One wet day on Tiree we had been sheltering in the warehouse behind the Co-op in Scarinish and we had been tempted to buy unsliced loaves and had found we were unable to do anything with them other than hack them into chunks. We were intending to prepare this meal on the moving bus to Stornoway and I knew that without sliced loaves it couldn't be done.

'Could you lend me a knife?' I said. 'If we could just slice up the loaves on the counter that would be fine.'

'Surely,' answered the most obliging shopkeeper in the British Isles. She brought a hugh knife, quite the sharpest bread knife I have ever handled. She was delighted to help. We sliced up another six loaves and put them into bags. Few problems are unsolvable.

'I'll tell my daughter you've been,' the shopkeeper smiled and we shook hands. 'We'll be seeing you again next year, if we're spared.'

It's the timelessness which makes things so easy; the complete lack of urgency which allows shopkeepers time to wrap up each loaf of bread in newspaper and to tie the parcel with a piece of string. Some of their serenity dilutes our Mainland instinct to hurry. It is very relaxing and creates a feeling of superb well-being. It makes a working holiday into a restful, rejuvenating experience

Once we leave the island shops behind we must rely on the excellence of our stores, or deplore their limitations until the bi-weekly van visits us on our remote corner of the machair. His progress is slow for he serves the dual purpose of provisioning the isolated townships and entertaining the crofters with Gaelic banter and local gossip.

The message that he has arrived in the village is no indication that he will soon be at the campsite. It may take him an hour or more to visit the few crofts. Time is unimportant. It is late when he arrives and his van headlights catch the red of the setting sun falling behind the island of Taransay. It seldom needs the hoot of Murdo's horn to bring the children tearing across the beach and flying from the sand dunes to squander their remaining spending money on sweets, crisps and chocolate biscuits. It always amused Calum that, when wishing to buy liquorice, our children always asked for Spanish. Though the van comes late it does not compete with the butcher we once waited for until after midnight. Resigning ourselves to a meatless few days Margaret and I finally crawled into bed only to see the lights of his van flash over the hill.

'I was thinking you were needing meat,' said our crofter next morning, 'but you were no at the van.' We are not used to keeping such late shopping hours.

I can never wait for the sweet buyers, who always outstrip me to the van, to finish their purchasing. I consider it the Divine Right of Skippers to jump the queue shamelessly, buy two dozen loaves, hundreds of apples and oranges, pounds of butter, cooking fat, sugar and flour and then to commandeer slaves to hump everything back to camp. My patience is not consistent. Behind dozens of sweet toothed children it is prefixed with 'im'.

'Let me come,' I say expecting to be allowed to pass. 'I've got to get this lot back to camp and see to the fire if you lot want any supper tonight.'

Should those in front of me be islanders my patience is profound. I find I can sit placidly on the roadside listening to the Gaelic and the laughter which accompanies it, wishing only that I could understand and share the joke. I can wriggle my bare toes in the sand, forget the fire and wait indefinitely.

'If you had the Gaelic I could tell you many things,' said Grannie. She found the English difficult but many Hebrideans are quite bi-lingual and change from Gaelic to English almost in mid-sentence. The joke, however, can be just as amusing in English.

Margaret and I stood behind an island housewife in the cosy space between the steering wheel, the boxes of bread, the van steps and the counter and listened to the teasing of the van driver whilst the woman paid for her groceries. She was paying her bill with an unusual number of pennies. There was much laughter and she turned to Margaret and said, 'I took those singing in the hotel bar last night.' We know she seldom leaves the croft except to go to church.

Pat Roberts and I were being given a strupag in the same good lady's house one very stormy evening during a very wet camp.

'Och, Chean,' she said. 'I cannot tell what Pat is saying at all!'

'Neither can I when she is on the phone,' I confided.

Pat wanted to know why. The answer came in Gaelic and there was laughter. 'My mother says she doesn't know how to say it in English,' said Morag. 'She's thinking that Pat has a lisp.'

'Not a lisp,' said goodnatured Pat. 'I cannot roll my 'r's. I wanted to call my first baby Rachel but everyone said I couldn't have a Wachel Woberts.'

Many of the elderly crofters' wives have hardly travelled at all. I knew one old lady who told me she had never been even to the other end of her own small island let alone visit the Mainland, but the world does not seem small to them. An old Tiree woman was asking after a friend who lived on the east side of the island. Tiree is flat and treeless and no more than four miles across at the widest point. She was told that her friend was not well at all.

'No more she will be, living on the east,' she said. 'She'd have no trouble at all if she were to live on the west.'

The old people of the Hebrides have great character. It exhibits itself in the lined and weather beaten faces and in their tenacity for life. One such friend of ours used to be the house keeper at Salum House and she made the best treacle scones I have ever tasted. When she retired we used to visit her annually in the small, white cottage perched on the edge of Salum Bay. We were sorry to hear that she had had a stroke, a 'shock' as they say in the islands. She recovered sufficiently to carry on at her cottage but took another 'shock' sometime later and this time it happened when she was on the machair, some way from home. Unnoticed by anyone she spent the whole night outside unable to move.

'Och, put it was a peautiful night,' she told us. 'It was a peautiful night indeed. I'm sure I don't know what I would have done at all if it had peen wet. There was plenty of stars.'

That was several years ago. A contemporary of mine and I visited her recently. She knew me but Joan she had never met. Her eyes kept wandering from me to my friend until, at last, she commented with unembarrassed admiration, 'That girl has got peautiful teeth.'

Joan was delighted to be referred to in such youthful terms and laughingly revealed the beautiful teeth to better advantage. She was complimented again and again in the next few minutes and, in fairness, I told the old lady that it was a dentist and not Nature that had created those 'peautiful teeth.'

'Och, well,' she said, 'and I would never have known,' whereupon all the subsequent conversation was punctuated by, 'That dentist has made peautiful teeth, I'm sure I thought they were your own.'

'I'll tell him when I see him, shall I?' asked my delighted friend.

'Och yes, you do chust that,' said Bella. 'Tell him he should come to Tiree if he can make peautiful teeth like that.'

There are those of our island friends who have given so much more than we can ever repay and some who have died so that it is only by cherishing their memory that we can ever absolve some of our debt.

Among the most colourful characters was Calum MacLean of Salum to whom, above all, we owe the growth of our courage and knowledge to return again and again to the Hebrides. In the first learning years it was Calum who gave us the confidence we needed. It was born of the security, wisdom and welcome he always extended and it was through him that the children first learned to love dancing and singing and to appreciate honesty and accept trust.

When he died we lost a true friend, a kind and honest gentleman and our tribute to him hangs in the old people's home at Scarinsh. For those who knew him each happy camp is an act of remembrance. Not only was he our friend he was also our benefactor, providing us with the necessities of life, water, food and shelter. Just outside the house at Salum stood a wooden shed which was Calum's shop and, if you knew where to find it, he sold everything; food, clothing, wellingtons, paint, cattle food, toilet requisites, lamps, earthenware, buckets, fishing tackle, sweets, medicines and bottled gas.

Our friend was not a tidy gentleman. He never cleaned out his old stock or swept his floor. We did this for him every year. Seldom did he even man the shop. The till was always left open and many is the time I have gone behind the counter to serve the children with sweets.

The slate bearing our purchases was an open pad on which we were trusted implicitly to record the cornflakes, sugar, porridge oats, eggs, flour and tomatoes; the butter, cheese, tea and cooking fat; the tinned goods, oranges, bread and salt and jam and coffee we needed every day. The trust he put in our honesty gave us stature and there was not one child who neglected to pay him or would have taken advantage of his absentmindedness.

I repaid him as best I could in kind. When the day of our departure came the grocery bill had grown to many pages. I would take out my cheque book to pay and from the 'deep litter' (his name for the clutter on his desk) he would take the pad and flick over the pages, marvelling at the enormity of our appetites.

'Och Chean,' he would say, 'I was going to add up this bill for Buckingham Palace last night but I had a visitor.' He would begin a tale which took long in the telling and then he would say, 'I'll need a little time to add up a thing like that!' and I would sign the cheque and offer him the otherwise blank piece of paper. He would take it without a word. He was not afraid to be trusted any more than I was.

We have found this unique relationship, this mutual trust, throughout the islands and there is no feeling so warm or so rewarding. There was another gentleman to whom I owed money and who did not have the bill ready for me when I wanted to pay. I also wanted to borrow some money from him for we had unwittingly gone to the bank on a Scottish Bank Holiday and I desperately needed some cash for the journey home. My friend was only too pleased to let me have twenty-five pounds.

I left him with a blank cheque and instructions to add up my bill, increase it by twenty-five pounds and fill in the cheque. Many weeks later I got my statement from the bank and, not having heard anything from my friend and wishing to get my accounts straight, I looked up the number of the cheque. The amount beside it was so small I felt sure the twenty-five pounds had not been added on at all so I wrote at once. I received a letter confirming this but saying I was not to worry as it would not be long before I was back on the island. I sent a cheque straight away.

Margaret hired bicycles from a shop near the pier and when she returned them the owner was very loathe to ask his price. Like many of the islanders we know he was very embarrassed by money transactions. 'Och, well,' he said with a shake of the head and a gesture which dismissed the subject. 'You'll be here next year anyway.' She had to take the money out of her purse and press the point. I do believe, however, that the islanders are shrewd. I think they would know at once if someone were not to be trusted and I do not think they would be doing business with him at all.

Children swarmed round Calum and he loved them all. They leaned on him and told him their secrets, sitting on his knee, fingering his bagpipes and treating him as they would a favourite uncle or a beloved grandfather. He knew how to talk to them but when he turned to an adult his conversation was mature, often intellectual, frequently profound. And beneath his wisdom there bubbled the most delightful humour which made him the ideal host.

He was paternally proud of his native island, knew what fame had come to her sons and daughters and was never tired of talking about them. It pleased him to tell us over and over again that Tiree was famous for its sea captains, its ministers and its men. He had played host to important visitors to the island and he could entertain a listener until well into the small hours with his stories, serious and amusing.

It grieved us to see him failing and becoming crippled with varicose veins in his legs and we took pleasure in helping him. Many is the time I have milked his cow. She was a temperamental old lady and though I milked her I never loosed her from the stall and let her free onto the machair.

One day Calum's housekeeper complained that Calum was away and the cow had not been let out. 'Och, she's that terrible with her horns,' she grumbled. 'She'll be lifting me off my feet!'

My sister spends all her life with animals and an old cow was no problem even if she did have horns.

'Well, I'm warning you. That's a terrible cow Calum has chust now,' said the experienced lady feelingly.

64

Margaret is only small. She went to the byre and leaned over the docile old lady's neck to release her and for the first time in her life found herself wrapped round an animal's neck and her feet well and truly off the floor.

'Wasn't I after telling you that would happen,' laughed our friend. 'That's a terrible cow chust.'

Calum had trouble with her too. According to our veterinary friend he had increasing difficulty in taking her to the bull as his own walking days were over. Determined not to be beaten by a 'galivanting' cow Calum was trying to persuade her to enter his van by pulling on a rope through his front window. A neighbour had come down the lane on her bicycle. 'Och, Calum,' she had said, 'for why are you trying to get the cow into the van?'

'Well,' he'd answered. 'She's needing to go to the bull and she canna ride the bicycle.'

It seems Calum's cows were no strangers to his van. One had been a litter making passenger one afternoon when Calum was reminded that he was to meet a guest from the plane. Unembarrassed by the odorous and bespattered state of the delapidated vehicle, the owner of Salum House drove out to meet his paying guest at the airport and found her already waiting.

'Would you be wanting Salum?' he enquired. 'If you'll chust be getting into the van now.'

She was silently shocked by the state of it, mechanically and hygienically and asked timidly, 'How far is it?'

'Och, well,' said the good man, 'and it will chust be approximately about eight miles.'

Having no alternative she carefully seated herself in the passenger seat and resigned herself to the smell of cow and the rattle of the bone shaker. They had travelled about half the distance in silence when she asked, 'Do you work at the House?'

There would be a twinkle, I'm sure, under the heavy eyebrows. 'Well,' said Calum, 'I'm what you might call a Knockabout. If there's a chob to be done I'm more than likely to get it.'

Later, when his visitor saw him wandering about the house she enquired of a fellow guest if the workmen were allowed the freedom of the house.

'That's not a workman,' she was told. 'That's the proprietor.'

Calum was telling us one year that Tiree had been used as a garden for Iona by the monks. 'They would not have a woman on the island,' he informed us. 'I believe they would not have a cow on the island either on account of its being a woman too. They kept their cows on another island and I'm thinking that they would have women there to look after the animals.' His eyes suddenly began to twinkle. 'I believe the monks were very good swimmers,' he said.

Calum himself was a bachelor but he had a great respect for women and he was very kind. He was amazed at the strength of the island women and was telling us of one island lady who had given birth to her fifth son during the night. Wishing to be helpful he had gone early to her croft to offer to milk her cow. He arrived too late for

65

she was already in the byre. The job was just finished. 'You're a daft woman,' he had said. 'You should no be up at all.'

'Whist'.' she had replied. 'Can ye no see I'm not up at all. I'm still in my night gown.'

We only knew this lady at a much later date but her indomitable spirit we admired tremendously. It was her fear that she might one day lose her independence. When the only son to remain on the island decided to emigrate with his young family to Australia, she rented his adjacent cottage to summer visitors.

One year I had promised to take my family for a 'cuppan' one evening late in May. My mother, a few years younger than the eighty year old Mrs MacLean, was distressed by the fact that we had spent longer on the Tràigh à Bheidhe, at Balephuil, than we'd intended. Undaunted by the late hour we found this determined woman painting the concrete floor of the cottage ready for the season.

'Whatever do you think you are doing at this time of night?' I remonstrated.

'Shaw,' she replied, 'my bed's not ready for me yet.'

I had great difficulty in persuading her to let me finish painting the floor its gay pillar box red whilst she put on the kettle. She was always busy and died as she would have wished, suddenly, whilst working in her kitchen.

Calum had working for him at that time an enormously heavy man called Big Neil. He was an infinitely gentle man who loved the myriads of daisies which flourish on Tiree. Calum was telling us one day that, in spring, a sparrow hawk had chased an unfortunate victim and it had flown for safety into the exhaust pipe of the tractor that Big Neil was using.

'He's a patient man, Big Neil,' marvelled Calum. 'He spent all morning taking off the exhaust and he was that gentle the wee sparrow flew out alive.'

Gentle, maybe, but Big Neil was strong. When he tightened the ropes on our skips you could feel them go taut like bow strings.

There was nothing Calum enjoyed more than to take us to the small, United Free Presbyterian Church. On these occasions he would be 'dressed' as the islanders say. We do not use the verb unqualified as they do and it always amuses our Yorkshire sense of humour.

'Would that be John MacLeod I saw yesterday?' I said one day to an island friend. There are hundreds of John MacLeods. 'He was looking much heavier and very prosperous.'

'Aye, that would be him all right,' said Angus. 'I'm thinking you'll have seen him dressed. You'll no' have seen him dressed before.'

The service in the little church on Tiree was conducted by an island man with the happiest face I have ever seen. Calum led us in as if we were all his family. Then he proudly sat beside me and his great voice rang out the psalms. I do believe we gave him as much pleasure as he gave us. After the service he would always ask, 'And did you echoy the service, Chean?'

I generally had for the preacher generated happiness all the time he was telling us that if our names were not in the Lamb's Book of Life we would be cast into a sea of fire. Perhaps we will but his name will be in the book, I'm sure. I never met the man but what I felt the better for it.

Too many of us would pile into Calum's ricketty old van and he would drive slowly home as was befitting for the Sabbath. The van would not respect the day but would make the same dreadful noises that it made on weekdays. There would be the same terrible grumbling from the gear box and the same loud reports from the exhaust.

Deeply religious though he was Calum could laugh and make light of it too. We were going to a film show in the Church Hall on the other side of the island and we intended to swim at Balephuil and not return to camp before the show. Margaret was worried in case shorts in the Church Hall would be frowned upon and asked Calum if we should take skirts. She was no doubt remembering that day on Harris when we had unknowingly clambered onto the Communion Bus, bare legged and encumbered with rucksacks. We had tried to cover our knees but rucksacks make poor skirts and we were most embarrassed.

Calum's eyes had twinkled with merriment and wickedness. 'I believe it says in the Good Book that a woman should wear something on her head,' he said. 'I don't believe it mentions bottoms at all.'

Since then we have often gone to church in shorts, if the weather has been wet, and we have taken our skirts in plastic bags and shuffled into them on arrival. There was a very wet day when the two miles to Kirkapol seemed endless. I can still see Simon trudging along with the water dripping from his cagoule into his outsize boots. Arriving at the church we exchanged our shorts for the dignity of skirts and in the confusion of the moment Amanda whispered, 'You've gotta laugh!'

The electric blow heaters had been switched on below the pulpit, on the square of carpet in front of the first pew. When we sat down for the sermon I glanced, from my side seat, at the rows and rows of children and noticed that those on the front row had all silently removed their shoes. They had unobtrusively placed the soggy articles before the fire and a hundred bare toes curled up, pink and clean in front of the heaters. I saw Helen smile and wriggle hers contentedly.

The rest of that dreadfully wet day we spent in Marian MacLean's cottage enjoying a Sabbath calm, a contentment, a warmth and a security, safe from the driving rain which beat incessantly on the window panes. Willie MacIntosh and his wife Janet and their three small, kilted boys came and Janet played her accordian for our favourite hymns. Many children cluttered the floor of the small living room. Others filled the bedroom, the kitchen and the passageway. Rebecca read to us from the Bible and Willie talked to us in his soft island lilt, whilst outside the clouds broke. Only semi-darkness came for a full moon rose to guide us back to camp.

Jackie and Judith were sensitive to the peace of that wet Sunday. For the morning service the next day they wrote,

'Do we ever stop to think how much we have to be grateful for? We take everything You offer and give little in return. You give us eyes so that we can see this wonderful island, You give us speech so that we can praise You, ears that we may hear Your Word.

When the cold came we found warmth, when the rains came we found shelter, from the wind we found protection and when the sun came we found strength to enjoy it.

We take part of our day to thank You, Lord.'

The last time we saw Calum he was sitting up smiling in his bed in the old people's home at Scarinish. As County Councillor for Coll and Tiree he had been instrumental in the building of it and Willie became the gardener. It was fitting that he should be taken there to recuperate after a vicious nose bleed.

It happened two days after our arrival. He had seemed so well and had made a great fuss of the children and fed the usual crowd whilst we had waited for the lorry on our arrival. When I made an early call, two days later, I found him still in bed. The room was in a shambles, the sheets and bed covers saturated with blood.

Calum had suddenly become a very old man. He was taken to Scarinish and we were left in the unenviable position of having to get water from his house and food from his shop in his absence. We did everything we could to leave all neat and tidy for his return. It was a wet camp and we had to use the barn frequently. He insisted that we should hold our usual barn dance and Charlie offered to come and play the accordian for us. We had lost our piper and in a way we were glad there was none other to take his place.

Every one of us went to Scarinish to pay him the highest mark of honour that we knew. By some premonition we had come prepared with a Thanks Badge of the Guide Movement to which most of us belong. I can see them all, Grace and Janet, Loraine, Alison, Stuart, David, Julie, Viv, Joanna, Prue and Jonathan and another forty more.

Because of his weakness the masses collected outside the big French window. Tall Sylvia and Linda and Julia, Hilary, Barbara, Gwen, little Doreen and Marta and Kathryn. Their singing, smiling faces were arranged in tiers so that everyone could see and be seen. A few of us went inside. Wendy was chosen to present the Award. Paul went into the bedroom, too, because his affection for the old man was suddenly a thing which hurt and he wanted to shake his hand and wish him well. Paul had been with us since he was ten and he looked a man now at sixteen. Hazel was there too. It was a moving moment. We were all in tears.

Then the singing chorus from the window began a special song, composed just for him, about his beloved Tiree. They finished with 'For he's a jolly good fellow, and so say all of us.' I do not think we could have pleased him more.

Calum recovered. We had a letter from him later in the year to say that he'd returned home and was even doing a bit of gardening. The letter was very verbose, full of extravagent adjectives and a little pompous. Though Gaelic was his language he wrote English well.

A few days later he was dead. He was preparing to go to a dinner on the island where he was to be speaker. He had a sudden heart attack and died shortly in the old people's home. We felt bereft of a true friend, a real island gentleman and it was sometime before we could bring ourselves to go back to Tiree.

Calum left us and so did Angela. He was old but she was incredibly young and so kind that we all loved her. We were grateful to her for the meals she gave us and the strupags sitting on her kitchen floor but we loved her most of all for the barn dances she organised in Leverburgh Hall. No one was gayer than Angela nor more uncomplaining. Her house was always full of visitors and relatives. Children and all were welcome. She taught us a great deal about Hebridean hospitality and courtesy.

Whoever calls at the farm on which we live, coffee is offered, or a cup of tea, or a meal. There is no limit to our hospitality but we always ask. Should the offer be accepted the abundance of our table could not be surpassed but if the offer is declined, on account of the visitor having recently eaten or being just on the point of going home to a meal, his refusal is accepted. In the Hebrides we are never asked. Immediately we enter the house the kettle is put on the stove. If we have just had a meal we say, 'Don't bother with a cup of tea. We've just eaten.' Our refusal is never accepted.

The islands are full of people whose hospitality is so positive that it cannot be stemmed. The plates they give us to hold on our knees are so temptingly full of pancakes and scones piled high with crowdie that few could resist for long. There is no hospitality to compete with that of a crofter's wife and in the process of doing justice to her excellent cooking and her delicious butter and crowdie we have often eaten far too much and put inches on our waist lines.

Angela taught us that it was gracious to accept without question for nothing gives the Hebrideans more pleasure. Margaret and I arrived in Northton one evening after an excellent meal at the little cafe which used to be in Leverburgh. It had been a pleasant tea party and we had been especially invited to it by a friend from Strond.

Full to bursting point with the good food, we'd driven no more than a couple of miles to Northton to see Angela about the barn dance she was organising.

'We've just had tea with Annie,' we announced hoping to prevent her from putting on the kettle she was filling.

'You'll have a strupag,' she said.

'Honestly Angela, we're bursting!'

'Och, it's only a wee bit in your hand,' said Angela, busily cutting slices of bread. 'I believe everyone in Harris knew you were at the cafe and I said to myself Chean and Margaret will be coming and we can talk about the céilidh.' She was opening a tin of meat and making sandwiches. We knew her very well and tried to prevent her. It was no more than an hour since we had eaten.

'Och,' she insisted, 'the sandwiches are so small. Do you remember the time, Chean, when all the Guides were sitting on the floor and we fed them all? I've got the piper for the social, and the singers and Neil will play the accordian.' She put out some scones. 'There's crowdie and cream. I know you like the crowdie.' And there wasn't a thing we could do about it.

Whilst we were eating she asked us if we were going to see a very old lady we knew who lived further down the township. Mary MacKay has since died, too. She was very frail, her sight was poor and she often cried when we went to see her and talked a lot about the days when she had been fit enough to entertain a score of us, sitting cross-legged on her floor.

'Come with us, Angela,' I said. 'It'll make things easier.'

So, shortly after we'd eaten, we put Angela into the landrover and drove to the old lady's house at the end of the straggling township. Though almost blind she knew and clung to us. Then she spoke to Angela in Gaelic and though we do not speak the language we understand some of it. We knew with certainty that she was telling Angela to put on the kettle and make a strupag. And, without a word, Angela followed her instructions and we ate it unprotestingly whilst the old lady beamed her pleasure.

Dear Angela. We could not believe it when we heard that she had died. She was younger than I and her laughter still rings for us in Harris.

We first met our friend from Strond fifteen years ago when we came to Harris with Janet and Ann and found the place so many have since called Paradise. She was working alone at the peats and we had just had an unusual ride on a bus. We had been walking from Finsbay towards Leverburgh along the inland road that goes by Loch Langavat. The empty bus had pulled up behind us and the driver had called, 'Would you be wanting a lift? I'm away to the peats.'

It was a very hot day and we were taken several miles along the road before the driver stopped by a lonely peat bog and said that this was as far as he was going. We took out our money to pay our fares.

'Och, I do not want any money,' he said. 'I was going that way anyway.'

A mile or two further along the road we saw a lady working alone at the peats. It was very hot and she was struggling single handed. We called to her asking if we could help and she was delighted. There were four of us and it made a tremendous difference to her. We all worked together for an hour until the job was completed.

She was excited and grateful and her generosity and delight have effervesced ever since. Her kindness has put us forever in her debt. No camp is complete without her vivid and colourful presence at one of our campfires when she arrives like Father Christmas with a bag full of goodies for the children. No Harris céilidh is complete without her, no sing-song finished until we have sung 'Amazing Grace' for her. No visit to Harris is over if we have not seen her in Strond or Leverburgh, Northton or Tarbert or Luskentyre. She is as much a part of our visits to Harris as the mountains and the sea.

It was on our first visit to Harris that we found the two bachelors who were to provide us with a camp site for so many years. They uncomplainingly put up with our continual drawing of water from their tap, each year they cut extra peat for us to burn so extravagently and like John Lachie, on Tiree, they plant more rows of potatoes for our hungry appetites. Only once have they been unable to supply us with potatoes.

'I'm afraid they are too small this year,' we were told. 'We were terrible late with the planting. Och, the airlies were not planted airly at all.'

As I write this I am suddenly afraid we take too much for granted. They work long hours on our behalf and I hope they know how grateful we are. The two men are alone now but I remember a time when both their parents were alive. The old lady was confined to her wheelchair but she was excellently cared for. She had a delightful sense of humour. I remember her youngest son expounding one of his theories at great length. Suddenly the old lady's face broke into a hundred smiles and she said, 'Och, Iain, I'm sure you speak like an experienced man!'

Their croft stands on the edge of the world where God has suddenly excelled himself with His paint brush. As soon as we saw it we could not resist the impulse to bring children there and asked immediately. The men were at the hay and they leaned on their scythes and talked to us about the possibility. They are kind, strong men who have each spent some time alone, shepherding sheep on the island of Pabbay. One of the most interesting evenings we have ever spent was in their company listening to Donald Alick tell how he was once asked to take Peter Scott out to St Kilda.

Before we left, on our first visit to Harris in 1962, we bought tweed woven on a Hattersley loom, a loom manufactured in our home town. In so doing we began a much valued friendship with a family who live only a few feet from the shore. Katie and Angus live in a warm and lovely cottage with their daughters Ann and Kathleen. The view from their window surpasses all other and their hospitality is second to none. We have seen their children grow from babyhood and it was the youngest, Kathleen, who astonished us with her bi-lingual skill at the age of five when she began learning English at school. The two children were intrigued with our tents and we, in turn, were fascinated with their agility on the rocks, with the ease with which they changed from English into Gaelic and the wonder of their being able to read both languages at the age of six.

From Katie we, and our Yorkshire children, have bought yards and yards of tweed and innumerable pairs of socks and pom-pom hats; tweed woven from the wool of the Blackface sheep in Angus's flock, dyed with natural dyes scraped from the rocks at the foot of the Ben and socks and hats knitted from wool spun and twisted on the well worn spinning wheel. For fifteen years we have dressed almost exclusively in Harris Tweed, appreciative of its warmth and durability and loving the unique smell of hill and sea and peat bog which clings to it and proves it genuine.

One day, during our stay, when weather and programme permit, the adults in our party will accept an annual invitation to Katie's for an evening meal. They will relax at the well filled table, enjoying a civilised meal, watching the sun gild the hills of Seilebost across the estuary and counting in double figures the colours of the rising tide.

Angus's parents occupy the house next door. The twin cottages lie close together for protection. We met the older couple on our first visit and have loved them ever since. On a hillock beside the house the old man invariably stood, gazing out across the bay, remembering his long years at sea and the seven times he had been round the world. Remembering, too, how he just missed the 'Iolaire' on the last, fateful journey to Stornoway, at the end of the first World War, when so many island men were lost returning home from active service.

We saw him often in the years that followed and he eventually became housebound but, now he is no longer with us, it is on the hillock that I will always remember him, standing motionless as a captain might stand on the bridge of his ship. His cheerful wife has a sense of humour unsurpassed by any other person I know and if I had but one more hour to live I would judge it well spent in her company. Her open arms welcome us to the house and to the country and no matter how many children follow us into her house they are welcome.

It must surely be the laughter which has drawn us back again and again to the Western Isles. We are so bored with the coarse apology for humour which is fed to us day by day on the television that it is refreshing to meet a people who have not lost the art of real mirth, to be with a group of children who have learned to generate it and to work with colleagues whose laughter is so infectious.

Perhaps it is the islanders' excellent but strange use of their second language or perhaps it is the reflection of laughter in their eyes but when I am introduced to an 'English wife from Glasgow' I know instinctively that in a minute we will all be laughing.

'But Glasgow is in Scotland,' I say.

'Ach, she's English right enough. She's no the Gaelic.'

If we comment on the late hour at which the good lady goes to bed we know before we hear it that the reply will be worth remembering. 'Ach, I would not go to bed at all were it not to give my teeth a rest.'

Nowhere am I more sure of our safety and this is no small comfort when we have so many children. Ian Hillcrest once offered to lend us his house at Balephetrish if the bad weather continued. Not many people would lend their house to three women and fifty children. If our beds are wet because of storm in the night I know that they will be dried. If we have to abandon camp and take shelter for the night whilst the tempest rages, I know that I have only to ask the crofter and he will bring his old van into the field and we will be able to pack it tight with sleeping bags for our temporary exodus. The fact that the van will not start does not perturb me nor am I unsettled by the calm, 'By g-golly, I do b-believe she's out of petrol!' Petrol comes from some-where. People in these isolated places have grown resourceful.

If the weather makes it impossible to sleep out I only have to ask one of our dearest friends. 'Yes, yes, the children can sleep in the house, Chean. Oh yes, dear. Chust bring them in. They can sleep on the living room floor and in the sitting room and in the bedrooms too!'

Until recently Grannie sat by the stove in this hospitable house. Had she lived just a few more years she would have been a hundred years old. She was still able to tell us of her childhood in Eileananabuich and of the early years she spent at Lusken-tyre as housekeeper to Lord Dunmore. And even at her great age she was still able to make beautiful pancakes. It was her greatest sorrow that we had no Gaelic for she found the English difficult. Her own mistakes amused her.

'Take another of the pancakes,' she coaxed us one day. 'I made them tomorrow.' I can still hear her laughter.

There was so much that she wanted to do for us that she kept her daughter busy. 'Make them a cloutie dumpling,' she would order.

'I'll show them how to make one,' promised Rachel. 'Send the girls up and I'll show them how to make a cloutie.'

The next day Prue and Joanna would go to their cooking lesson and after they had put the dumpling in the pot to boil they would return to camp full of importance and satisfaction. Later in the evening they would go to collect it and they would bear it hot and steaming into the D'abri, like Mrs Cratchit and no dumpling would taste better.

Rachel is our taxi, our telephone our postman, our bottled gas agent. She is our hotel, our messenger and our haulage contractor. But most of all she is our friend. Just a few days ago we planned a surprise for her. For some time a Thanks Badge had lain in its little box within the muddle which accumulates in my handbag. We only awaited the right opportunity. It came.

The midges have been pretty bad this year and I am sure she thought we had all come to take refuge from their vicious assault when fifty of us, along with a good friend, Elsie Mackie from Tarbert, invaded her living room.

'I've brought you some visitors,' I announced unnecessarily. It is a big room which will hold fifty people even if most of them sit on the floor and when we seated her on the chair nearest the stove she looked down on a sea of expectant faces. Catherine pinned on the silver brooch with the same affection with which Wendy pinned on Calum's, seven years ago, and Rachel accepted it graciously.

'I feel like the Queen,' she said. The award had been deserved a hundred times.

There are, I know, families whose friends keep away because of the children. People come to us because of our children and they have made many of our friends for us. Not only island children but adults who give them lifts in cars. Fellow campers and hikers find their way to our fire via our children and in their turn the children go to the crofts, they help feed the calves and pet lambs, play with the pups and dig the potatoes. At the thatched, white cottage on Tiree where we get our potatoes, carrots and milk, Janet was a daily visitor to milk the cow.

I remember watching some crofters dig potatoes. I was accompanied by Jean, a little girl who followed me perpetually because she was rather insecure and a long way from home. She also talked continually.

'These potatoes are just like my mother's in her garden,' she informed me. Then, unexpectedly she made the outrageous suggestion. 'Skipper, do you make your own manure?'

Few islanders cultivate a garden in the sense that we know it. I know one excellent gardener, Ted Cadden of Horgabost. Chris and Viv and Margie picked half a hundredweight of gooseberries from his bushes one year. Neil was a fine gardener too. He loved his flowers and he loved children. There were three that could not keep away and his wife was always feeding them. They had no children of their own but it never mattered how many children were sent to dry their wet hair before night fall, nor how many little ones I sent to shelter from the rain whilst we struggled with a difficult pitch.

One day I found Pat, Denise and Linda saying 'Goodbye' and having a strupag before leaving. It was a beautiful evening, silver and green and gold. One on which to leave, for then the longing to return is a living, breathing need. The girls were in tears, moved by their happiness, their sadness and the almost ethereal beauty.

I was a little harrassed by the strike and distubed yet rewarded by the children's tears. I was in no mood to taste what Annie placed before me. 'How do you like my date and walnut cake?' my hostess asked and I had to confess that I was all of a do-dah and didn't know what I'd been eating at all. We all laughed but the episode has never been forgotten. I have eaten many date and walnut cakes there in the years that have followed and made sure that I enjoyed every one. Our hostess is a widow now, but we still crowd into her kitchen just as frequently, use her bathroom and employ her nephew as accordianist when we have our barbecues and dances.

The most rewarding bath I take each year is the one which comes immediately after the strike. The islanders have lovely bathrooms and their luxury is increased when the only competition is our 'uncivilised loo.' On Harris the good lady who provides our milk and crowdie and our rhubarb jam also provides us with our bath after the strike. A few of us are very dirty for the black billies have to be cleaned, the ashes removed from the fire and the sods replaced.

Not every strike is dry to the end. Incredible though this may seem we have only taken down two wet tents in twenty years, but sometimes we have had to hurry and before we have finished every job that has to be done, the heavens have opened. I remember that on one such occasion I was offered a lift when the only dry article of clothing I wore was my shorts. But the rain had taken the car's owner by surprise too and his passenger window had not been closed. A lake had formed on the leather seat which my shorts soaked up like blotting paper.

On these occasions a bath is luxury indeed. I remember the first time I was offered one. Lexy brought me warm, clean towels, whiter than I had ever seen before. 'I can't use those,' I said, displaying my dirty hands and knees. 'They're far too clean!'

Security is a rare gift when one is five hundred miles away from home but it is ours. Fortunately we have had to call the doctor on very few occasions and each time he has been willing to help no less than the crofters themselves. We called the Tarbert doctor to visit one of our Canadian girls at close on midnight. We were spending the night in Tarbert school and she did some unsuccessful gymnastics, in her sleeping bag and came down very heavily. The noise her head made when it crashed on the floor and the headache which followed made us anxious. We need not have been and the doctor enjoyed a long chat with her about Canada.

Another Canadian girl we had, Fiona, suffered a very swollen foot, the result of being sat on by quite the plumpest member of our party. As we were in Stornoway we played safe by having it X-rayed only to find no damage had been done. We took Jessie Kate to see the Tiree doctor. She had journeyed down to Yorkshire to spend a week with us, she and the Cathy we always call Cathy Harris. They had then returned with us to Tiree for the summer camp. She complained of a sore tummy. We did not know how to interpret 'sore' as it was obviously an inadequate translation form the Gaelic.

As we were to pass the surgery at Baugh, on our way to a film show, we decided to ask his opinion. There were cows on the machair in front of the doctor's house and I am still sheepish about the fact that I, a farmer's daughter, left the garden gate open and every cow had to be chased out. Inside we found the surgery somewhat cluttered. It amused us that the doctor had to remove eggs from his examination table before he could lift up Jessie Kate. He found little wrong but we made the acquaintance of a doctor who was soon to become a practitioner in our own town, with a daughter, Chris, who was to become one of our campers.

Jessie Kate had never seen pigs before she was on holiday with us. There are no pigs on Harris and when I asked some children how big they imagined a pig to be they thought no bigger than a sheep. When Jessie Kate saw our sows she thought they must be elephants.

'Why don't you keep a pig or two?' Margaret asked a crofter one day.

'P p p pigs and Members of P p parliament,' he stuttered in disgust. 'Shoot 'em!'

A previous doctor on Tiree had kindly left his surgery one early evening to rush to Julie. She began camping with us when she was only seven. In those days the Lone Ranger was a very popular television programme. Julie could imitate his unique leap onto his horse's back and she continually practised this technique on us. She would take a long run on the beach, leap courageously into the air and land on our backs whether or not we were expecting the sudden burden.

One afternoon we had been visiting an old lady up at Upper Vaul, about a mile away from camp. We had just begun the return journey when our energetic baby took to the air and mounted me with vigour. In doing so she twisted something in her tummy which put her into considerable pain. It was, and still is, the worst fright we have ever had. Julie is my god daughter and she has spent all her holidays with us since she was a baby. This was her first camp.

The pain was too severe for us to touch or carry her and our progress back to camp was frighteningly slow. As soon as we could we sent for Calum, with the van, to take her to Salum House and we sent for the doctor. He drove quickly over from Baugh and within minutes of his arrival Julie was very sick, so violently so that whatever had been twisted untied itself and when the doctor came he could find nothing wrong.

He was not angry. He did not criticise us for calling for him, nor dispute that there had been an urgent need but I did get the impression that he thought me all kinds of a fool to bring a seven year old, four hundred miles away from home, five hours by sea from Oban, to camp under canvas.

Perhaps I was, but now, thirteen years later, I have no regrets. Julie has camped with us eleven times and her enjoyment and ours in her presence, has been indisputable.

One year we visited a doctor in Tobermory who treated the cut on Jane's foot and then discovered that he had been at Leeds University with her father, had played on Keighley Golf Course, practised in Hebden Bridge and knew one of our friends at nearby White Windows Cheshire Home. It's a small world. We called out the Portree doctor very late at night for Joanna. She was wheezing alarmingly. She was possibly alergic to something, maybe the excess of sheep's wool when she had been helping with the shearing at the Fank. He was a kind young man who produced just the right remedy to ensure a good night's rest and gave us an excellent prescription for the morning.

But quite the most unusual visit to a doctor we ever made was because of Mandy and her sore foot. It had been bothering her for a few days and when we struck camp it was quite painful and swollen as if she had something lodged in the sole which had gone septic. We tried putting it in very hot water in the wash basin of the Ladies' Room on the Hebrides, but it aggravated rather than helped.

I decided to see if there was a ship's doctor on board and Mandy and I were taken on to the bridge to see the Captain and the Mate who was responsible for the First Aid on the boat. We had a very interesting half hour watching the controls and listening to the wireless operator whilst the Mate investigated the foot, dressed it with disinfectant and advised us to see a doctor.

The bus driver on the next stage of our journey said he knew a surgeon on the island who would attend to it. He reassured Mandy that we would not be long before we reached the house where he lived. The surgery was an annex on a modern bungalow somewhere on Skye and the door was closed. On it there was a notice which said, 'You are entering a smokeless zone.' We were readily admitted through the kitchen door.

The surgeon himself turned out to be a patient, poor soul. One leg was completely encased in plaster and he was convalescing in his dressing gown by the kitchen fire. A locum was doing his practice for him. We were fortunate to find the elderly doctor in and were taken into the surgery for Mandy's foot to be inspected. The doctor looked excited and surprised by what he saw.

'Come with me, Amanda,' he said. 'I want my friend to see this.' He led her, hopping on one leg, into the kitchen and left me to imagine all sorts of things. When they returned he seated Mandy and took a very thick volume from a well stocked bookcase. He flicked through the pages becoming more and more delighted by his discovery.

'Yes, yes,' he kept saying. 'Amanda's got orf.'

'Orf,' I said, 'what's that?'

'It's a sheep disease and very rare,' said the doctor. 'Sometimes a shepherd gets it on his hands when he has been shearing sheep. Perhaps Amanda has trodden on some infected wool. Has she been barefoot?'

Barefoot! None of us wear shoes on the islands.

'There is no known cure,' he informed us, 'but it is self healing. It will clear up in a few weeks. I will give her something for the pain but unfortunately these pills might make her constipated.' He was obviously pleased with his diagnosis. 'I've only seen it once before,' he said.

We thanked him gratefully and returned to the bus. Our driver, cast in the kindly mould of all Hebridean bus drivers, had phoned through to Armadale asking for the boat to be delayed against our late arrival.

'What's the matter with you, Mandy?' everyone wanted to know.

'I've got orf and something to make me constipated,' was the dour reply.

Indebted as we are to so many friends our only consolation is that the islanders seem to enjoy our visits as much as we do. There was an old man on Barra to whom we owed a great deal. Seven of us had used his field, accepted milk and eggs, warmed ourselves by his stove and eaten at his wife's table. On some of these luxuries a price cannot be put, but every camper can pay ground rent and milk and eggs are saleable commodities. But he would take no payment.

'Not at all,' he shook his head emphatically. 'The pleasure of your company is all the payment we required.'

There are, I'm pleased to say, other ways in which we can repay such kindnesses.

As we trek along together, as we trek along,
Shall we sing a song together, shall we sing a song?
Though the road may be weary, still our hearts will be cheery,
As we sing a song, as we trek along.

We'll go singing on together, we'll go singing on,
As we trek along together as we trek along.
Love, live, laughter and sorrow, who knows what comes tomorrow,
Who knows, who cares, as we trek along.

Chapter Seven

BARRA IS a beautiful island. We arrived there at five o'clock in the pouring rain after a very long journey. Margaret and I had just five youngsters with us and two one wheeled carts. Together we wandered over a jigsaw of islands.

We borrowed the carts from Miss Dorothy Clough of Steeton Hall whose long life has been spent in the service of young people. She taught me my camping skills when I was a child and has been friend and counsellor ever since. The carts were collapsable with one detachable wheel, similar to that on a bicycle, and two pole shafts. They were useful vehicles though they looked somewhat ridiculous and caused much public interest. On them we could strap our bedding rolls, rucksacks, tents and kitchen equipment and we pushed them on Tiree, Barra, South Uist, Eigg and Rhum and Skye.

When we needed to travel by bus we just unscrewed the wheel and unslotted the poles and everything went easily into the boot. When we went on board we took off the wheel and carried everything on like a stretcher. It was easy and between us we had the holiday of a lifetime, an adventure never to be forgotten. Had my life offered me more time I would have repeated this kind of expedition every year, but time for me is limited and when the choice is between fifty and five the fifty must take priority.

If you want to make friends, we have found, the best way is to do something odd, even daft, and everyone shows kindly interest and amusement. Do the odd thing with children and you have friends everywhere.

We began our journey on the friendly soil of Tiree and pushed our two wheels from Scarinish, along Gott Bay to Salum. We camped in Happy Valley, on the shore and spent four blissfully happy days wandering about Tiree accompanied by many of the island children we already knew so well.

We were eight when we journeyed from Yorkshire because one of the fourteen year old Tiree girls had just spent a fortnight's holiday with us and was returning after her first spell on the Mainland. It had been her first introduction to trees and trains and cities.

I had collected Mary two weeks earlier from the boat in Oban and had brought her by train and bus to Yorkshire. She was very composed, only occasionally giving away the fact that this was all as new to her as the moon was to Neil Armstrong. She would not, could not, bring herself to cross the unstable passageway between two carriages on the train and when we arrived in Callander she was convinced we had reached Glasgow. On arrival in the busy station at Buchanan Street she was very quiet and when we visited the Ladies she saw no relationship between a disc and a slot and fumbled with her penny.

She must have been afraid. She was shocked by the traffic and the ruthlessness of the crowds. She shook her head over the occupants of the high tenements, leaning out of their windows to get some breath of fresh air from the warm summer evening and she hated Sauchiehall Street. I was glad to be bringing her to the clean Dales and the quiet farm.

Mary returned with us to Tiree at the beginning of the trek and when we arrived at the thatched, white cottage which was her home, the table was laid for a full course meal. It was not the first time, nor the last, we had eaten a meal with our good friends Effie and John Lachie. We go to their cottage like going home. They were our first friends on Tiree and Happy Valley belongs to them. Without them there never would have been a first time. It was on their land that we planted the acorn which grew into the enormous oak.

The island girl we first knew as a barefooted ten year old, won a scholarship to Oban High School. She graduated from Aberdeen University taking an M.A. degree. She spent some time teaching in Canada, married a boy from Tiree and they have been living in Hong Kong ever since.

There were four children in the family, Mary, Ellen, Christine and baby Hughie. There were also four boys at the post office and Mary Ann MacLean and wherever we went they were with us and when we slept the last night in John Lachie's clean, whitewashed barn they slept there too. Our girls did not want to leave and if we had changed our plans and said we would stay the whole holiday on Tiree I think they would have cheered. But I was silent and we packed our bags and went to Barra.

It would have been more encouraging if the weather had not been so stormy. The Claymore tossed all the way across the Minch. When we carried our stretchers down the gangway at Castlebay ours was a bedraggled and dejected party. There is a small waiting room on the pier. It is an incongruous, concrete shed quite out of place among the Hebridean houses with their peat smoke drifting horizontally and all the conglomeration of fishing tackle, lobster creels and herring boxes.

The waiting room door was open and we dashed inside out of the rain, stacked our peculiar equipment against the wall and took stock of our position. The first thing we needed was food but long experience on these islands has taught us that you can seldom get anything whilst the boat is in. Almost always the shops are shut so that the owners can go down to the pier to collect further supplies. We waited nearly two hours, once, on Jura in blazing sunshine but then we had the novelty of watching the whisky barrels being rolled up the slope outside the distillary at Craighouses. We waited for a shop to open in Coll in a similar deluge to the Barra one. Oh, yes, we knew very well we would get nothing until the boat left for South Uist and there was nothing we could do about it.

We knew, too, that once we left Castlebay we might find no other shop until we reached Northbay so we waited patiently in the little concrete room, glad of its temporary shelter. We spent some time adjusting our equipment, securing our oil-skins and stamping our feet to keep warm.

Eventually, heads down to the wind, we ventured outside. The Claymore was turning and heading north for Loch Boisdale. The shops in the Main Street were still closed but by the time we reached the Co-op there were signs of activity and we were able to replenish our larder. Laden with awkward tins and packets and loaves of bread just unpacked from the steamer, we went back to the waiting room.

We fumbled with the door handle, streams of rain water running from our sou'westers, finding illegal entry and trickling coldly down our necks. The handle was unyielding, the door was locked. This is something we had not expected on Barra where house doors are not bolted. The one remaining human being on the otherwise deserted pier told us that the Pier Master was, 'Away to Norsebay' and suddenly the enormity of our plight could not be disregarded.

We had tins but no opener, bread but no knife. We had no cooking equipment, no tents, no sleeping bags and no personal gear in which to find some dry clothes. A crowd began to gather. There was a lot of Gaelic and much rattling of the lock but, unlike a station master's room we know, it held firm. We and our kit were parted.

'Well, well, and the man's away to Norsebay,' said one of the men. There was a great deal of Gaelic and our interpreter turned to us. 'They're saying he'll no' have gone straight home. He'll be having a strupag right enough.' He named a small township on the Northbay road. 'They're to take the lorry and go after him for the key.'

Several men climbed into the lorry. We had bought unexpected and welcome entertainment. Northbay is seven miles away on a road so narrow and winding that we settled down and prepared ourselves for a long delay. The depression which had enveloped us when we left Tiree had gone and our incredible five, Janet, Ann, Toots, Margaret jun. and Foxy were already in high spirits and laughing at our predicament.

A crofter's wife waved to us as she passed on a footpath below. We watched her go to one of the fishing boats and return with half a dozen fish in a string bag. She made a detour and came towards us. She showed anxiety over our plight and could not understand our amusement and lack of concern. She generously offered us the use of her home, wanted to feed us and said we could stay the night.

We could not accept even shelter from the rain whilst men were still dashing round, in a lorry, trying to find us a key. We thanked her for the supremely generous offer and have never forgotten the sincerity with which it was made. She walked away slowly and looked back several times.

The pier master was located as our friends had prophesied, supping his strupag not far away and when the lorry returned he was with it. The men were delighted with their success and stood around watching whilst we screwed on the wheels and prepared to push the two carts up the steep Main Street. They followed us to the top where we turned left for Tangasdale and we thanked them sincerely. They all stood waving as we set off at a spanking pace, heads bent against the weather, confident once again in the benevolence of islands and their people.

It must have been close on seven o'clock. We decided to cross the island and make camp as soon as we reached the sandy machair which we prefer. We were all very hungry. We reached the summit of the road in a lather of sweat and rain and after that the downward trek into Tangasdale was easy. The bicycle wheels were running freely and we reached the shore in good time.

We never pitch without asking permission. For one thing courtesy demands this. For another we generally need to use a crofter's water supply and, especially if we have children with us, we like our presence to be known and accepted. We never know when an emergency will mean we need help.

So we asked at a small cottage on the shore, white and thatched, for permission to pitch three small tents on the machair. We were told that the land belonged to a crofter who lived half a mile back along the road. It meant a further delay and everyone was tired by this time. A sea mist obliterated what Margaret and I knew to be one of the most beautiful Hebridean shores. All Barra's magnificence was completely hidden. I did not want to press the youngsters beyond the limit I knew they could go.

'You stay here,' I said. 'Flim and I will run back along the road. We won't be long.' They sat down in their oilskins, leaning on an upturned boat, their sense of humour somewhat exhausted.

Margaret and I hurried back up the road to the house we had been shown. We must have looked like shipwrecked marriners, cluttered as we were with waterproofs and sou' westers. The rain was dripping from our noses, running down our legs and soaking the socks in our hiking boots. We felt embarrassed to be knocking on someone's door.

A woman opened it and I asked the simple question I have asked so many times. 'Could we please have permission to pitch our tents on the shore and may we fill our water carrier?'

'You are wet,' said the woman, immediately concerned. 'You must come in and get dry.'

We explained that we couldn't, that we had left five girls on the shore and that we were all ready to pitch our tents if that was all right. The woman turned to her daughter and there was a discussion in Gaelic.

'Himself is not at home chust now,' she explained. 'You must come in and get dry and when he comes we will ask him about the tents.'

We told her that there were seven of us and that we were all too wet to go into anybody's house but that as soon as we could pitch our tents we would be all right. We would soon be able to get dry and cook something to eat. To her this was unthinkable. We were wet and must be dried; hungry and must be fed. Tents were quite outside her comprehension.

'Take off your oilskins,' she insisted. 'You must come inside. Himself will soon be back from the hill.'

Her daughter had understood about the teenagaers we had left on the shore. 'Run down to the machair,' she prompted Margaret. 'Bring the others. You can get dry whilst my father comes home.'

We were helpless. We had genuinely tried to save this good lady trouble and she had refused to listen. Margaret went down to the shore to collect the others and bring up the carts. There was nothing else we could do.

Never have we felt so wet or so cluttered with oilskins. We left them in a pile outside the door believing that they could not get any wetter at all. Never have seven pairs of shoes looked so many as they did on the floor of the small entrance porch. We seated ourselves beside the stove, some on chairs and some on the floor and began to steam. We toasted ourselves until we began to tingle and our bare toes to curl up in pleasure.

The two women began to be very active. The daughter was busy in the kitchen and her mother began to fuss around the living room. She scrubbed the wooden table quite unnecessarily and laid a spotless cloth. There was not much conversation. I felt she would have talked had we had the Gaelic. It was being spoken fluently in the kitchen. The atmosphere, however, was easy. We were in no doubt at all about our welcome.

We watched, intrigued, whilst our hostess lifted a carboard box from the cupboard and began to unpack a lovely china tea service from its protective tissue. We were deeply honoured. In England, had this happened, I feel certain that we would either have been turned away or have received permission to camp and would have already been pitching. Had we had the goodfortune to be asked into the kitchen I think we would have been given our tea in mugs which would have been quite suitable for wandering, wet strangers.

But here, on this remote island in the Outer Hebrides, on the worst night of summer, the best china was being unwrapped, the newest of delicious scones were being spread with the morning's fresh butter. Fresh cream was being folded into the crowdie, slices of new, brown bread were being cut and homemade oatcakes piled on a plate.

'We have been fed,' as Joanna so aptly puts it, many times on many islands but never more liberally than this, never with more grace and dignity and our hearts warmed to this born hostess.

Himself was slow to arrive and when he did he disturbed the calf which was enjoying a meal of oilskins at the door. It had eaten a big square out of Ann's long gas cape. When the man came into the house he greeted us as warmly as if we were known and expected guests. Apparently such were far too rare to send away at once. He was much more garrulous than his wife and he completely ignored my request about the tents. Instead he apologised for being unshaven and proceeded to remedy it at once.

'Och, first I must take off the whiskers,' he decided, lathering his face in front of the mirror. 'I do believe the rain will stop. Ach, there's plenty of time I'm sure.'

He was so obviously enjoying himself. I should have wanted to get the tents pitched and the business of unpacking over, the groundsheets down and my family settled down for the night. Instead, like my retinue, all I wanted to do was to sit by the fire, within the friendship of this family circle and listen to himself.

He was the most entertaining of hosts. Having shaved he took his mug of tea, drew up his chair and prepared to enjoy this unexpected and obviously very welcome céilidh. He was full of stories of the island, of folklore and superstition and he held us spellbound. He believed sincerely in the second sight and told us stories of lights and premonitions and visions; of life in a crofting community, of treasures washed up by the sea, of shipwrecks during the war and of survivors washed ashore with their dead companions.

When we rose to go he insisted we sat down again and he turned the handle of an old gramophone and played us Gaelic songs. He begged that we would sing, so we did and darkness fell and still the gay céilidh went on.

Finally I forced him to talk about the tents. 'Well,' he said, 'and I'm sure you could camp by the lochan were it not for se sistles.'

'Blow the thistles,' I groaned silently. He took me out to negotiate the land. Across the road, below the house, was a sloping field with a lochan in its hollow. The thistles were pathetic apologies for the sturdy Scottish Emblem and were only sparsely scattered.

'This is perfect,' I said.

It was long past midnight and the rain had stopped. Our genial friends stood in their illuminated doorway and waved both arms in salute. Headlights flashed along the road and we clung to each other. 'It's a light!' someone gasped and we all laughed.

Barra gave us no more rain. We never left the little Loch St Clair with its ancient dun, for the thistles were no trouble and the fresh water was beautiful for swimming. What's more, Tangasdale was a good place from which to explore the island.

It seems to me that the early days, which were so full of mistakes and bright ideas that went wrong, were much more fun than the near perfection we know today. To boast is to tempt disaster we know all too well, but the fact remains that we have solved a lot of our problems. And so we should for we have been at the game for a long time.

'It's a wise man,' Margaret tells me often, 'who can change his mind.' She and I have to do a man's work on the farm. We began when we were children with Father as our mentor but he is old now and issues his instructions from the armchair. Harry is handicapped so it is we who have had to be builders, plumbers, electricians and architects as well as farmers. We have built and pulled down what we have built so many times that we are experts at learning from error. We have laughed at our first attempts so often that we have learned to take this sequence of events for granted and I have heard Margaret say with feeling, 'Don't put in too many nails. It'll be easier to pull down when we decide to move it!' Some failures stay more vividly in one's mind than others and one of these was the lightweight lat I invented specially for the Trek.

In those days lightweight equipment was not so easily come by. We borrowed Itisa tents from Steeton Hall but Miss Clough had no lightweight lat suitable for treeless islands, so I made what was probably the first and last of its kind. It was an 'A' line lat, very narrow at the top and wide in the skirts, no more than a very small tepee, really. It was big enough to enter but, though one's identity was concealed one's presence and one's purpose were both very obvious. In wind the walls wrapped themselves round the user and in rain they clung to her most embarrassingly. More often than not the whole thing fell on the unfortunate person who had then to cry for the help of a friend to hold the pole. Who cared? On the islands we occupy the machair alone and there is plenty of privacy.

We left Barra as reluctantly as we had left Tiree.

84

Several years later I returned with a dozen sea rangers and camped on the beautiful Tràigh Vais. The din of the Atlantic rolling into this shore can be heard from the lagoon like waters of the Tràigh Mhòr, that incredible, two mile stretch of sand where the plane lands. The dunes which separate the two strands are narrow yet there is no greater contrast between calm and tempest throughout the Hebrides.

On this occasion too the windy weather turned wet and I have never known it rain harder. It beat painfully on our faces whenever we had to leave the tents. That year we had left twenty five children with Margaret and Enid Shackleton on Tiree and I struggled to the phone at Northbay, in the face of the most appalling weather. I had to reassure myself that the younger ones were all right. Both Margaret and I lied to each other, both giving assurances that all was well when tents were blowing down over our heads.

Next day, hoping that the weather would improve, we struggled over to Tangasdale to see Himself and our kind hostess. It was their great joy that they were able to loan us the use of an empty cottage. We found it dry as a bone and not one puff of wind entered it. It was a typical Hebridean house with two dormer windows and we occupied it throughout our stay. The weather improved but little and it would have been ungracious to vacate it.

There are many instances and anecdotes to tuck away in our memories, to be frequently aired in the years that have followed and the Trek, with the seven and the trike carts supplied so many of them.

We left Barra, that first time, on the early evening boat, somewhat limping because the wheel of one of our carts had buckled and we could not get it mended. Arriving in Loch Boisdale we were rather hungry and decided to find somewhere to brew up.

All roads are flat on the Uists and the land on either side is waterlogged and spongy. Everywhere there are Lochs covered with water lilies which are at their best in July and August. Houses dot the landscape, built on islands of rock amid the bog. It is a hard land, a land which will appeal to only a few but we love it. There are few places more beautiful than Ludaig on a peaceful evening when the sun turns to pink all the houses on Eriskay.

No suitable eating square of ground presented itself and in desperation we stepped into a wide and miraculously dry ditch, just off the main road. We lit the primus and became busy. It was, I know, a makeshift meal, not one of our usual standard but it sufficed. We had thick slices of bread and butter and hot baked beans. We finished with a dessert of Cremola Rice pudding, a favourite that year.

We remember feeling acutely embarrassed when an officer from the boat passed along on the road above our heads. 'You all right in the galley, girls?' he called cheerfully. We would have liked to offer him a delicacy, or even a bowl of rich Scotch Broth but our menu was very limited.

We were just sitting enjoying the meal when we had another visitor who left us feeling that we had committed a crime of great discourtesy. There being so little activity on the peat bog, the man on the bicycle was noticed immediately. He was riding very purposefully towards us and our attention followed him all the way.

85

When he reached the road, above our ditch, he dismounted and asked us why we were making a meal by the roadside. For a moment I wondered if it could possibly be prohibited. I said I was sorry but that we had just got off the boat and the children were hungry.

'But you could have asked for food at any of the houses,' said the man. 'Chust anyone on Souse Uist would give you food. Children need not eat on the road side. Whateffer you want the crofter will give you.'

I assured him that we did know this. That we knew the extent of Hebridean hospitality but that we could not ask for food when we had plenty. 'We're quite alright,' I said. 'It's a lovely evening and we are warm and happy.'

But we couldn't convince him that it was not a shocking thing for visitors to the island to have to eat in a ditch. In the end we partly satisfied his conscience by accepting some hot water to wash our dirty dishes. We had an uncomfortable feeling that we had unwittingly offended a gracious people and the pain of that meeting is still there everytime we think about it. But how were we to know and if we had known how could we ever ask for more than a campsite and water. We have received much more but we have never asked for it and we never will.

From Uist we sailed to Mallaig and left our buckled wheel and useless cart in the left luggage office before taking the Small Isles boat to Eigg. Our stay there was wholly enjoyable. We fell in love with a softer, greener island of fields and farms, cliffs and caves, bracken and blackberry bushes. Margaret remembers it most because it was the only time and place where she has ever imagined she had a brain tumour. She awoke in the velvety darkness with such a severe pain in her ear that she could hardly bear it. The agony was intense. She could not lie on her ear without excruciating pain and she was only fractionally easier sitting up. The pain was so great she could barely cope with it let alone worry about being ill on a small island at which the boat called only twice a week.

After a long time she ventured to put her fingers inside her ear and discovered a feather. Obviously it had escaped from her sleeping bag and the quill must have been pressing on her ear drum.

I remember Eigg for quite a different reason. We had to land in a small boat which came out to the anchored steamer for the Eigg passengers. The exit from the big boat to the small ferry was through doors which open from the lower deck and those alighting are helped down the steps into the unstable, dancing boat below. All luggage and rucksacks are thrown down afterwards with carelessness and complete lack of respect.

Three youths were alighting on Eigg, obviously intending to camp as we were and one of them must have had a bottle of tomato ketchup stowed insecurely in his gear. As this flew through the air, from the steamer, the bottle fell out of his rucksack pocket and crashed onto the gunwhales above our kit. It broke into pieces and bespattered everything we had. My only consolation was that it was not salad cream. I could not have stood the smell of that for the rest of the Trek.

Rhum gave us our first real experience of midges. Fortunately we have only had to battle with these militant insects twice in all the twenty years; on Rhum in 1958 and on Harris this year. We had a brief experience of them in Tobermory but we were only staying there overnight. Because my experience of them is very recent, and many of my 'family' are still nursing bites, I feel I know all about them but the truth is we have been lucky 90% of the time.

They were very bad on Rhum because we could not get away from them at all. The only camping area allowed by the National Trust was close to the water's edge. There was a lot of seaweed which no doubt harboured them. On Harris we could escape if we went onto the sandy shore and if we trailed our feet in the water we could forget about them.

On Rhum the only place we could escape them was in the hills. Round the campsite they settled on us like an inky cloud and our little tents were black inside. They did not even go when we cooked on the primus inside the tent.

So we fled to the hills as often as we could, stalked the deer and made friends with the wild, dun-coloured Rhum ponies. Only Margaret could ever get near them but she is our St Francis; she has a way with all animals.

Our first experience of stalking deer ended in hysteria. There being just seven of us, that year of the Trek, whatever we ate nothing divided properly. I had four Mars Bars which, when cut in two, gave us a spare piece.

'This is for the first one to spot a deer,' I said feeling quite sure that fifteen hundred deer on one small island could not remain hidden and elusive for long.

I was the first to see the stag. Alert and poised it stood against a backcloth of trees. We froze, expecting it to take our scent and disappear. Janet decided to try to take a photograph, the arrogant creature remained so still. When I remember her crawling, Indian fashion, through the heather the laughter in me is always irrepressible. She came surprisingly near it for a 'white squaw' then, unexpectedly, she stood up. We heard her give an exasperated ejaculation of annoyance and stamp back to the road.

'Deer!' she stormed. 'That's not a deer! It's a target!' I was set upon for the extra half of Mars Bar I had prematurely and illegally claimed and 'Skipper's deer' is now a legend. But the deer on Rhum were to give us a great deal of pleasure as we wandered among the foothills of the Red Cuillin.

I am accused of many things. Absent mindedness is one of them. If Hazel did not come to camp I would lose all my possessions. My toilet bag disappears, my glasses, my watch. I never have a biro to sign cheques and I keep the one so kindly loaned to me. I do not know what I did with my camera or where I put the matches. She always knows.

I am also accused of asking questions and not listening to the answers and of talking too much which may well be true. I talk if I am visiting or entertaining but I also need long periods of silence and I need often to be alone. I am also guilty, they say, of big headedness, of liking to air my knowledge and throwing out the names of islands with the confidence of one who thinks she knows. Margaret and I have been on twenty-four of the western islands and have taken children onto sixteen of them.

When the seven of us sailed for Coruisk, on Skye, I was sarcastic about the rest of the passengers on board who were looking prematurely up Loch Scavaig when

Eigg and Rhum, Muck and Canna were lying dreamily on our port bow. I was so busily pointing these out that we never enquired what the other passengers found so interesting. Therefore we never saw the Royal Yacht Britannia and missed our one and only chance of seeing our Sovereign at sea. I was in danger of being thrown overboard.

It was on our last sail back to Mallaig that a fellow passenger asked if we were Guides, said she was a Commissioner and wanted to know all about our travels and adventures with the one wheeled carts. She celebrated our brief meeting by inviting all seven of us down into the dining room for a lovely meal. We did not refuse.

The generosity of the people we met so briefly seemed never ending. We left the Mallaig to Fort William train at Banavie believing that we would find a quieter campsite than the one in Fort William. Unfortunately our three small tents were too many for the postage stamp piece of grass Margaret and I once camped on between the station and the Caledonian Canal. It had been very private and after the isolation of the islands entry back into the gregariousness of the Mainland is sometimes too sudden. But the campsite in Banavie village was uncrowded and we spent a comfortable night. Our wanderings were over.

We woke to a sun drenched Sunday, breakfasted and took down our tents, folded and packed them for the last time. We set off in the direction of Fort William with plenty of time to catch the bus to Oban. The busy little Highland town was full of tourists and we felt out of place, weather beaten and travelled. We began to meet the congregation of a little church which stands on the outskirts of Fort William.

'Do you folks feel a bit daft?' I said. 'Cos I certainly do.' It's an odd thing to do on a Sunday morning, to push a one wheeled cart, piled high with expedition equipment, along the edge of a pavement filling with worshippers, just out of church.

The Manse was just across the road and the smiling minister, whose congregation had been pleasantly swollen with summer visitors, was leaning over the gate. We tried to look nondescript and normal.

'Good morning,' he called out. 'Are you coming or going?'

'Going, unfortunately', we replied.

'Where've you been?' he asked.

We stopped. He knew Calum and all our friends on Tiree and many of our beloved islands. He invited us in and his wife put on some coffee and buttered and jammed some scones. It was a rare and vivid encounter and would have proved to us, if we had not already known, that gracious hospitality is alive on the Mainland too.

It has always been a great sadness to us that when we put away the strange vehicles we put them away for good. We had hopes, as we journeyed south, of other adventures on other islands. We stayed overnight at Loch Gilphead with friends we first met when they lived at Salen, on Mull. Vi and Dave MacAllister made us so welcome that Janet cried. She couldn't help it. Enormous tears fell onto her tea plate. Everyone had been so kind and Janet was overcome.

'We must do this again,' said Foxy. We never did. Children are as numerous round us as the Rhum midges and I would like to take them all to the Hebrides.

Since then I have taken many and an adult Foxy has taken many to Coll. The disease is infectious.

So the small moving camp came to an end and too few years remain to selfishly live it again.

The McInnes family in front of their home before their new extension was built

Oh, the Lord is good to me,
And so I thank the Lord,
For giving me the things I need,
The sun, the rain and the apple seed,
The Lord is good to me.

Chapter Eight

HAVING RETURNED home I have no interest, whatsoever, in food. We arrived in the silence of the early morning only a week ago. At three o'clock we wakened them and helped them into their anoraks and lifted down their bags from the racks. How funny they look asleep on the train, limp and flushed and very young. They sprawl all over the seats and each other and us, brown and clean and secure.

The train pulls into a crowded station and fathers handle equipment and mothers hug their children. Within five minutes there is no one there but the three of us. It is cold in the early morning but colder still because we are bereft of children. We shrug our shoulders, smile at each other and think how nice it will be to get to bed.

And for days I have no interest in food. It is lucky that I return when the tomatoes are ripe and I can pluck one for my breakfast and two for my tea. I eat my school dinner because I must set a good example to the school children but apart from that I have lost interest. I have seen far too much food prepared, watched far too much of it consumed and eaten far too much of it myself.

My mother is an excellent cook. Her cakes and pastries, her puddings and crumbles are delicious so it is natural that I should ask for her recipes. Unfortunately they begin with six ounces of flour. The puddings we make for fifty must begin with four pounds of flour and a large multiplication sum must be done. When we make pastry we empty a three pound bag of flour into the bowl and three half pound packets of fat. We make a dozen fruit pies, drop a hundred dumplings into the stew and scrub a whole pailful of potatoes. Each day we make a gallon of custard and every time we fill the coffee billy we make two gallons. We eat fifty pounds of biscuits and countless apples and oranges.

There were Scouts, one year, camping on Tiree, over Balephetrish way, and we invited them all over to Happy Valley for joint sports and an evening meal followed by campfire. We frequently have visitors but not usually another thirty all at once.

'Eighty for supper tonight, Skip! What on earth'll we have?'

'Scouts have whopping appetites,' I was told. 'We'll have t'have plenty.'

'We'll be hungry too,' they hastened to remind me.

We filled both four gallon, stainless steel billies with rich stew and emptied in what seemed like a sack of potatoes. When they were both boiling merrily we lifted them from the heat and topped them up with countless dumplings. The intense heat from within was sufficient to cook both potatoes and Yorkshire dumplings without our returning the billies to the fire, a dangerous thing to do with rich stew. If just one square inch burns on the bottom the whole dish is tainted and perfection lost.

We are careful not to burn things. We no longer attempt to boil milk for custard. The bottom browns very quickly. We mix dried milk with the custard powder and pour on boiling water. Once, long ago, Margaret slightly burned the custard. The taste is unmistakable and nothing will camouflage it. There was only one thing to do.

Before the sweet course was served I used a little diplomacy, psychology, call it what you will. It seldom fails. 'We ought to give three cheers for Flim' I announced. 'She saved the custard. She ignored the flames and the heat and rescued it. Hip, hip . . .' The cheers were noisy. After that there was not even a whisper of 'It's burnt!'

I would like to think that children are happy for a more positive reason than that they are full. I am not suggesting that food is the only ingredient in the recipe for happiness but it is a primary one and therefore we have developed our skill in this field perhaps more than in any other.

I am reminded of a céilidh we all attended in Crossapol Hall on Tiree. It was a long céilidh with many Gaelic songs and a great deal of piping and foot tapping. It was too long for many of the little ones. It was scheduled to begin late and, like all island activities, did not begin on time. It was after eleven when it ended. The children's behaviour, as always at island gatherings, was irreproachable. They could not have been very comfortable for they were sitting on side seats and, after the fresh air of the shore, the hall was stuffy and warm and soporific.

'Haven't they behaved well?' I bragged as we tiptoed out. No one had giggled or chatted or shuffled, few had wanted to go to the toilet, none had felt sick, many had enjoyed the singing and the strange language. Feeling rather proud Hazel and I said, 'Goodnight,' to our friends and followed the quiet, obedient children to the bus which would take us the six miles back to camp.

We were deceived. We did not own a company of angels. Each and everyone of them was a hungry horror and when we put our first foot on the bus steps the loud chorus began.

'We want food! We want food! We want FOOD!'

'Start up the bus,' I urged our bus driver, 'before everyone hears this unruly mob.'

The sober faced angels of the céilidh bore no resemblance to the laughing, demanding youngsters shouting for their supper. They started to sing for it too and began with the noisiest possible songs.

Oh lord, I thought, It's nearly morning and they're not one bit tired. They've had to be still too long and now they're ravenous. The fire will be out and the D'abri in darkness and somehow or other they will have to be fed. I will not pretend that the prospect never alarms me.

The anticipation of the preparation of a great deal of food is worse than the activity. That is routine and once the team is set in motion it is not the mammoth task it would first appear to be, even in darkness. By the time beds have been unrolled and occupied the fire has been coaxed into a heat intense enough to boil two and a half gallons of water for hot chocolate and coffee, or to hot up previously made soup.

The lamp is easily lit in the D'abri, skips are opened, cakes are cut and biscuits emptied from their packets. Older, experienced members take round the big jugs, the bucketful of mugs and the heaped trays. And fifty are fed.

We do not have a menu. We used to, long, long ago. Now we live a meal at a time. If we feel like baking we light the oven and go baking crazy. If it is hot we conjure up a buffet comparable to that served in any Lyons' Corner House. If the fire is right we toast, or on a sudden inspiration we make two hundred pancakes.

I have many helpers. Their motives are not sincerely honest. I sit by the fire and half a dozen servants run my errands, 'Fryingpan, cooking fat, fish slice, tray, tea towel, desert spoon.' They run backwards and forwards between the fire and the store. The news gets round.

'Skipper is making pancakes . . . pancakes . . . pancakes.'

'How do you make pancakes, Skipper?'

'What's the recipe?'

'Well, I put three pounds of flour into this bowl and a pinch of salt, some sugar and some eggs and milk. Then I beat the batter until bubbles rise on the top.'

I could not tell anyone how much sugar or how much milk or even how many eggs. Such a lot of camp cooking is intuitive. We have no scales or measures. The mixture will make two hundred pancakes.

The smell attracts attention and everyone wants to help, believing that helpers will get preferential treatment. Everyone wants to sample. No one will take anyone else's word for it that the mixture is right. There are the most ingenious excuses.

'That's a funny shaped one, Skipper. It won't do. I'd better eat it.'

'That one's a bit burnt. Nobody will want it but I don't mind.'

'There're too many on the tray. One's fallen off!'

'I won't eat any for tea. I promise.' I've heard that one before!

'I like mine hot!'

'Mrs Belsey says I can have one,' says one ingenious soul believing that I will not dispute Hazel's authority.

'Flim's hungry!' says another, equally glib.

Is it surprising that the tray is continually depleted? It can be easily understood why I station Brigitte, our French girl, with a mallet and authority to use it on any subsequent thief.

Frequently we have to change our menu at the last moment. Carrots can be grown very successfully in sand and where they are we do not use tinned. But they cannot always be produced for the desired meal. Potatoes too have some times to be lifted by ourselves.

'Could you spare us any carrots?' I have often asked.

'I'm sure you can have carrots, Chean,' I am told. 'They are beautiful carrots right enough. They'll be chust melting in your mouth.'

I have displayed my pail and indicated that I have brought it specially for the carrots.

'And how are you all enchoying the potatoes,' I am asked.

'The potatoes are lovely.'

'Och, they only need a wash. They are chust tasty in their chackets.'

And so the conversation would go on and on and our crofter would stay in his seat by the stove, settle himself more comfortably and his wife would put on the kettle for my strupag. Then she would continue with the business of preparing the mid-day meal for her family and I would anxiously remember that I had forty to feed

93

but my host would settle himself for the day and no carrots would be forthcoming. I would periodically bring the conversation round to carrots and each time I would receive the assurance that there were plenty of carrots and they were 'chust beautiful.'

Having had my delicious strupag I would give up, leave my bucket for the carrots when they were eventually lifted, which they always were, and hurry back to camp to hastily open a canteen sized tin of peas. You cannot hurry an islander and what right have you to do so anyway. We are visitors and they are providers and there is, indeed, plenty of time.

On the other hand food often arrives so unexpectedly. I remember a day when a quarter of a sheep was delivered. Another morning, when we were on North Uist and were still sleeping after a late pitch in an unknown place, the door of the tent was pulled aside and a lady, we had never seen in our lives before, peeped in.

'Would you be offended if I gave you some eggs?' she enquired. If she had seen our arrival the night before it could only have been in the light of our torches for the bus driver had set us down very late and had pointed out a suitable place. We learned that the place was aptly called Sollas and there is no more peaceful place in the world.

On a clear, cold evening we had just crowned the year's Miss Tiree and the judging of Mr Wonderful had begun. Peter, his chest tattooed with 'Geordies forever,' could not compete with well padded and super-muscular David whose sister had stuffed his shirt with potatoes. Paul had been out fishing on the spit of land between the twin bays of Salum and Vaul. Though aided and abetted by Susan and Cheryle, he had caught not one morsel for breakfast.

The competition was interrupted by the announcement, 'Someone's coming, Skipper.'

Donny MacInnes was struggling over the hill with a heavily weighted bucket.

'I was out in the boat chust now, Would you be wanting any fish?'

The bucket was full. He was given a warm reception and his catch was emptied with a shower of silver into the biggest pail we had. Donny would take no payment.

'Och, not at all,' he said. 'I chust fish for the fun of it.'

Paul stood there in wistful sheepishness. Donny was half his age and size but Paul had nothing to show for his dilligent search for bait on the shore and his long vigil on the rocks.

We wondered how to cope with thirty three, beautifully fresh fish which, we were told, were saithe. Fortunately we had the use of Mrs MacLean's cottage that year. A small fridge is a non starter for the family of fifty five. Indeed a deep freeze would be hard pressed to cater for us. Nevertheless there is a time when almost anything can be put to use and the Day of the Fridge had come.

A number of the seniors, led by Elaine, Chris and Shirley turned the little kitchen into a fish factory. Afraid of having the smell of fish on their clothes for the rest of camp they gallantly took off their shirts and tucked tea towels down the waistbands of their shorts. With much laughter they cheerfully removed heads and scooped out guts covering themselves and their neighbours in scales and blood splashes and creating such a fishy atmosphere in the kitchen that any amount of scouring powder and detergent were needed to remove it.

The fridge accepted the evening's catch, grateful of a job to do at last. A few days later Linda and Viv tackled the even greater task of deboning and frying but all declared that the evening meal was delicious. Time consuming and messy but undoubtedly delicious.

A box full of tinned food and innumerable fresh rolls is sent annually from Katie Morrison on the Harris shore, biscuits, packets of tea, bottles of milk, batches of scones and many pancakes find their way to our store tent.

I can never understand why other leaders, camping with large numbers of children, do not use an oven. I have tried in vain to interest all the ones I know. Our oven makes all the difference in the world to our cuisine and our purse. With it we can have a low cost, varied diet, far more appetising than continual top stove cooking and it looks so professional and mouth watering before it is cut and served. Our meat and potato pies are made in dishes, two feet in diameter. The pastry crust is thick and golden brown and the gravy bubbles hotly through the air cuts and around the sides. Because there are artists among us there are pastry trefoils and tents to adorn each lid and the fork marks are the initials of the cook.

They are taken ceremoniously from the oven and carried down the whole length if the D'abri being exhibited first to port and then to starboard, all the way down to the waiting cooks who will carve them up and share them out. Incredible noises are made throughout their journey. 'Oooohhh' and 'Aaahhh' and 'Sssslooop' and 'Ynm yummm.' The cooks are then named and three cheers are shouted. Tell me any child who will not eat a large helping after all that?

'Can we have shepherd's pie,' we are asked perpetually. Meat and onions, carrots and rich gravy covered with mashed potatoes generously decorated with knobs of butter, grated cheese and tomatoes. The finished result is so scrumptious that willing hands and greedy stomachs scrape out every tiny morsel from the huge pie dishes. Some corny person always wants to know which shepherd we have eaten.

We make fruit crumble rich and golden and sickly enough to satisfy the sweet toothed and pies so full of fruit one would think we had a whole orchard at our disposal.

An oven is possible in any camp. Where it can be built into the sand it is simple. Ours is big enough to receive our two large pie dishes and we lower it into a rectangular hole cut out in a sand bank. We ensure a good flow of air underneath by placing a grid on four canteen sized tins filled with sand and raise the oven above the grid on four more tins. We leave a 'chimney' at the back so that air can flow under the oven and out up the back of it, providing enough oxygen for the peat to burn well. Then we pile sods and sand over the oven to bury it and preserve the heat. Our door opens downward so that when we look in the oven, or lift things out of it, we are shielded from the intense heat below. It is so simple. We can cook ten plate fruit pies in it at a time and the joy that it has given, over the years, is incalculable.

Seldom are we tempted to eat out of doors. If there is sunshine on the islands there is no shade for most of them are treeless. Many of the island children have no conception of trees. One year we brought thirteen year old Ellen back from Tiree to spend a holiday in Yorkshire. She not only wanted to see trees but, like a blind man, she wanted to touch them. She wrapped her arms round their trunks, fingered their bark and stroked and held the leaves.

Commenting on this one day, to a visiting school adviser, he told me of a colleague he said he had who, on a visit to Uist, had found it difficult to believe that the children really were ignorant about trees. Yet when he had asked them what a sycamore was they had had no answer and when he had asked them if they knew what a beech was he had been told that a 'Beech' was a bad women. I cannot vouch for this being a true story but certainly the islands are bare of trees and many children do not visit the Mainland until they must seek work. Sadly the islands do not provide enough jobs for their children.

Because there is no shade we generally feel that it is necessary to eat indoors and get out of the sun for half an hour. If there is no sun, food keeps warmer when served inside. In any case we recognise the D'abri as an excellent place for learning to show appreciation and enjoyment of food and for learning patience and tolerance.

There is no sight I love to see more than the double row of barefooted youngsters enjoying their meal and asking for more. I marvel at their self control and patience in the small space where all movement is limited. One day I decided to test their tolerance. I was barefooted myself and I walked the whole length of the tent with a tray of cakes. Purposefully, yet discreetly, I stood on every pair of feet and not one grumbled or even commented.

This tolerance of one another in the D'abri and sleeping tent, in crowded bus or small ship's cabin, around a crofter's stove or within the limited area of the safety rope when bathing, is something I notice and appreciate and consider to be one of the indications of our success.

Each year it offends me to have to bring food from home. I would much prefer to buy all from the islands. Heavy freight charges make this impossible. Also in the Hebrides I cannot get the canteen sized tins which feed so many so cheaply and we could not cope with hundreds of small tins. Unpacking our food on arrival is like stocking a small shop.

One year we were careless in the packing and neglected to put our many packets of biscuits into a closed tin. They should always be packed into the oven, or the hot water cylinder or the four gallon billies. On this occasion we packed them into the skips as they were, just in their sealed cardboard cartons.

'Mrs Belsey,' said someone when unpacking the skips on the evening of our arrival on Harris, 'Something's eaten our biscuits!'

Something had indeed gnawed its way into the cardboard box, through the cellophane and waxed paper and devoured many packets of biscuits. We congratulated the thief on having the courtesy to eat up one packet before starting on another and marvelled at the spiral effect of the half eaten one of the most recent meal.

'Mice!' said Mrs Belsey.

A group had gathered round her and they proceeded to finish the unpacking. In the bottom of the skip was a nest. Two in fact. In a flash the adult mice darted into the grass leaving two families of babies wriggling and squirming in the clutter of paper shavings.

'Aren't they gorgeous?' said Mrs Belsey. A dozen heads leaned over the skip marvelling at the little pink bodies with their blind eyes and flailing limbs.

'What'll we do with them, Mrs Belsey?'

'They'll die without their mother,' said Mrs Belsey. 'We'll have to find her.'

There followed a hunt which had so little chance of success as to seem ridiculous unless you have watched a small, brown, farm mouse courageously return for every one of its babies from a nest you have just disturbed with a muck fork. The pitching of tents had only just begun. There was kitchen equipment and food everywhere but the mother never went far from the nest. When she came creeping back she was caught and put gently into a peg bag, which was quickly emptied for the purpose. The rest of the family and the paper shavings were scooped up and slipped into the bag too.

The operation had taken a valuable half hour of our precious time. I had kept out of it. There seemed to me no possible happy ending to the story but I was incapable of interfering in a mission of such gentleness for such small, unfortunate creatures.

But Mrs Belsey is a resourceful woman. A van was being driven onto the field. Our bread and fruit and perishable goods were being brought by the crofter's son, a blonde and handsome sailor who is everyone's favourite.

'Please', said the ingenious Mrs Belsey, 'We have a bagful of mice we could not possibly kill or leave to die. Please take them and put them somewhere where they'll have a sporting chance.'

The young man's face was a picture. His big hand dangled the bag with its ridiculous contents, and around him clustered a bevy of adoring females begging him to be merciful.

We did not ask him what teasing he had to take from his family nor did we ask him what he did with the mice. What happened to the evicted family of thieves we do not know, but the big, blonde man is still our hero. We have had other thieves in our store tent but none so much fun as the mice. We wondered if they were Yorkshire mice or if they had boarded the skip in Glasgow or Tarbert. Perhaps they had even been sailors and had suddenly found themselves ashore. We wondered if they approved of the beautiful islands as much as we did. One of the escaped adults remained with us. We saw him a few times and saw him disappear for good when the last skip was packed for home.

We had a mouse in camp once, who was neither a thief nor a stowaway. He was white and he came with a child called Margaret. We did not know that she had brought him until we had arrived for a three week camp on Arran. We were surprised and amused when we heard the news.

'Whatever made you bring him?' I asked, not knowing whether to be cross or just exasperated.

'Mi mum was goin' t' kill 'im if I left 'im behind,' she explained. He caused a great deal of trouble and fun. The cry would go up, 'The mouse has gone!' and there would be a frantic search in rucksacks and kit bags before the little creature was found again and put safely back into his box. Eventually the call of the wild was too great for him to resist and he disappeared completely. Perhaps there are still off-white descendants on Arran just as there are half white rabbits on Harris because Catherine's pet wandered freely in the field below their house.

Because everything has to be squeezed by experienced hands into the six skips for transport, ingenuity has to be exercised. Sometimes it has dire results. One year I packed the coffee billy with two large packets of jelly crystals. On arrival on Tiree I asked my sister to put the billy on the newly lit fire so that we could all have a hot drink. Because the billy was heavy she naturally thought it was full of water so she just lifted it on without looking inside.

Shortly afterwards there hung over Happy Valley the strangest fragrance of freshly picked strawberries. The lovely smell became more sickly, like jam, and finally there was a definite smell of burning fruit. When we eventually tracked it down to the coffee billy the mess was indescribable. We almost thought our lovely billy would be a 'Write off'. The jelly crystals certainly were!

We do not often make jelly. The weather must be very cool for the large bowls to set. We tried it once, on Tiree and the next day it still hadn't set. In desperation we poured it into a large, rectangular billy and carried it down to the sea. We placed it at the edge of the incoming tide and instructed Stephen to sit on it until it set. It was, perhaps, a monotonous task for a nine year old boy but Stephen was a bit of a 'loner' in his first camp and seemed to enjoy sitting on rocks just dangling his feet in the sea thinking whatever thoughts nine year old boys do.

Nevertheless Margaret and I were a bit shamefaced, nearly an hour later, when we came back from Calum's with some groceries and saw him still sitting there. As we neared a bigger wave than most unskittled his seat and turned it completely on its side in the water. We watched him calmly right it and resume his vigil.

'How many times has that happened?' we asked, laughing and not particularly concerned.

'A few,' he admitted.

We investigated the contents. The jelly had set beautifully and at lunch time Stephen was cheered so much for his gallant part in the sweet course that no one had the heart to comment that the orange flavour was decidedly salty.

It would not be one hundred per cent accurate to say we never make a mistake but we do not waste much food. We had to learn the hard way that you never make rice pudding or try to hot up tinned rice except in a double cooker. Similarly scrambled egg is only delicious when cooked in a covered bowl over boiling water. We have learned that when cooking steamed pudding the fire must roar all the time and that if the cook does have to go to the shore to supervise the swimming she must jolly well leave a competent person at the fire to see that it is stoked.

There was a day I remember vividly on Tiree, when our local vet, a native of Tiree, and his sister-in-law, Mairi, and family were coming from Cornaigbeg. In honour of their coming Joanna cleaned the kettle. She cleaned it very well indeed, inside and out, with Brillo pads. It shone like it had done when first brought from the shop but the tea it made was undrinkable. The taste of Brillo completely masked that of Typhoo.

Our guests were very nice about it and waited patiently for more water to be boiled and a fresh brew made and they did not hold it against us. On the contrary they brought us a gallon tub of icecream later in the week.

The boys didn't get any of it! We had threatened that they must help with the washing up that day and the horrible creatures scarpered. They could be seen on the beach a safe way from the camp.

When the unexpected icecream came someone took pity on them and ran calling on the shore, 'Come on boys, There's icecream for everyone in camp.'

'Huh,' called back Paul. 'We're not taken in with that one. Do you think it's April Fools' Day, or something?' Nobody bothered them any more and when they found out they'd missed a treat they were very sheepish.

It's quite amusing how my orders can be so mis-understood. Alison was making Instant Whip. She was very plump and liked her food, especially the sweet things. Whenever there was cooking she was there to help.

'What kind shall I use, Skipper?' she called from the store tent. 'Strawberry, lemon or butterscotch?'

'You can use a few of each,' I called back. 'Use ten.'

So Alison took a big bowl of milk and mixed in a few of each and the result looked revoltingly grey and tasted decidedly odd.

Instant food sounds ideal for camping with large numbers. Perhaps it is but it is also expensive and mostly we leave it severely alone. One year we were rash and brought a large tin of instant potatoes to make cheese cakes.

'Mix some instant potato,' I called from my vigil by the fire. Whereupon the cooks, with Mrs Belsey in charge, proceeded to mix the fine powder with cold water. I was very sarcastic. 'Cor!' I said, 'I thought everyone knew how to mix instant potato.' I really thought they'd ruined the whole tin. I had to take back my words, however. The fried cheese cakes were delicious. I don't know everything, that is perfectly obvious!

Of course they say that the few mistakes we make are because I don't explain properly and that they have to have imagination to know what I am talking about at all. Thank goodness Mrs Belsey is usually around.

'Fetch me the er,' I say with authority.

'Take her some more fat,' says the other half of the telepathy act.

'Get me er,' I say with both hands full. Someone hands me a tray.

'Not that,' I say in exasperation. 'I want er,' and Mrs Belsey sends me the bowl I am so desperately in need of. I say it is because I am harrassed by so many billies on the fire and if they were observant it would be obvious what I wanted anyway. They say it is old age or mental deterioration or some such uncomplimentary remark.

Compliments seldom come my way. Fortunately I appreciate that children seldom show their gratitude and affection in well chosen words. It is far more likely to be hidden in sarcasm, in wit and teasing. To me it is equally acceptable and sincere.

I was surrounded by fifteen year olds, one cold evening when I was making pancakes on the gas fire in the D'abri. Hazel was aiding and abetting their purloining of the hot pancakes and in spreading what I call 'unnecessary' butter. She was therefore very popular. I do not know how the subject of baldness came to be discussed.

'Was your father always bald, Skipper?' someone asked.

'No' I defended him, 'as a matter of fact he used to look like King George VI.'

'Mrs Belsey won't remember that,' someone oozed.

Hazel was delighted. 'Oh no,' she said. 'That was long before my time.' There was silence. The compliment was a stunner. It took everyone's breath away.

'What do you want?' I asked suspiciously.

'Another pancakes,' they chorused.

'Then isn't it Skipper you should compliment?' said my loyal friend. 'Not me. Say something nice about Skipper now.'

There was a long, uneasy silence. Apparently there was so little to compliment me for that even to think was arduous.

'Oh, come on,' she hurried them as the next panful of pancakes neared perfection. 'Surely you can think of something nice to say or you'll get no pancakes.'

The fifteen year olds smiled vacantly, unable to supply the necessary flattery. Then, at last, Catherine hit the Jackpot. 'You are number one with Prince Charles!' she said and the pan was emptied.

Cooking must be quick if all the other joys of camp are to be experienced. Life cannot be all meal making. Therefore the fire, whether it be under the grid or under the oven, must be very hot indeed. A great heat is necessary to bring a bucketful of potatoes to the boil and cook them in the same time it takes on the Aga at home and that is all the time we can spare.

We get milk for our porridge, on Harris, from the crofter on the hill. One year there was grave danger that we would get no milk at all. The Ministry bull, which is brought to the island every spring and returned to the stud every autumn, took a fancy to our milk cow and suckled her dry every morning. The crofter was at his wit's end. He brought the cow off the hill and tried keeping her close to the croft.

Margaret was not with us that year and I suggested that we send home for some device to prevent him suckling. We had several steel discs which can be clipped into a yearling's nose if it persists in suckling the dam when her next calf is born. We also had a harness and string bag contraption which enclosed the whole udder in a calf proof net. I wanted to send for a disc as these are successful and easy but the crofters declared that they would be in trouble if they tampered with the Ministry bull. He is evidently a very sacred animal.

Hazel was ringing home to her husband that night and offered to send a message direct to Margaret. 'Tell her to send a string bra for Dolly's cow,' I told her. 'She'll understand.' She knew exactly what was meant and a few days later the strange parcel arrived. The poor old cuddy looked somewhat ridiculous in her unusual underwear, but we got milk for our porridge.

The islanders work more by the calendar than we do. On the fifteenth of August, each year, the herd comes down from the hill and with it the Ministry bull. They roam the sand dunes where the children play, the beach where we swim and they eat the machair on the other side of our somewhat flimsy fence. Normally we camp in

100

July and I had some mis-givings when our camp dates had to be changed to the last fortnight in August. I shuddered at the thought of allowing so many children to leap and scream and shout on the sand dunes anywhere in the vicinity of so large a bull as the Ministry's Aberdeen Angus. I was reassured.

'Och, the bull is very quiet. He will be lying on the shore and strangers will walk right beside him and he will not be getting up at all.'

'If it were last year's bull, that would be different. There was not a fence at all that could keep him out but this bull is quiet.' I was still aprehensive.

'The bull will hurt no one at all, Chean,' I was told. 'He's not dangerous at all. It's the sea that's dangerous. Forget about the bull and watch the waves.'

We had an Aberdeen Angus bull at home and he was so quiet that we could step over him. Indeed we had to do so often because he would sleep near the front door or just in the entrance to the barn. I have fed calves with my legs so near to his head that I could feel his hot breathing and yet he moved not a muscle. But should anything strange happen he was a different animal altogether and I would not have trusted him one minute with fifteen white tents on the other side of a fence that would not hold him.

'The bull will not bother you at all,' said our own crofter. 'If you will not wear the red. Any bull will go for the red. Chust tell the children not to go on the beach wearing anything red and he'll not be troubling you at all.' What a suggestion! At least half our cagoules were bright, bright red and every towel and bikini were scarlet. We tried but it was well nigh impossible. Perhaps even the Ministry bull is colour blind as they say all bulls are. Maybe he is just a nicer one than most, inspite of his size. Perhaps he is contented like all Hebrideans, natives or visitors. Look at it as you may he caused us no trouble at all. The cows were much more precocious. They sadly depleted our store of tea towels and on no account dare we leave a bikini on the fence.

We have had great fun trying to cook local dishes and using food gathered from the field and shore. We were given a handful of dried carragheen on Tiree and successfully warmed some milk and thickened it with the dried seaweed to make an excellent blancmange. We flavoured it with a little raspberry jam and it was delicious. We have eaten mussels and cockles gathered on the shore and tried, but did not like, a bowlful of limpets.

We came on a fieldful of mushrooms on Arran, when we were camping for three weeks at Machrie Bay. The hospitality of this island is not in dispute. It is a beautiful land, full of generous people but it is the only place we have ever found where we could not pick field mushrooms, or rather that when we had picked them we had to forfeit them to the owner.

Mushrooms grow here in our own fields at home and they belong to whoever finds them. I must confess it is a little galling to see someone out early, gleaning the fields of every mushroom on our land but that is the way of it. 'Finding is keeping' where mushrooms are concerned. Bilberries and blackberries belong to everyone and elderberries can be taken from every tree. It therefore never occured to us that we were doing anything wrong on Arran.

We came upon the field unexpectedly. The footpath we were taking ran gaily through it. The fungi did not appear to have been gathered recently for the field was full of old, decaying mushrooms as well as new growth. Perhaps that was why there were so many, because, ungathered they had been able to reproduce in quantity.

We were intoxicated with our find and thought of the delicious soup we would make for supper or the mushrooms on toast we would serve for breakfast.

'I'll cook them in best butter,' I promised.

We improvised so that we could carry them, repacking the picnic baskets so as to leave one free for the field treasures we had found. It was a beautiful day and we felt as if we had struck gold.

'We'll have some fried for breakfast,' I continued there were so many. 'I'll put some of them in the stew.' Margaret and I had never gathered so many at once.

'Are you sure they're mushrooms?' asked an unbeliever.

'Quite sure,' I said. The earthy and quite distinctive smell of them covered my hands and the taste of them was already in my mouth.

We were still gathering in the harvest when a lady came across the field from the house and told us we could not have them! We did not protest. How could we! We were stunned and disappointed but we could not argue. The field was not ours. I don't think we have been more flabbergasted. We said a silent, sad 'Goodbye' to all hopes of delicious soup and buttered mushrooms on toast and emptied the basket into a delectable pile. We said we were sorry and took away only the story to laugh over in the long winter evenings at home.

It is mushroom time as I write this. I marvel that such busy people as Margaret and I still have time to hunt for the odd pound of mushrooms which other people are not sharp-eyed enough to see. An hour soon goes and we seldom get more than a small bagful. Mushrooms do not grow here with the abundance with which they grow in the Hebrides as we have since learned but the satisfaction of even a few, and the delicious meal which follows are worth all the lost minutes.

We have gathered mushrooms in plenty on Tiree. We gathered two pails full to the brim behind the thatched, white cottage where our friends live. Hebrideans on some of the islands will not eat them at all and think they are poisonous. A friend with whom we stay will not even cook them if we gather them. We found enough for breakfast at the Butt of Lewis, one day, but she just laughed at our foolishness.

We were so busy picking them, that first time on Tiree, that we did not see the sea fret coming in from the Atlantic with incredible speed. I remember the gatherers suddenly shouting and running towards camp as if to protect it from a fire breathing monster. We picked up the two full baskets and ran after them.

Washing was snatched from the line in great haste, brailings unrolled and doors closed. The mist enveloped everything and in the sanctuary of the D'abri, wearing our warmest sweaters, we pealed off the skins and scraped the stalks for a truly delicious meal.

There was a year on Tiree when mushrooms grew so plentifully that we ate them for breakfast, dinner and tea. They sprang up overnight in their hundreds and were gathered in preference to the shells and beach flotsom the children generally find so attractive. We gathered them greedily when our larder was full and there was no need. We put them in stews already so rich and delicious that to add mushrooms was mere extravagance. They accompanied mixed grills which were amply satisfying in themselves and no one grumbled at the extra billy which was to wash. And we took 30lbs with us to Yorkshire at the end of camp.

Certainly we were not in need of another plastic carrier bagful but Susan, Rosalind and I filled it in a field at Balephetrish before climbing the three 'peaks', Beinn Hough, 388', Ceann a Mhara, and Ben Hynish, 460'. It was sheer greed, double greed because first we had to empty the plastic bag.

Some of the walkers were trailing and whilst I waited for them to catch up I called to see some good friends at Tullymet. A few days previously the good lady had fed a group of our children on their way home from Scarinish. She had seen us passing in great numbers and wanted to give us something else. I found her busy parcelling up a sponge cake and emptying biscuits into a plastic box. I remonstrated but she would not be deprived of her pleasure. The trailers arrived and gladly accepted the biscuits and I set off again, a strange hiker carrying a sponge fit for the cake stall of any garden fête.

Half an hour later I had left the trailers behind and overtaken Susan and Rosalind, eleven and nine respectively and already beginning to weary.

'Just let's catch up the others and we'll eat this cake,' I promised. Thus bribed they lengthened their steps until we could see the other walkers half a mile away.

'Wait you lot,' yelled the healthy youngsters. 'We've got food.'

No one heard. Heads down, ears muffled by their cagoule hoods and the softly falling rain, they pressed on unheedingly and the distance began to grow between us.

'That field is full of mushrooms,' Rosalind suddenly announced. We leaned over the fence and knew that the temptation to pick them was too great. No matter how we emptied our pockets we could find no plastic bag in which to put them other than the carrier bag containing the sponge cake.

'We'll have to eat it!' said Susan.

'We can't eat it all,' I said.

'We can!' said Rosalind and we did, every delicious crumb of it and we filled the carrier to the brim with mushrooms.

The 30lbs we took home with us at the end of camp travelled farther than we did. The picnic skip containing them was never lifted off the train when we arrived home. It continued happily on as far as Skipton. Our possessiveness towards mushrooms is such that we created havoc in the station until we were reassured that it would come back on the next train. I collected it very late that night and we sat up until morning preparing them for the freezer.

We were at Calum's one day when we were able to sample fresh prawns, caught on the rocks below Salum House and on several occasions we have been given lobsters. The most memorable one came from our over generous friend at Strond. She gave it to us especially for Hazel who loves them so. It was a lovely lobster, quite the reddest I have ever seen. We took it with us on the island bus to Stornoway and I must confess we intended to eat most of it alone, when we had sent the children off on their shopping spree.

We did not bargain for it being the day of the Stornoway Procession and Gala. We heard the news when we stopped to buy ice creams at Balallen and of course everyone was excited. We decided to send everyone away, on arrival, to get what shopping done they could before the prematurely early closing of the shops.

'Let's go for a coffee,' I said. 'Then come back quickly and prepare a meal for the kids. They'll be ages.'

We are seldom alone. There are always hangers-on who feel more secure with us. We rarely go into a coffee bar without one on each hand. It was inevitable that there would be some to share the lobster and indeed we could not have eaten it all between the two of us. We did not, however, bargain for the shops to close as early as they did, even if it were early closing day and Gala day, and we had not even started to eat the lobster before the crowds came back carrying the presents they had brought for home.

Like the loaves and the fishes that lobster had to feed a great many people. On each palm was placed the minutest pink and white offering and three cheers rang from the bus window, and out across the harbour, for our generous benefactor.

There are many occasions when we have tried to treat ourselves and found it impossible. There was the morning after the dance when everyone was sound asleep and Hazel and I were wide awake. There are few things I refuse to cook in camp but fried eggs happens to be one of them. Fifty fried eggs! To use Cynthia's phrase, the mind boggles.

'All I want to go home for,' says Viv every year, 'is for fried eggs and bacon, tomatoes and mushrooms for my breakfast.'

'I'll tell you what,' I said to Hazel on that beautiful morning after the dance, 'How would you like bacon and eggs for breakfast?' I was sitting up in bed remembering mornings like this with Margaret, a little white tent and no children. 'There's no one awake. Let's leave them be and have a civilised breakfast. Just the two of us.'

The body in the next bed sighed blissfully. ''Sounds lovely,' it said.

I dressed and crept out of the tent and into the D'abri, put on the gas, sat on an upturned bucket and began to fry. I had just finished a perfect egg and lifted it, with crispy bacon onto my colleague's plate when the D'abri door parted and Julia poked her head in.

'S shhh,' we hissed. 'Don't make a sound. Come in and join us. We're being selfish.'

She took a plate and I lifted out the second breakfast from the pan, laid in more bacon and broke another egg. It was hardly ready before the next early riser caught the delicious smell in the air and came to the D'abri. And the next and the next . . . I served twelve breakfasts before I finally cooked my own. Robert Burns knew what he was talking about when he wrote, 'The best laid schemes of mice and men . . .'

Crowdie is our favourite cheese but we always drink all the milk we can get on our porridge and cornflakes and have none left to solidify for crowdie making. In any case we could not make it half so successfully as the dear lady who provides us with a huge plateful every two days.

'Can we have crowdie this year?' I am asked innumerable times. I explain that crowdie is a gift I cannot order because no payment will be accepted but the crowdie adicts are never disappointed. The beautiful white mound is carried carefully down to camp by Catherine, or Morag, or Morag Ann or Ishbel or which ever daughter happens to be at home. There are cheers to greet her. Any excuse excites all children to cheer. One day a parcel of food came too. In it we found the daintiest sandwiches, fresh scones and pancakes. We were told they were left overs from the shepherds' picnic at the fank. I include this because I want you to know that the shepherds of the Western Isles are married to the best of Britain's housewives.

One would think it impossible to eat such vast quantities of food and still have appetites for sweets and crisps and whatsoever mama sends in the innumerable tuck boxes which appear with each morning's post. The red van hoots his horn loudly and whatever we are doing there is a sudden flight of Yorkshire starlings towards the road. One thoughtful person only will run for the cornflakes box which satisfies our need for a camp pillar box. It rattles all the way to the van because it is full of loose change. Few have the right stamps and the good man has the patience of Job. He sorts out the assortment of coins each day and buys the missing stamps.

Almost everyone gets a tuck box except Margaret and I who have no husband to send a box of chocolates like Hazel has. The contents of these mystery parcels are eaten at midnight at forbidden feasts. We ban them in the certain knowledge that they are no fun unless they are illegal. We know also that there is no fun unless my voice shouts from the tent, 'Who's making all that noise?' We are seldom deceived but we have no wish to join them. We are far too tired and too old for midnight capers.

If necessity should will it and national disaster bestow upon me the job of feeding many from a camp kitchen, I believe I could do it for a great length of time. I never weary of my job or count the days hoping that they will pass quickly. But immediately I am home I want no part in the preparation of food for many a day. I want to make no decisions about what we shall eat or drink and I am more than willing to eat it raw.

The strange thing is, and this I can never quite understand, when I weigh myself on the bathroom scales in the little house where I have my most welcome bath of the year, I have always lost weight. I have eaten three big meals a day instead of two, I have consumed snacks and strupags galore. Much of the food has been of a fattening nature and yet, praise be, I have lost weight. There must be a lesson in this somewhere.

9

Wind, wind, heather gypsy
Whistling in my tree,
All the heart of me is tipsy
At the thought of thee.
Sweet with scent of clover,
Salt with breath of sea,
Wind, wind, wayman lover,
Whistling in my tree.

Chapter Nine

'I HOPE you get good weather for your camp!' say all my friends before we go as if this matters more than anything.

'Oh, blow the weather,' I reply. 'Just pray that we have no accident and that everyone is well.'

We can cope with the weather! It does put us severely to the test, we admit, and we take care never to underestimate the violence of the westerly gales, the horizontal, stinging slant of the downpour when it rains, the cutting sharpness of blown sand from the dunes and lack of shelter in blistering sun. All are trying, to say the least, but weather is something we cannot order or alter. Wisdom, we know, is in changing what can be changed and accepting what cannot without question. The happiness and safety of our children is our responsibility and the weather is not, so we concern ourselves with the one and take the other just as it comes. It is much less traumatic to learn how to cope with its extremes than to worry oneself sick beforehand.

Weather will never spoil our fun and it is much more likely to increase it. Contrary to most people's suppositions the most difficult weather can be the heatwave. If it comes at the end of a good summer it can do little harm for the children are already browned and immunised against too much sun. If it descends unexpectedly after a long winter and a cold spring it can be disastrous, especially under canvas, on treeless islands where there is no escape from its glare. Our work is considerably harder in heat and we return home more tired after a hot camp than a wet one. It may sound silly but it is so.

Heat brings sun spots and midges, sore arms and legs, headaches and smaller appetites. It saps energy, necessitates our standing for long hours in the water, holding the safety rope, and makes every job round the fire and oven very much harder.

But it has its compensations. It makes bedtime routine incredibly easy. There is no need to slacken guys or to wander round in the early hours to make sure that no one has rolled under the tent wall and is getting a wet bed. No clothes line hangs in the D'abri, dripping wet swimming costumes and towels coldly against your face and no pile of wet cagoules litters the tops of the skips in the store when we are eating. We can turn a blind, uncaring eye on the wader in the sea who is not so agile as her relative the noisy oyster catcher and allows seas to break over shorts and shirt. We can allow Kathy to swim in her knickers and vest and go into hysterics at the sight of her astonished face everytime the seas run back and leave her semi-decent because the knicker elastic is not tight enough and the sea is in a teasing mood. Neither shirt nor shorts will take any drying. Ten minutes in the blazing sun and all will be well.

We have known fortnights in the Hebrides when there has been no rain in the forecast at all, when day after day had dawned with cloudless skies and Julia has pulled her sleeping bag out onto the machair to watch the sun rise and then slept some more in the open.

We have known Tiree so dry that even the sand has lost its absorbancy and spilled water has stood in pools, like mercury, or as if the earth has become water-proof. One year we knew that if it rained water would pour down Happy Valley in the same way that water will rush down the waddies in the desert when the rain comes.

'If it rains at all we must trench round the tents,' I warned, 'or water will just run through them.'

I can only presume that I dreamt that it was raining. If it was an illusion it was a very noisy one and very real. It was dark and I distinctly heard rain falling on the roof of the canvas.

'Rain!' I shouted to Margaret in her cocoon. 'We'll have to trench or water will run over the groundsheets. We'll have forty wet beds in the morning.' She hates getting up during the night on holiday for she has many broken nights, in the long months before Christmas, when she is busy rearing calves.

Pour soul, she was half asleep. Not so me. I was wide awake and worried. We pulled on heavy oilskins and sou' westers, (the kind that keep you very dry and make you very deaf) and went outside. It was pitch dark.

All our actions were mechanical and reflex. Taking a spade each, to ease up a line of sod around each tent to take away the water, we went our separate ways. We did not talk, no one wakened. Our oilskins were stiff and dry, our sou' westers fell over our faces obscuring vision.

We met at the D'abri, half an hour later, the job completed. I remember my sister pushing back her sou' wester and wiping the sweat from her face. 'Are you sure it's raining?' she said.

'What?' I shouted. It's very difficult to hear in oilskins.

'Are you sure it's raining?' she shouted, careless of waking children. We pulled off our sou' westers in the darkness. The air was crisp and dry.

'I don't believe we are wet at all,' she observed incredulously. 'Look, the canvas isn't even wet and our feet are dry!'

It was true. The ground was dry. The burnt up grass was too short to catch the dew. We couldn't believe it. For half an hour we had sweated in oilskins, looking like the Skipper on a tin of Norwegian Bristlings. We'd been unable to see, or feel, or hear properly. We'd had no thought but to trench and we had done it mechanically, in a semi conscious state half-way between sleeping and waking.

My sister was suddenly very wide awake and what she said reduced my stature several inches before we both burst out laughing. We saw the funny side of it to-gether, in the middle of the ghostly, white tents of the sleeping camp. It never did rain. My sister thinks it never had!

All too often, though, it does. We have lain in our sleeping bags believing every minute that the flapping, riotous canvas above our heads must surely tear itself free of guys and poles, hurtle into the night and leave us to drown. All of us know the sound. Christine wrote in her first essay back at school, 'I lay in my tent listening to the wind howling and a loose guy flapping against my tent.'

She received a good mark, having written well about something she knew, but the essay would have been forgotten, lost to the memory like hundreds like it, if it hadn't been for the amusing fact that the teacher had scored out the word 'guy' and written 'rope' instead. She had used red biro.

One wild night on Tiree, Margaret and I lay in our little white tent on the very edge of the machair, at Salum Bay. We were more exposed to the elements than the heavier tents in the hollow of the sandy valley. We had just had a hectic hour trying to secure the tents against a rising gale sweeping straight in from the Atlantic. We had driven pegs in deeply everywhere, double pegging where there was greatest strain. We had locked all runners and securely laced the doors.

Because the wind continually took our lid from the water bin we had stowed it away in the D'abri and risked the drinking water being full of sand in the morning. We had braved the gale swept beach to bring back more water than usual to give weight to the washing up water bath, for the wind threatened to steal that also.

Unable to do more, other than pray for a drop in the wind speed, we had fought our way into the tent exhausted. Wearily we had undressed and crawled into our sleeping bags. We had not talked at all. We both lay there silent, listening to the din. The noise in the canvas of the little white tent exceeded any we had ever known in camp before. The canvas crashed above our heads like a dozen whip lashes.

Suddenly I saw the funny side of it all. What chance had so small a tent, against such a gale, on an island as flat as Tiree. The wind was just laughing at me for presuming to make such a flimsy tent and expect it to withstand such fury. It was just chortling with mirth ridiculing us, laughing at our frailty. It was playing a game with us and thoroughly enjoying itself. I began to shake with uncontrollable laughter and I could feel the other sleeping bag shaking beside me. Margaret was laughing too. We have the same sense of humour.

'Is there any hope of sleeping in a racket like this?' she hooted as if she thought the mere idea was outrageously funny.

'Oh, I don't know,' I said, 'we've slept in some queer places before. Remember Islay when we slept so close to the sea it made our few yards of camp an island when the tide came in? Remember Mallaig?'

'We'll never forget Mallaig!' she agreed.

We'd asked permission to pitch a small tent which had only held the four of us, Janet, Ann, Margaret and me, providing the fly sheet was used and on condition that we did not turn over. But we had had a night to spend in Mallaig, and we are of the breed that sleeps in tents and not on the platform seats of draughty stations as we've seen some people do.

A dear lady had said we could put our tent on an almost impossibly small piece of grass, so close to the seaweed strewn shore as to be but a foot away from it. We had pitched and eaten and listened to the wind rising and howling outside.

'We're in for a right night,' Janet had prophesied.

'When it's high tide the sea'll be awfully close,' Ann had remarked. 'They're

109

high tides. The seaweed's wet.'

We had been asleep when the storm broke. It woke us with its violence and the incoming tide seemed to shout angrily at us for daring to come so close. There had been thunder too, and torrential rain; the kind which makes you think that the tap in heaven has been turned on and the jet of water directed through a colander. The tide had seemed to come in with great speed and vengence and the waves to boil in front of our tent. Suddenly there had been a new noise. One of running water.

'Is there a stream nearby?' someone had asked. There hadn't been one on arrival but a torrent of water was blazing a trail down the hillside, cascading over the rocks and leaping into the sea.

With the din of angrily falling rain on taut canvas, we had re-slept and would have remained oblivious, I think, till dawn had we not been noisily awakened by the lady of the house. She had appeared outside our tent, flashing her torch and soaking up the rain. She was calling to us to come into the house.

'I canna sleep for worrying about you!' she had called.

'But we can't do that,' I'd told her. 'It's very kind of you but we are dry and if we come out there we'll get wet.'

You have to be a camper to know the security of a tent. She hadn't understood. I'm quite sure she'd thought we were crazy. Nevertheless we had wakened next morning dry . . .

'Yes, I remember Mallaig,' said Margaret and we both turned over and went to sleep. It was a bad night but no worse than one we spent in a small plantation of a dozen pine trees at North Bay, on Barra and certainly no worse than nights we've had at home when, at danger to life and limb, we have nailed back flapping corrugated sheets on shed roofs.

In retrospect it was no worse either than the very first night we ever spent in the Hebrides with children; that wonderful first time we had with Sheila, who was a student, a singer of Lonnie Donegan songs, eleven year old Ian's best friend and our first Queen's Guide. That was a terrible night, on Tiree, twenty summers ago and we were glad to find the tents still there in the morning.

We'd pitched in the face of a rising gale but in brilliant sunshine. The raising of each tent had to be a major operation in which all took part and we had to hang onto the canvas of each in turn as it billowed out like a full sail. Double pegging and locked guys were insufficient and we had, in desperation, tied six foot bark strippings, brought from Mull to feed the fire, onto the sod cloths and weighted them down with pebbles carried from the beach.

Calum said that, according to the radio, the gale was expected to rise even more and he was gravely concerned about our safety. 'I'm sure you should not be sleeping outside tonight,' he said. 'Och, if I were you, Chean, I would bring them all into the barn tonight. The night is to be very wild indeed, if the man in the box is right, and I'm sure he is for it looks awful stormy.'

'Even so,' I said, 'we cannot leave the tents unless we really have to. We've got to be here to catch them if they decide to give up the struggle and blow away.' Our houses are very precious indeed.

'Ach well,' said the worried man,' I'll not be sleeping very well thinking of all these children on the shore.'

It was a very wild night, that first one with children in the Hebrides and we were glad of our previous camping experience and the tough way we had been brought up on the farm when we were children. Brute strength was needed to hold those tents down.

Almost everyone wore pyjamas in the early days. They are of course, snug and warm in a sleeping bag but they are impossible if one has to get up in the night. No cycling cape, oilskin or cagoule will protect the lower half of the trousers. If one has to wander round the camp in the middle of the night, which is not uncommon, hammering in pegs and securing or slackening guys, the only alternative to wet pyjama legs is to remove them first and leave them behind in the warm sleeping bag. Bare legs can be easily dried on a towel. Nowadays almost every girl has a shorty nightie and I have followed suit, finding one a great deal more convenient. It is bad enough having to get up and go out into the cold and wet without having to take off warm clothing besides.

We used to take a storm lantern until we found that there wasn't one on the market, that we could afford, which would withstand a Hebridean gale. Within seconds the light used to be extinguished. A good torch meets most of our needs but it was a lantern I had to struggle with that first night on Tiree.

We took turns, all night, walking round the tents repairing wind damage. Reluctantly I would drag myself out of bed consoled only by the knowledge that next time it would be Margaret's turn. Off came the warm pyjamas and over my head went the cold cycling cape. Modern cagoules are just as cold and pretty horrible when wet.

It was just like being on the deck of an aircraft carrier when the Bay of Biscay was at its worst. Flat and treeless there was no shelter at all. The only way I could keep the lantern in was to hold it beneath my cape. There is nothing so dark as an island when cloud obscures the moon and stars. On the Mainland there is usually a light from a house or a village street or a glow sent up by a distant town. In the Hebrides we have come out of lighted houses into darkness so impenetrable that we have experienced blindness and have clung together and groped with our feet for the pathway. For this reason we have always bought and made white tents, for even on the blackest of nights they are vaguely luminous.

I battled my way from tent to tent on that first, wild, July night, amazed that they were still standing, blessing the logs and pebbles which anchored them against the gale. I returned, after a particularly long session, to find Margaret awake. When she saw me she burst out laughing.

'Have you seen what you look like?' she shouted above the gale. 'You couldn't be more illuminated in a goldfish bowl. For goodness sake either risk getting your trousers wet or don't hold the lantern under your cape.'

Next morning Calum was down at the campsite almost before we wakened. 'Och it was a terrible night, Margaret,' he said. 'I'm sure I could not sleep at all. I chust kept coming down to the camp to see if you had all been blown back to the Mainland.'

If he had also seen a transparent, yellow ghost flitting round the tents the good man was too discreet to say so and I was too embarrassed to ask.

The storm which did us most damage was on Arran. We were camping on peaty soil which has none of the qualities of sand but it was a beautiful place. We were very happy there and Mr and Mrs John Frew were extraordinarily kind to us. The lats were a nuisance because when it rained they became flooded, something we had not experienced before.

We had a long way to walk to the church and, as the wind was very strong, we dare not leave the camp absolutely deserted. We therefore left two seniors behind and battled our way along to Shiskine, to the morning service. I remember singing, 'We need thee every hour, most gracious Lord,' and watching the white clouds chase each other madly across the sky through a small window in the church.

We had to fight our way back to Flag Point and with every minute the wind increased. Our re-entry into camp must have looked like a Giles Cartoon or something from the Golden Silents' era. The tents were heaving and flapping and the ridge poles were creaking ominously like masts of tall ships on a stormy ocean.

'Secure your tents,' I bellowed, seeing the urgency. The two who had been left in camp were nearly exhausted. They had fought for two hours to keep the camp safe but even forty were unable to do that! We had only just got back in time.

The wind was roaring up the Kilbrannan Sound bent on complete destruction, lifting the waves into mountains and looking with scorn and anger on our flimsy houses. Within minutes of our arrival the first ridge snapped. We know what to do when this happens. We have had plenty of experience camping on windswept beaches. There were willing hands to hold the uprights and stalwart bodies to lean against the inside canvas to take the strain and ease the weight off the main guys. Plenty of experienced help came to unpeg the main guys and draw them and repeg them fore and aft, double peg the guys and lock the runners. It usually works. If a ridge goes in the middle of the night fore and aft pegging will hold till morning but not in an Arran gale.

Everywhere people were hanging onto uprights and pressing their weight against the billowing walls of tents, trying to ride out the gale with everyone as anchor-man but it was of little use.

'Listen to the D'abri creaking,' someone warned.

'Our ridge's gone!' the cry came from beneath a second sagging tent.

'Ours will be next!' forecast another struggling group.

We were to be on Arran for nearly three weeks and only one week had gone by. We dare not be foolhardy. We had too few spare ridges to risk them all. 'We must have a weather forecast,' I yelled. 'Run to the farm, June, and see if they know when the wind is likely to drop.' June fled, the wind giving her the speed of seven league boots.

'Perhaps it will drop with the turn of the tide,' said Valerie.

'The wind is to continue and to increase,' was the message from the farm. Fortunately it was not raining and we have learned to be grateful for small mercies. I told everyone to take turns in packing personal belongings and pile them in the centre of each tent. We put all kitchen equipment into the skips and sealed the lids. We have never ever been so quick.

Then, without more ado, we lowered the tents, rough-rolled them and began a massive evacuation to the barn. Everything unanchored became airborne. Trays and plastic bowls hurtled through the air, water bin lids, plastic bags and comics chased each other madly. Someone's playing cards spilled and flew away. Billy lids, the notice board and even a formica table top rose like kites. Lats were flat and toilet paper unravelled and blew away. Buckets fell over and rolled in animation and all the while we laughed as if it were a huge joke, the funniest thing of the year.

We had lost three ridge poles. The whole field was a shambles and believe it or not everyone was enjoying it. Some were even stealing a precious moment to photograph it believing that they might never see the like of it again. The only things to remain standing were the flagpole, for some reason, and our little white tent. The barn was a very small, two storey building. The lower half was filled with our equipment arranged as neatly as we could, considering the frantic haste, and the loft looked ridiculously small to accommodate so many people.

We spent the afternoon evacuating and the evening retrieving things from fields away. Then we spent some time on the shore watching the enormous seas disturbing the Kilbrannan Sound. We ate hungrily after such exercise and everyone slept soundly except me. I was too over anxious about us having to sleep so closely together and I was continually stepping over bodies to see that no one was in danger of suffocation. The inert children never stirred and in the morning everyone was still breathing.

By dawn the gale had spent itself and, after breakfast, we were able to repitch, improvise new ridges and begin again. Everyone reckoned we had had an experience worth having. I hoped it would be one we never had to repeat but the weather remained unsettled all camp and, on the next to the last day, the dry gale came again and the tents began to take an awful battering. We decided to say 'enough is enough' and struck camp even though it meant a second night in the loft. It was a relief to be going home and not to have a repitch in the morning.

We never abandon camp unless we are absolutely sure there is no alternative and even then we seldom leave no one to guard the tents. Never do we leave them over-night with no night-watchmen. We have had many ridges snap and we have had canvas tear but never again have we had to drop all our tents as we had to do on Arran.

We have had rain which threatened to persist all day and Sundays seem more vulnerable than other days to storm and tempest. One Sunday, on Harris, it began to rain soon after breakfast. We were unable to have our morning service out of doors and congregated in the D'abri for our hymn and reading and prayer. This morning service, which we have each day, is now entirely in the hands of the children and some have found delightful and profound stories to read.

On this particularly rainy day we had the short service and then we proceeded to sing every hymn in our small hymn book. Having exhausted its possibilities we sang every campfire song we knew and the rain continued to beat upon the roof. We

113

played every guessing game we could think of and were surprised at our extensive repertoire.

Our singing had made us thirsty and hungry so Linda and I donned oilskins and went out to make a meal. We put on enough billies to completely cover the fire, it being the only way we could protect it from the deluge. The heat from it was like a furnace. We made gallons of soup and hotted up tinned steak and two lots of tinned vegetables. We boiled a bucketful of potatoes and made custard to put on tinned peaches and enough coffee for a multitude.

Satisfied with our efforts we carried the steaming billies into the D'abri and the cheering children and we all ate until we could eat no more because every scrap was gone. We tried to make the meal last a long time for there was little left to do but eat. At last we carried a big bucket of steaming, soapy water into our midst and the washing up patrol had a gay audience whilst they immersed the dirty dishes in the rich suds and polished them dry.

Eventually even that entertainment came to an end so we chatted for a while and the children played cards and read comics and still the rain beat upon the roof as if there were no end to its din. We played with string, wrote letters home, made up songs and played charades. The afternoon wore on and we began to think we were there for the day. The rain bounced off the canvas and tightened the guys so that we slackened and reslackened again and again and watched the canvas shrinking alarmingly.

We were all rather amused by this time. Witty remarks were thought to be hilarious. We began to wonder if the rain in the Hebrides were intoxicating.

'Tell it to stop, Skipper,' somebody challenged. 'Go to the door and tell it we've had enough!'

'Okay,' I promised, 'I'll fix it.'

Everyone was listening; any entertainment was appreciated. The unity in the tent was unique. More than forty children had been confined for several hours and boredom could have been an enemy but there was no room for it in the full tent.

'Right,' I said dramatically in the doorway, 'we've had enough, thank you very much. You may not believe it, to hear the noise in here, but we are definitely not amused!'

There were shouts of laughter. Of course I have no supernatural powers. The rain does not stop when I tell it to nor when I beg it to. That has been proved a hundred times, but on that wet afternoon, when the smell of hot bodies in the D'abri had become strong and cramp was being felt in every muscle, the rain did stop. A short time later there was a lull in the noisy chatter and we were conscious of a silence.

'It's stopped raining,' someone breathed. She was right. When the D'abri doors were opened wide it was like the opening of the Ark. Like released animals the children tumbled out and leapt about in a wild desire for activity. Everything was very green and wet but the blessed, sandy machair was firm.

'Let's go for a walk!' they said.

So we did, or rather we went for a run. There was a mad helter skelter for the shore and in the direction of a new sound, one we had not heard there before and which we could not immediately identify.

'Blimey,' shouted the boys who were always well ahead, 'there's a fantastic waterfall!'

The lochan at the foot of the Ben must have overflowed, suddenly having to cope with a deluge of water from its contributary streams. Overflowing it had filled the burn with white water. Just above the croft it leapt several feet into the creek which is so often dry. Now water was carving a deep ravine 4 feet deep in the sand all the way to the sea. We slithered up the slope, marvelling at the cascade, tossing in bits of marram grass and watching them hurtle down to the sea. The activity was infectious. We began to toss in shells and bits of driftwood until the novelty palled and the stampede for the shore was resumed.

It is interesting to note that only one person got wet on that very rainy Sunday. There was not a wet cagoule nor any article of clothing. The shelter of the D'abri had remained absolute. We emerged from it completely dry and only I did not remain so. I slid, unexpectedly, down a wet and moss covered rock at the foot of the mountain and landed fair and square in a foot of water. I was as wet as if I had been in the sea fully clothed.

There was a wet day when we went to Stornoway. Just as the D'abri is a sanctuary when the elements have no mercy, so is a bus. There is the same safe feeling that everyone is together, warm and dry. There is the secure feeling that food is available without having the chore of cooking it and there is the knowledge that, because we have left camp for a while we have also left it in order, like a house tidied and left and locked for the day. Neat and deserted it will keep dryer than with the disturbing presence of children continually delving into rucksacks and crowding into tents.

Sometimes weather descends on us unexpectedly and we have left camp unattended. On these occasions we may expect to find anything on our return. Without someone to slacken the guys in wet weather they become taut enough to pull up pegs, snap ridges and tear canvas. It is not unusual to return to find lats flat and loosely flapping tent doors. If the weather threatens before we leave, a couple of volunteers will stay behind. It is a luxury to be alone in camp with only meals to prepare for two and leisure to fill selfishly. Volunteers know this.

On the wet day we went to Stornoway Linda stayed behind alone for it was sincerely hoped that the weather would clear and as she was staying on Harris for a further week, after our departure, she knew she would get another chance to go to Stornoway.

It was a grey start to our journey but even so the weather deteriorated rapidly and heavy, black clouds hung low over the mountains of North Harris which so effectively divide Harris from neighbouring Lewis and make of them different peoples.

'The bad weather is here and not in Lewis,' we said optimistically. 'The sun is shining in Stornoway.'

We could see a ribbon of blue on the northern horizon and believed it to be an omen, but the blue sky was travelling northwards faster than we were. It was like tomorrow, always a little way ahead and there was nothing we could do about it.

We had an incredibly peaceful day travelling slowly through the rain, wandering gently round the shops and eating fish and chips within the steamy interior of the bus. Then we crossed to Bravas on the western coast and pottered around the shop that sells local crafts.

For some years I have worn a leather clasp in my somewhat untidy 'bun.' It had become shabby and camp had not improved it and I knew I could get a replacement in the little shop. I was about to buy one when Mandy and Julia came up behind me. 'Don't buy one of those will you, Skipper?' they begged.

'Why ever not,' I said insensitively.

'Well, we can't tell you, cos it's a secret,' they said in embarrassment. If it was a secret it was a very transparent one. I did not buy and showed surprise and pleasure in my present at the end of camp.

Surely, we thought, after we had spent a pleasant half hour in the Black House at Arnol, enjoying the snug little dwelling and sitting for a while round the peat fire burning in the centre of the floor – surely the rain will have stopped before we get back to camp. In our experience wet weather seldom lasts all day in the Hebrides. Sooner or later there will be a break in the clouds and we can get ourselves sorted and dried out. The Hebridean summer may not be all sunshine but it is certainly not all rain. Provided there is some wind a change in the weather is not very far away. Without wind there is less hope. We attended Sheep Dog Trials in Tarbert, one year, when a dirty, black cloud settled overhead and refused to move. It was like being under a holey umbrella all afternoon and we could see the sun shining all around us.

There was cloud over Harris and Lewis on that memorable day that even the strong wind failed to move. There was premature darkness on the road under the shoulder of Clishan. the highest mountain on the island. Mist hung heavily and encircled us, swirling eerily in front of our windscreen. Great torrents of water emptied themselves down the corries on the bare, black mountains, fell in gushing waterfalls over the ledges and continued boiling into the lochs. It was the worst and most sinister weather we have experienced, breathtaking and wonderful and we rubbed the steam from the windows to see the magnificence of its blackness.

Into the sea the rivers poured water so rich and brown with peat that the ocean turned from turquoise to the colour of strong tea, as golden as if it had been gilded. Streams we never knew existed tumbled white water down the hillsides and lochs overspilled angry water into the burns that led to the sea.

From the dry security of the bus Pat Roberts and I were fascinated. Margaret and I would have enjoyed it tramping but the thought of fifty dry people stepping warm from the bus and walking the half mile back to a wet camp was not inviting. I knew, however, that the driver could be persuaded to take the bus up the impossibly narrow road and turn on a postage stamp sized piece of ground. Even so it would be a cold, wet world in which to unload children.

So I asked the driver to wait while I ran to see if we might sleep in the long disused schoolroom whose only function nowadays is to house the Sunday Service every fortnight. It wouldn't hold everyone but the overflow, Rachel said, could sleep in the house. It seemed a sensible thing to do.

The excitement of the waterfalls rushing down the corries and the mysterious mountain mist had given way to a reluctance to face the elements and there was an unaccustomed solemnity and a little anxiety abroad. The atmosphere changed completely when I told them that they were to sleep indoors. Immediately they were singing and cheering and the sun was shining, figuratively speaking, for everyone.

We emptied the bus of everybody except one person from each tent and coaxed our patient driver up the narrow road with its many pot-holes now overbrimming with water. Linda, who had been left behind, had made a tray full of cheese sandwiches and a billy full of soup. We took these, and all the bedding rolls down to the schoolroom in the bus and thanked our kind driver. We were immeasurably grateful to him.

The fun then began of sleeping the night in a new hotel, packed together like sardines in the little schoolroom and all over the house. An inexperienced onlooker would think that order would never be restored. In the early days of our camping it never was. We spent the night in a barn at Rylstone, after a week of rain, and next morning there was a pile of lost property enough to supply a jumble sale. Some articles were never claimed at all. We had a lot to learn twenty five years ago but the children were the same. 'You'll never camp again,' I had said to Toots in the downpour.

'Oh, Skipper,' replied the ten year old 'It's lovely!'

Chaos does not happen now. Though the scene looks like that of a disaster area, for half an hour, each knows what he or she is doing and is soon in bed. Similarly in the morning one would think it impossible to tidy up but within twenty minutes all can be away. It is important not to look at the conglomeration as a whole but to see it as fifty individual problems, small ones, which can easily be solved and to have a motto which says each must do a little more than a fair share.

Dear Rachel! The fun those children had and the security and warmth in which they slept were all due to her unique and generous hospitality which brings out the best in all of us.

The seniors slept the night in camp and during the darkness the dirty weather continued its journey to the Mainland and left drying sunshine for our awakening.

Severe weather, we believe, is necessary for the building of character and the cementing of personality. This is the true nature of our job albeit well camouflaged. Many people could cope with their every day problems far better if they had only been to camp in the wind and the rain and the blazing sun; if they had but learned how much fun it is to make the best of things and how much satisfaction can be gained from coping with difficulties.

It is only after struggling all night against wind and rain that one really appreciates the sun on awaking. If we had fair, calm weather all the time we would never know each other's endurance or potential or ability to share and we would never know the strength and loyalty and generosity of our friends.

117

Who are these living beneath the sky,
Whilst the shimmering sun and the pattering rain
And the clouds pass by?
They will dine beneath the boughs
And their leader always vows
That they're never afraid of wasps
And hardly ever afraid of cows.

10

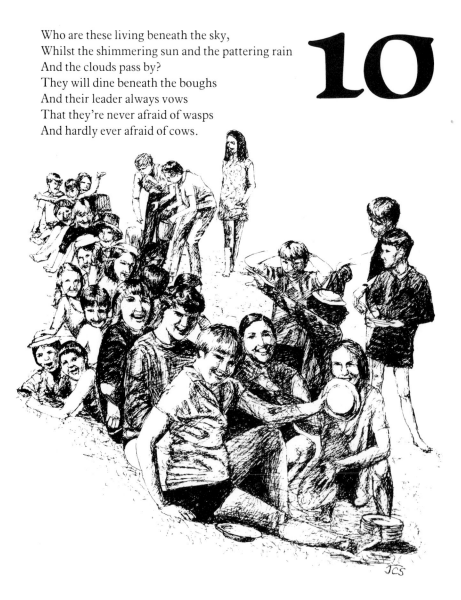

Chapter Ten

QUITE THE most ingenious people in the land are the Yorkshire children in camp in the Western Isles. By accepted standards they have nothing and everything they make, or play, or do involves invention and imagination and creativity of a very unique kind. There are few sources of entertainment other than what they provide for themselves and because they start with nothing and achieve such fantastic results they derive a great deal of pleasure. They approach each activity with a rare humour and a wit with which I cannot compete. They are subtle and quick with their repartee, are so ready with their answers and so quick to respond to suggestion that gaiety and laughter are our constant companions.

They are creatures of repetition needing the same activities year after year, but bringing fresh humour and new ideas so that only tradition is old and every play is new.

There are some more ingenious than others. Nellie and Gillian were as droll and as creative as any pair could be. Hazel and I returned to camp after a visit to our friends John Lachie and Effie in the thatched cottage on Tiree. We had eaten so we could not criticise those who were tucking into biscuits in the store tent. I left Hazel doling out more food and went into our tent to exchange my visiting skirt for a pair of shorts.

I thought it strange that my companion's blanket should be already laid, not very smoothly, over her lilo. We are very particular about keeping beds and blankets in our kit bags until we get into them at night. The evening air is always damp even after a hot day. The dew falls quite early and there is no sense in having a wet bed to sleep in through negligence. I pulled back the blanket intending to fold it and put it away and inadvertently I uncovered a skeleton.

On first appearances it was a human skeleton. It stretched the whole length of the lilo and was made of bones too numerous to count. Animal remains had been picked up from the shore and strung together with skill and patience and sensitivity to make the most human skeleton imaginable. I had no wish to spoil the fun. The evening light filtered greenly through the tent giving the bones luminosity and the effect was quite startling.

More suitably dressed I returned to the D'abri.

'I think you ought to go and look in the tent, Mrs Belsey.' I said solemnly.

There was a ripple of excitement among the children, an air of expectancy and an electricity which communicated itself to Hazel and made her alert.

'Oh no,' she groaned. 'What have they done? Is it my bed?'

'I'm afraid so.' I despaired.

'In it?' She was wary. I nodded.

'Not dead?' she feared. Visions of dried starfish, crabs, or even jellyfish rose to torment her.

'Very!' I admitted.

Too many followed her to the tent and they were unable to crowd inside. Most of them were shaking with laughter. Hazel was suitably impressed and sufficiently indignant to please everyone.

The skeleton was carefully removed and reappeared at the Fancy Dress Parade. Somehow or other Gillian managed to clothe herself in black. Then the skeleton was hung and tied against her and the effect was superb.

'Make a useful gadget for your tent,' I suggested one year. I did not estimate their powers of inventiveness. All day buckets and bins and culinary utensils were disappearing from the store and there was infectious giggling from the tents and loud warnings to, 'Get out or else,' to curious intruders who wanted to know what was going on but would not indulge their secrets in return. Where children are concerned lats are as amusing as false teeth and unwelcome donations from flying seagulls. It was to be expected that 'proper loos' and 'portaloos' would feature in the competition line up.

A stout, three-sided framework appeared in one lat which, said Catherine and Kathryn, was, 'To help you get out of the lat when you fell in.' Linda, visiting the lat in the dark, fell over the contraption and thereafter declared that, 'The bally thing makes sure you do.'

There was a comfortable chair, a front door bell, a washing line of twisted string which dispensed with the need for pegs and a system of string and pulleys in the boys' tent which operated a travelling waste paper bin. More ingenious still was a washing machine in a water bin. It had an extremely efficient agitator made from a pole and many cross lashed pegs.

But the invention which caused the photographers to gather in great numbers was THE BED. Made by the Riddlesden Lot, it stood a foot from the ground and it, and the neat bedding rack behind it, almost filled the tent. What a bed that was. It was as firm as a rock and its base was made from six foot lengths of pine bark strippings from the forests of Killiechronan, on Mull. All five members of the tent community could sleep on it provided they lay 'spoons' and all turned over at once. During the day it was tested by all, lounged upon, jumped upon and shaken by those wishing to disprove its stability. For two and a quarter nights it was slept on soundly. In the early hours of the third night there was a scream as one protesting leg finally gave up the struggle to support five robust teenagers and the saga of THE BED ended ignominiously. By torch light we investigated the shipwreck and sadly cut the many lashings which had held the wonderful thing together. Then we silently handed out the scores of poles which had been used to make the wonderful thing as if we were mourning the passing of a friend.

Leaving things in our tent has brought us amusement and much pleasure. Amusement because their wit is seldom corny and pleasure because there is respect in their confidence in our ability to see a joke.

The seniors found out that it was Mrs Belsey's Wedding Anniversary, whilst we were in camp, and they left a box of chocolates on her lilo and a bunch of flowers.

With them they left a note, prettily decorated with pressed harebells. It said, 'A very happy Wedding Anniversary from three very happy spinsters.'

This prompted the happy recipient to involve a colleague in the early morning making of spinster caps. My old lawn sleeping bag inner had begun to tear, so it was used for this amusing occupation. They gathered up the frilly edge with blue nylon, binder twine and painted polka dots and kisses with coloured felt pens. At the evening campfire they crowned the 'Three Happy Spinsters.' We wonder how long it will be before they send us wedding invitations!

Our children would find no difficulty in producing a wedding cake. They can improvise anything. They decided to commemorate my long years of taking children to the Hebrides by making one year an important anniversary. I had taken a packet of icing sugar to camp intending to have a bun making and icing competition, but they requisitioned it in secret. For the same ulterior motive they purloined two fruit cakes from the camp store. Both were square and one being smaller than the other suited their purpose fine.

Only one had a coating of almond paste but they craftily sliced off the top half inch of it and transferred it to the naked one so that with the stolen icing sugar they were able to do a professional job. The wife of a neighbouring crofter provided them with some colouring which enabled them to make an efficient job of the piped message and tiny rosebuds. Incredible as it may sound they managed to buy cake candles on the island.

A silver tent and mallet were cut from a foil pie dish which disappeared from the tent when I was not looking and four pegs were neatly covered in silver. Pressed into the larger cake they supported, somewhat shakily, the second tier and a masterpiece of confectionary was achieved.

Quite by accident I was seen to be approaching when Operation Cake was at a tricky stage and I was waylaid by a stooge strategically placed to intercept and divert me from the hive of industry. I remained quite unaware of what was afoot and when the secret was complete and ready for the unveiling and the lighting of the candles, they were rewarded by my genuine surprise and pleasure.

Taken away from material things there grows in children a natural humour which is spontaneous and clean and brings constant merriment and a stream of ideas. It has been a tradition for many years to hold a 'Miss Camp' competition. Our Beauty Queens have few 'glad rags' with which to adorn themselves, but that does not deter them. Unassuming Joanne was our most beautiful. Many have been amusing.

Eleven year old Judith appeared in the line-up dressed in bed socks, nighty and stocking cap. She was questioned by an interviewer who spoke clearly through a spoon microphone attached to a very long piece of string.

'And who have we here? What is your name?'

Clutching a well worn teddy bear, Judith replied, 'I'm Miss Dozy.'

'Oh! I see, and what is your ambition, Miss Dozy?'

'To own the biggest bed in the world.'

'Really!' said the senior with the improvised microphone. 'And what do you do for a living?'

'I test beds in a bed factory.' was the glib reply.

Claire teetered in the D'abri incredibly elegant after a wet week in camp.

'Your name is?' enquired the 'Michael Aspel' of our show.

'Miss Fussy. I'm afraid you'll have to adjust the microphone.'

'Is that better?' The spoon and string were shaken vigorously.

'Yes, yes, but the lighting is poor.'

A difficult customer this. The audience was in suspense.

'And should you become Miss Tiree, what will you spend the money on?'

'Ohw,' the accent excruciating, 'on nail varnish, of course. Ohw, undoubtedly.'

One year we decided that the Sex Discrimination Act allowed boys to enter the Miss Tiree Competition and girls to make a bid to be Mr. Wonderful. This announcement kept our seniors Viv, Elaine and Shirley fastened in their tent for an hour turning, with the help of sheep's wool, tall Shirley into stooping Grandfather. Grandad joined the Mr Wonderful line up with a somewhat senile and vacant expression which won all our hearts. Asked the usual questions he merely smiled and presented his ear to encourage his interviewer to speak up.

All went well until he was asked what he would do with the money should he be lucky enough to win. His face lost the charming smile. With a bewildered and wholly convincing stammer he asked, 'Is it a c-c-competition?'

One would have thought that, returning as often as they do before college or university, nursing or marriage claims them, they would run out of ideas for fancy dress and idiotic games such as the annual 'It's a Knockout.' One would think that they would run out of tunes for our yearly Eurovision Song Contest, but no. The fantastic use of natural materials, everyone's limited wardrobe and the contents of our handbags, is unending. With a few safety pins and sellotape Sarah becomes a punk-rock singer. Within half an hour the indomitable seniors are transformed into scarecrows of the gayest variety. Their cheeks are ruddy and their locks are of straw and their over-coats covered in patches. They commandeer the use of an old piece of rusting farm machinery, drape themselves over it in a crazy fashion and with guitar accompaniment and a bold notice announcing that they are 'THE WORZELS' they give us a superb rendering of:

'I've got a brand new combine harvester,

I'll give you the key.'

It is calculated to send us all into hysterics and succeeds completely.

Campers who can laugh at midges have a rare sense of humour indeed, for of all creatures the midge is the least amusing. It is too small for retaliation and produces mountains on bodies and faces thousands of times its size. It can drive the most placid of us to insanity and make us declare that though we neither smoke nor swear we will be doing both before the end of camp.

'You could win a war with midges,' said a train companion once and I'm sure she was right.

Our laughter loving children can laugh at midges.

One evening we returned to camp, after having a strupag with Rachel. and found them all engaged in a noisy and energetic dance.

'We do the Okey-Cokey?' they sang.

'What brought this on?' we asked.

'Oh, we're just avoiding the midges!' laughed Lyn.

In this year's hot camp two Eurovision songs were written about the midge.

'I'm taking home my Harris midgie,' sang one lot.

'Won't my Mummy be surprised at me?'

One group reverently extolled the wonders of the 'Amazing Midge' to the very popular tune of 'Amazing Grace.'

Before the subject of the Eurovision Song Contest is left behind, I must record the 1975 winner or I will never be forgiven by the masses who voted for it and cheered so loudly and called for its encore and pronounced it 'Song of the Year.'

It was extravagantly outrageous and unexpected and will, I am sure, be remembered when all else is forgotten. Its audacity cannot be surpassed and will, I hope, never be equalled.

The seniors had excelled themselves in wit and idiosy, in work and in affection and the Song Contest gave them an opportunity to reach a climax which was enjoyed by all except the victims. All camp we had been the butt for their witticisms and their sallies and they decided, in song, to make amends, say they were sorry and present us with a peace offering.

In abject adoration they kneeled before Hazel and me and honoured us in verse. And we were deceived. How were we to know that they had been to Joanna and asked, 'How far can we go with your mother?' and that the answer had been, 'All the way. Mum's a sport!'

The sentimentality of the verse should have been a warning to us for it was unnatural. Then they sang their song and its sweetness was out of character.

'Glory, glory how we love them,
Whatever would we do without them!'

It was odd, decidedly odd! A change of tactics so fundamental as to be revolutionary.

Then came the peace offering. A plate each of delectable strawberry Instant Whip, lovingly prepared, touchingly decorated with one bright, red strawberry. I vaguely remember hoping that they were going to allow me to eat it myself when suddenly the height of audacity was reached. Gerry's plastic plates, with their sweet dessert, leapt into the air and we found our faces buried deep in the blancmange.

Hazel's reflexes are better than mine, also, presumably, is her sense of self preservation. Before I had picked myself up and wiped the dessert out of my eyes, she had removed her plate and finding it still three quarters full of Instant Whip she had retaliated. Like lightning she had grabbed one laughing and unsuspecting face after the other, and buried it deep in the blancmange. When I opened my eyes I could not believe what I saw. It had all been so quick. Julie and Linda were victims of their own crime, beautifully plastered with strawberry mess and everyone in the D'abri was falling over in laughter and wiping away the tears of delighted merriment.

The four of us, whose respect for each other is infinite, sat wiping our faces with paper kitchen towelling and wondering how soon we could have a hair do. There was bedlam in the D'abri. Our audience was out of control. Everyone was cheering and yelling and shouting for more and for speeches and for an encore. The two culprits smiled rather sheepishly, regretting having under-estimated Mrs Belsey's quick thinking and so accurate aim.

The votes went overwhelmingly in favour of the Slap Stick comedy and of course they won the Contest and, because the winners always give a repeat performance, we had to endure the verse and the song again. I am eternally grateful that they allowed us to eat the second peace offering with dignity.

Where there are children and teenagers and students a certain amount of horseplay must be expected and borne. Is there a child, boy or girl, who has not played cowboys and Indians, cops and robbers, soldiers and briggands? Is there one who has not been to a circus and wanted to throw the custard pie, or one who has read of pirates and not wanted to take part in the mutiny? I think not. There is seldom a camp when someone does not get the urge to fly an alien flag from the flagpole be it no more original than a pair of shorts, a bikini or a bra.

Mutiny happened one year when Hazel and I were having a strupag at the small white house of Dolly and Lexy MacLeod above the camp. Seeing the unbecoming flutter from the flag pole in an apparently deserted camp, Margaret went to take it down whereupon the invisible army suddenly appeared and set upon her in grand style. Laughing gaily they put her legs into a tent bag and tied her to the pole. It is a wise adult who does not struggle too hard for children seldom know when they have gone far enough. Resistance is fought courageously and no one is happy if anyone gets hurt.

'Let's have a mutiny,' cried some dare devil. 'Let's keep Flim tied to the pole and lie in ambush for Skipper and Mrs Belsey.'

'I do hope they're not too long,' prayed Flim, nevertheless resigning herself to a long session in the bag, knowing she would feel rather foolish and wondering what she would say if the crofter should come.

All was so quiet when we eventually returned, we thought everyone must be on the beach and we strolled unsuspectingly and leisurely towards the D'abri. There was a sudden war cry as everyone dived out of hiding and we were unceremoniously pushed to the ground and sat upon.

'We're having a mutiny,' cried one, quite unnecessarily. 'We've got Flim and now it's your turn.'

They were all very excited and there were many blood curdling suggestions as to what they should do with us now they had got us. Obviously they had not planned beyond that. I let them rant and holler for a while and lay, decidedly flattened, wondering how I could bring this to an end without their losing face. In a lull in the noisy argument I suddenly shouted, 'Who wants food?'

It worked like magic and we had far more hands than usual helping with the supper.

'Bribery!' you may say. 'That is no way to control children who behave like a horde of savages!'

124

I dispute your right to criticise. It was my body which was being sat upon.

When the weather is hot we can go to bed at night without being obsessed with guy ropes and storm pegging. We swim a great deal and potter happily on the beach avoiding really strenuous activity. It is all very peaceful and enjoyable. When the weather is cool everyone is much more vivacious and in some ways there is a great deal more fun. Everyone takes part in 'It's a Knockout' or camp 'Sports' or the 'Best pair o' legs' competition. We love Treasure Hunts and sketching competitions, exhibitions – serious and amusing, shellcraft, toffee apple making and we write songs and make mascots, invent stunts and plays and generally get together a great deal.

Hot weather scatters children over a wide area and our constant task of watching to see that none is left out or lonely and a little bit homesick, is quite difficult. Cold weather gathers us altogether on the dunes for mad competitions or on the grass for a crazy game of rounders. The wind makes us very dependent on each other for entertainment and really bad weather, when rain threatens that it will never stop, drives us all ionto the D'abri where the most original activities are born.

'We'll entertain everyone this afternoon, Skip,' said a band of my Sea Rangers several years ago. 'Can we have the D'abri? Don't let anyone come in, will you?'

Everyone became intrigued to know what was going on in the Big Top for things were being carried in discreetly and a great deal of laughing and whispering was going on. When we were finally let in there had been a transformation indeed.

The tent was festooned and decorated to resemble King Neptune's Palace. Seated high on a seaweed-strewn throne was King Neptune himself with a crown on his head and a big scroll in front of him. Reclining among the rocks and shells and seaweed, with which the floor was littered, were a number of very beautiful mermaids. Their hair had been loosened and in it gleamed shells and bits of silver toffee paper. They wore bikini tops and had sewn up the gayest towels to make fishy tails from which their bare feet protruded.

It was a grey day outside but inside the tent there was colour and the air was electrified with children's anticipation and full of underwater magic. The spectators were silently curious and they leaned forward in order to see more and those in the back rows knelt or stood wishing to miss not one bit of this surprising entertainment.

Julie was only eight. 'What are they going to do, Auntie Jean?' she whispered.

'No one knows,' I shrugged. 'We'll just have to wait and see.'

'We've called you all here, to King Neptune's Court,' announced Barbara, 'to be judged. Most of you have committed dreadful crimes and must be punished.'

This was unexpected and it was awful. No one knew quite whether it might be better just to slip out quietly and disappear, pretend a call to the lats or the necessity to write an urgent letter. Curiosity overcome guilt and everyone stayed.

The scroll was unrolled and misdeeds began to be read and punishments given. I was accused of having had a button missing from my shirt since the beginning of camp and was required to sew on a cardboard monster which had obviously begun life as a cornflakes box. I was condemned to wear it until the elements softened the cardboard and the whole thing disintegrated.

Paul was accused of never having washed the dishes and was ordered to redeem himself at once. A bowl of water was carried into the tent along with some plates and mugs, dish mop and tea towel. Every piece he had to wash to the satisfaction of a jeering, sarcastic audience.

Flim's crime was that she talked to animals which was, said King Neptune, definitely prohibited. A poem had been written about the accused. It was definitely defamatory and she was condemned to read it in public whilst members of the spectating body were encouraged to throw wet bits of seaweed at her.

By this time Julie was very apprehensive. She had pressed herself very close to me and was obviously worried about being seen and called upon. She was a great favourite and camp pet and she guessed rightly that she would not be missed. The previous hot afternoon she had gone onto the beach not dressed for swimming but had been so tempted by the water, and the fun which was going on as usual, that she had been persuaded to swim in her knickers and vest.

So she was accused of swimming on the shore indecently clad and was condemned to put on at least a dozen sweaters. Being very small she looked exactly like Humpty Dumpty. Having taken her punishment and found it did not kill her to do so, or embarrass her beyond the point that she could take, she ran back to her seat beside me, heaved a big sigh of relief and proceeded to laugh heartily at everyone else.

The reading of crimes and the mad forfiets lasted all afternoon and made an otherwise grey day colourful and gay.

Mostly the suggestions come from the ranks.

'Let's have a Hairdressing Competition in camp this year,' said Joanna when plans were being made before the holiday. Unbeknown to me she took a wig to camp and on the evening which seemed just right for a Hairdressing session, she came to me.

'We want to give you a fancy hair-do, Skipper. Do you mind?'

They turned me into something elegant and sophisticated, hid my somewhat untidy bun under the wig and a good time was had by all.

We are, however, quite capable of doing some of the teasing and the leg pulling ourselves. It is not always one sided with us on the losing end.

'What's the prize for It's a Knockout?' the boys wanted to know. They had just put a great deal of effort into winning and had run up from the shore to announce their success and find out what their winnings were.

'You'll have to wait until Ruth and Rachel get back from Tarbert,' I said. 'They won't be long but they went specially to get the Knockout prize.'

'Yeh, but what is it?' persisted Peter.

'We're going to get it anyway,' said Jonathan 'so you might as well tell us what it is.'

I was busy at the fire and everyone was hungry but it was too good an opportunity to miss.

'I don't really know what it will be,' I hedged. 'I just made a suggestion. They might not take it up.'

'Aw, they'll get what you said.' Stephen was sure. 'What did you suggest?'

'I'm sorry,' I lied, 'but I honestly did not think you would win and I suggested toilet things. You know, talcum powder, soap, shampoos and things. They've lovely perfume in Tarbert.' I tried to keep a straight face.

'Aw, Skip, what'll we do with that sort of stuff? We wouldn't have tried so hard to win if we'd known! Blimey!'

They went off to their tent with long faces and humped shoulders.

'Let's have some fun with the boys,' I whispered to Hazel, knowing full well that Ruth and Rachel would return with tuck to fill a large box, just as I'd told them to.

We emptied our toilet bags and handbags for a collection of feminine cosmetics. When they had been arranged on tissue in a cardboard box they looked of presentation standard and when Ruth and Rachel returned we had our fun. We pretended to be sorry but the girls had been over ten miles to buy the prize and there was really nothing we could do about it. The girls were all in hysterics and the boys were masculinely scornful. Only when we had had our pound of flesh did we produce the real reward. Well! The boys should not have been so easily taken in. They should have known that we were a great deal more resourceful than that!

Only occasionally has a curb to be put to high spirits. There was a game with a tyre which came to an abrupt end but not before a great deal of fun had been had and a serious accident averted by a miracle. There is a slope in Happy Valley which appeared to have been made especially for rolling tyres down. The finders of the tyre merely rolled it down the slope but when more players came a game began to evolve and things became more complicated.

The finally agreed procedure was extremely uncomfortable and one wondered what fun there could be in it at all. They would lie, a dozen, even twenty at a time, down the slope and each took it in turn to roll the tyre over the bodies. The object of the game was to roll the tyre so straight that it stayed on the 'rails' all the way down. It was really quite ridiculous the fun it caused. It went to their heads like champagne and they rolled around in joy, or agony, and nursed their bruises and boasted their successes, day after day.

Until the day the tyre turned crazy and went walk-about. Enthusiasts were playing the game before breakfast. The porridge was cooked, the sausages fried and the cook-house whistle was about to be blown, when the final competitor released the tyre on its long and last journey. Somewhere near the top it left the rails and like some guided missile began to head straight for the fire, the breakfast and me.

'Look out Skipper!' someone yelled.

I leapt from the fire as the beserk tyre collided with the grid and flopped over the porridge billy. Tongues of flame began to lick round the sides of the tyre almost immediately. We pulled the offending object clear and that was the end of that!

Accidents at the fire must be avoided at all costs. Because of the large numbers, the fire has to be big and the grids must be safe. The fire is the focal point of camp. Everyone gathers round it, sits by it, pokes it and feeds it. Rubbish is burned on it when cooking is not being done, letters are read by it, elevenses are eaten by it and plans are made around it. Tears are shed and dried by it, confidence is restored there, potatoes are peeled or scrubbed beside it and washing water continually boiled on it.

Therefore it must be safe. Joanna was badly blistered once, when a billy of water overturned. The splashes boiled in the ashes and the hot sand, and angrily spat out all over her bare feet. Even though she rushed to the water bin for cold, healing water and spent a long time walking in the sea she was still in a great deal of pain and discomfort.

To be without fire is unthinkable. Gas is impossibly slow and we would never think of changing to it for cooking. We prefer the friendliness of the open fire. It's warmth and movement is comforting to a child who is feeling just a little homesick or who is trembling with cold after being too long in the sea.

The fire is the panacea for all ills. Its smoke can be blamed for many things. I received a letter one day. It was delivered with a flourish by the distributor of the pile of envelopes which arrives each day. I was involved by the fire with hands too floury to investigate it and minus my spectacles anyway. I seldom get letters in camp unless they are bills or notes from friends on the island, usually delivered with the van. This was obviously neither.

'Who's it from?' asked Hazel.

'Dunno,' I said. 'Open it for me.'

It turned out to be a grateful letter from a parent whose circumstances had been difficult because of illness.

'Shall I read it to you?' volunteered Hazel. Everyone else was preoccupied reading personal post.

'Please.' I said.

She began quite strongly but the letter was so touching her voice began to falter, then choked and finally she dried up altogether.

'I don't think I can go on,' she apologised, wiping her eyes. I was similarly engaged. It is useful to be able to blame the smoke for making ones eyes water when the rest of the gang suddenly appear demanding elevenses.

One other play had to be stopped but it had already gone too far and had damaging affects before we found out. Unbeknown to us the boys held a seance with a board and a glass of water and thirteen year old Stephen was petrified by the unlikely message that, during the night, he would go to the lats and twelve year old Jonathan would murder him. He was quite white and silent and all the reassuring in the world did not seem to help him.

Failing to break through the barrier of his fear I said, 'Look, Stephen, if you really don't believe me that it was only a game and not one tiny bit true, come and sleep between Mrs Belsey and me. You'll feel quite different about it in the morning because nothing will happen, I promise you.'

I fully expected that the prospect of sleeping between two middle-aged ladies would be the greater of the two evils and that Stephen would swallow his fear and say manfully that nothing would induce him to sleep in our tent. The enormity of his scare was only fully realised when he gulped and said awkwardly, 'I think I will.'

He brought his bedding roll into our tent and never went back on his decision to stay. He must have been very afraid, at thirteen, to risk the criticism of his contemporaries. They must have understood, for I don't think he was ever teased. –

They were sensitive to his anxiety and quite shocked by the intensity of it.

When he awakened next morning and found himself still alive, the look of relief on his face taught us how dangerous the silly game could be and how necessary it is to create a relationship which can offer security without the fear of losing dignity.

If the canvas walls of the D'abri could talk and recount the stunts and concerts and parties that are enjoyed beneath its roof it would have an interesting story to tell. Old Ma Bott's used to be one of our best loved evening performances. We had a group of teenagers, who, in their junior days, had belonged to a children's concert party, led by a capable lady called Mrs Bottomley. The songs and dances she had taught must have been well learned for they had been remembered in detail.

What had been amusing when danced and sung by little children was downright devastating and hilarious when resurrected by the same children in their late teens. We have seen a row of them, dressed in voluminous skirts made by buttoning yellow cycling capes round their waists, do the can-can as professionally as any Paris dancers. Beneath the yellow oilskins we have seen the most elegant legs and the frilliest of pantees.

We have heard nursery rhymes enacted in elaborately improvised costumes. We have laughed until it hurt at Giggles and Elaine when they sang, 'I've got sixpence' with operatic fervour, Elaine an octave higher than any soprano and Giggles, abnormally sober, sustaining a rich contralto.

'Where are you going to?' sang Kathy, handsome in striped pyjama trousers and a blazer.

'I'm going a-milking, sire,' sang Sandy, coyly shaking her curls under a frilly sunbonnet.

'My old man,' sang Penny, staggering round the D'abri with a 'meat safe' and an old cock linnet.

'There's a monster at the bottom of our garden,' confided Ruth, eyes bulging.

We have listened to all the old songs. 'Daisy Daisy' and 'If you were the only girl in the world,' and we have rocked with laughter at the leg kicking and the extravagent gesticulations.

One year Linda and Julia blacked their faces to give us an excellent selection from 'Hello Dolly.' I remember that 'Encore', was shouted several times and each campfire, for days to come, was incomplete without their act. Soon afterwards Linda went to Malawi and Julia to work in a kibutz in Galilee.

There is no end to our plays and the children's enthusiasm for every activity offered. Particularly have they enjoyed Treasure Hunts and their appreciation did not die, as we expected that it would, when one year they were convinced that all treasure must be buried and when they found a freshly dug patch, before completing the trail, decided that their luck was in and started digging like pups after a bone. They unexpectedly exhumed Calum's old cow and hastily had to re-cover it.

Always we have had other children too, islanders and summer visitors. Garry and Jimmy came down from their caravan to make their contribution in song and enliven, for us, a very wet camp. Charlie and Ian came every day and were so well behaved they always knocked on the tent pole before they came into the tent. From them we learned the 'Hiking Song' and 'The Road to Dundee.' From Garry and Jimmy we learned 'Two Highland Lads are we' and many more.

The MacLean boys were never away until they emigrated to Australia with their parents May and Hugh. Donald was our own piper. He came and piped on the hill above Happy Valley every day. There was Ewan from Glasgow and Hugh from Ayr who sang the 'Tiree Love Song' in Calum's barn and was so tactful about removing the boys when the girls had to undress. One year he travelled home with us on the boat.

'Where's Hugh going?' I was asked.

'He's going home, of course.' I answered.

'But he lives on Tiree,' they were absolutely sure.

'What makes you think that?' I wanted to know.

'We asked him. We said, 'Where do you live?' and he said, ''Ere.'

The mistake was understandable.

There were Mary and Ellen and Hughie, Ann and Kathleen, Donna and Mairi Christine Catherine and Faraquhar and Donny; Dolly, Cathie, Kenina, Joyce and Jessie Kate, Alice Ann and Mary Ann, Katie Ann and innumerable Margaret Anns. There were Rachel and Marjorie and Alison, Morrisons, MacInneses, MacLeods, Lamonts, MacLeans and MacLennans, MacVicars and MacKays, Campbells and Robertsons. Ruth from Findorn, Margaret, Jill, Ian and many, many more I remember but whose names are so similar as to be repetitive.

They were attracted by the fun, intrigued by the tents and eager to sample the food. Their contribution has been incalcuable and their integration complete.

It seems to me that there must have been many more than two hundred and fifty children. It is only a rough guess anyway, for unfortunately we kept no record. We only know that ten, or so, new ones join us every year. The other forty have all been before.

In retrospect it seems as if children have come out of the crofts everywhere to join us. It is as if some piper has played a tune and children have been unable to resist. They have been welcome. We have loved them all.

11

I want to live in a friendly world,
A friendly world, a friendly world,
That's good for folks like me.
If I run short of a bowl of rice
And my next door neighbour's in,
I want to know that she won't say 'No'
To the colour of my skin,
Or the church I worship in,
Or the place from whence I came,
Or my great-grandfather's name.
I want to live in a friendly world,
That's good for folks like me.

Chapter Eleven

SEASIDE RESORTS provide for the conventional holidaymaker the usual conglomeration of novelty shops, ice cream parlours, coffee bars and Bingo halls and for evening entertainment Shows and Fairgrounds and Dance Halls. For the visitor to the islands there are few of these things but that does not mean there is no entertainment on the islands at all. Far from it. A people so hospitable and entertaining as the Hebrideans cannot fail to provide both drama and comedy. They own Nature's most beautiful stage and a backcloth of undeniable splendour. The annual crofting activities need no production team, no choreographer. The pattern of the sheep being gathered on the mountain is better than any kaleidoscope and the movements of the intelligent collies are more expressive than any ballet. Also the humour of the islanders is more infectious than that of any stage comedian.

A great deal of the activity of the small community centres round the fank. Often it shelters in a fold in the rock or nestles against a curve in the road. Frequently it has grown from the shore and although man-made from driftwood stakes and corrugated sheets it looks as if it belongs. Its presence indicates that the community is thriving and the sheep droppings and wool which litter it tell, by their age, how recently it was used.

There is no sound more Hebridean than the noise of the fank. The rich, greasy smell of the wool at shearing, the strong disinfectant at the dipping are all the more odorous because of the contrast in the clean air. The smell of the fank lasts only as long as the animals fill it. The sharp air from the sea blows over it as soon as they are released, obliterating the smell of sweat and wool and droppings, but soap and water does not effectively wash away the grease from human hands or take away the distinctive smell of Blackface wool from the finished Harris Tweed.

We have been at many shearings, dippings, markings and tail dockings, helping and watching, captivated by the moving mass of sheep crowding together on the sheltering cliff or wall behind the fank. Many of the youngsters have come home tired, greasy and happy from a day with the crofters.

Margaret and I were helping one of the shepherds at a small fank in his lambing park, on the roadside, two miles out of the township. He was marking the spring lambs, docking their tails and administering worm pellets before releasing them with their mothers to summer on the hill. The dogs rounded them up with such skill it was a joy to watch and we were equally amazed at the accuracy with which the crofter could pair mother and lamb when scores were all packed tightly together and when, to us, each lamb was a reflection of another.

It was a typical island scene and we did not feel alien in it. Our skill in handling the lambs improved rapidly. We are cattle farmers, not shepherds, but we can easily adapt. We were releasing the sheep and lambs through a gate on the other side of the road and they were scampering away to freedom when we were interrupted by the arrival of a large bus. It came slowly round the bend, its enormous width filling the road.

'Tourists!' said Angus. 'Watch them now. They'll be out of their seats in a minute taking the photographs.'

He was right. Amateur cine photographers leapt out of the bus and started to film the fank. We pretended we did not see them. None of us is used to being a film star. Out of the corners of our eyes we could see them take up poses to film, to the best advantage, the crofting scene, so that they could capture it and take it home to view in their sitting rooms on dark winter evenings.

We were amused. 'Poor things,' I said. 'I wonder if they think they have filmed three Harris crofters.'

Angus laughed outright. 'Not at all,' he chortled. 'You would never be seeing Harris crofters in Hot Pants.'

I had forgotten we were wearing shorts. I am sorry if the movie makers realised too late and, when viewing, felt cheated.

A crofter's life in the Outer Hebrides centres a great deal round his sheep. His cow is only kept for the house and the calf is merely a by-product of the necessity to have milk and butter and the Hebridean cheese which is called crowdie. It will be sold at the Autumn Sales in Oban or Dingwall for as much, or as little, as the current market price for beef sucklers. The Tiree crofter keeps more cattle but to the Harris crofter the sheep are often his livelihood. They give his wife wool, to dye with the crottal and heather dyes and weave into tweed, and they provide him with meat. They also bring him an annual cheque with which to pay his nominal rent and buy the foodstuffs and household requirements he cannot provide himself. The islanders are good shepherds and each sheep is important. More, it would seem, than the passing of a driving test.

A friend of ours still sported an 'L' plate on his old car and I was moved to enquire kindly, as befits one who failed her test three times before final success, 'Haven't you got rid of that little decoration yet?'

'Well no, as a matter of fact I did not pass the test,' he said. 'Och well, it was rather unfortunate. I was driving across the island with the man from the Mainland beside me when I happened to see a ewe I had not seen for some time. I stopped the car on the roadside just to have a wee look at her. Ach, it took no time at all but I'm afraid I forgot to turn off the engine.'

Many of the islanders, down the Long Island, still weave in sheds alongside their houses. Few of our older girls have not tried their hands at twisting the one-ply wool on the well worn spinning wheels. Few have not leaned over the greasy loom and watched the hand weaver busy at the narrow width of good warm tweed and bought some of it from Katie afterwards. When their interest has waned they have knelt to play with a box full of kittens which invariably occupies a dark corner of the shed. Most have returned home with a toorie with its heavy pompom and its rich smell of Harris wool.

Whatever the island activity there are those who are falling over themselves to take part. There was a memorable occasion when a party went out to help with the peats.

'Are you coming too, Mrs Belsey?' they asked when she joined the procession to pile into the old van. It was her first camp and she was only just becoming known in the township.

'I'd like to help,' she said, 'and I also want some peat to take home for a peat garden.'

She had been collecting all sorts of peat bog flowers and plants and kept them in plastic bags just outside the tent. In the van she explained what she wanted to the crofter and asked him if he could spare any.

'I'm sure,' he said. 'But you'll be wanting the thatching peats. The dry peat for the fire will be no use at all. It's the thatching peats you'll be needing, chust.'

At the alighting place the van spilled its eager youngsters onto the road and they wriggled under the fence and galloped across the bog to the neat seam where peat was being currently cut. They clamoured to be told what to do. They were taught to stack the dry peats in piles about as big as a haycock and to thatch each with peats taken from near the surface and heather covered sods.

Everytime the crofter lifted a suitable peat he passed it to Mrs Belsey to be stacked separately. It was apparent that he did not know her name. Any child would have been more than willing to say, 'That's Mrs Belsey!' had he thought to ask, but he chose to enquire of her himself.

'And what would be your name?' he asked.

Christian names are used predominantly in the islands where all surnames are nearly the same, so Mrs Belsey answered simply, 'It's Hazel.'

The good man then proceeded to hand the suitable tufts to any nearby child saying, 'This one is for Hazel.' This amused the Yorkshire children no end for they would never use a Christian name and we do not use them in their presence. We do not think it is wrong. It is just the way we do in our part of the world. The children thought it amusing but they were quite unprepared for the next question when it came.

'And how old are you Hazel?' said our friend with complete absence of tact.

There was an expectant silence which Mrs Belsey broke by laughingly admitting that she was forty.

'Och, well well,' said the poor embarrassed man, 'And I was after thinking you were about seventeen. Oh well, and I'm very sorry to be asking a lady such a personal question.'

It is far from insulting to a lady to believe she is less than half her age. It is complimentary, to say the least, but he did not get over his embarrassment until the next time we went to that island. We had just arrived and were busy unpacking skips and putting up tents when he came over to shake hands and welcome us.

'Well, well,' he said, smiling and holding out his hand, 'And this is the lady who grows younger every year. And how is your peat garden, Hazel?'

The man was certainly to be commended for his diplomacy!

Compliments come in the most unexpected places. Two small boys were constant visitors one wet camp. They entertained us with their songs and their out-spoken, uninhibited remarks, the choicest of which was delivered as Pat Roberts and I sat on a green slope at the Tarbet Highland Games.

We had ordered the bus to meet us about half a mile from camp where the driver can turn much more easily. We had had to pass the caravan where the two boys were staying with their parents. In passing we had waved a cheerful, 'Good morning.' In honour of the games I had exchanged my shorts and shirt for a respectable dress and I certainly had not walked down the road displaying a pair of sunburned, hiking legs! Nevertheless the small boy with the lovely Scottish accent came up to me and remarked innocently, 'Och, my fairther was admiring your laigs this morning!'

I did not trust myself to speak in case I should explode. Pat was shaking beside me.

The brave child went on undaunted, 'Och, he said tae my mither, How would you like a pair like those?'

We could control ourselves no longer. The poor child sat staring wondering whatever he could have said that was so funny.

It is, and always has been, one of the greatest days in the year to go to the Island Games. Our arrival on the field invariably excites the man with the microphone to announce that, 'The party of Gerl Guides are from Yorkshire,' and then to extend to us a warm welcome and hope we'll have 'guid weather' for our stay on the island. He also asks foreign visitors to call at the marquee and as we usually have someone from France or Canada or America this is soon announced too.

The informality of the Games is its chief attraction. By just appearing at the start of the running track the children can usually compete and sports are no fun for them unless they can take part themselves. They run and jump and try putting-the-shot and staying on the slippery pole.

Margaret rather fancied trying to toss the weight. Though less than five feet and weighing only seven stones she is remarkably strong and would certainly have been able to lift it and it wouldn't have come down in the same place either. Her appeal to be allowed to compete met with complete disapproval.

'No, no, no, Margaret. You can't toss a weight like that,' the strong men shouted.

'Och, that's no fit competition for a woman.'

'Och, she couldna lift the weight at all.'

'No, no, Margaret,' they said. 'You'll do yourself a harm if you lift a weight like that.'

They dwarfed her with their height and broadness. She tried to coax them into letting her try but they were adamant.

'A woman canna lift a weight like that!' they said with finality. I'd have been willing to bet that she could but we never found out.

We were watching the high jump.

'That's the policeman jumping,' said Doreen. 'The one who was at the pier when we came.'

So it was. It is refreshing to go to a Gala and find the police have time to take part in the competitions.

Until the winning team celebrated too exuberantly and somehow lost the cup, we always took part in the Tug o' War. Deciding who should take part, who was heaviest for anchor man and who should be coxwain and goad the team on, used to fill a pleasant hour at least. Once we won the ladies' Tug o' War and had to compete with the men's winning team just for the fun of it. We found out how popular our young girls were by the number of handsome young men who hung onto the end of the rope and made sure we won.

Hazel, Margaret and I have spent hours sitting on the green slope at the edge of the field overlooking the Games, listening to Skye pipers and watching the Highland Dancing competitions and the tossing of the hammer. All the while we have continually buttered sliced bread, handed out apples and tomatoes and cut up fruit cakes for our compulsive eaters who come perpetually in search of food.

There is no more beautiful setting for any Games than the rectangular sports field of Tarbert School. It fills the floor of the narrow neck of land between East Loch Tarbert and West Loch Tarbert. On the left rises Ben Luskentyre, the highest mountain in South Harris and on the right rise the foothills of the North Harris mountains. At its feet lap the blue waters of West Loch Tarbert and behind it stands the cool white building of the school.

We were sitting thus enthroned one year, watching the idyllic panorama and the colourful scene below, when we were visited by a handsome, kilted Highlander, who had obviously been celebrating in the hotel bar. He was in a very benevolent mood and asked innumerable, somewhat slurred, questions about the children. He was, I'm sure, naturally fond of youngsters and he thought ours looked so healthy and bonny he wanted to do something for them.

'Och, I whant to shpeak to the pershon in charge' he announced.

I had been keeping well in the background but I was forced to introduce myself to him when he began delving into his wallet preparing to give away money.

'You've got peautiful children,' he told me. 'I want to give them a treat.'

He took a five pound note from his wallet and, just as if he were calling for drinks all round, he waved it at me saying, 'Treat all the children from Uncle Chimmy!'

Of course I remonstrated.

'You mustn't,' I said, as firmly and as kindly as I could. 'We can't take your money.'

'Treat all the children from Uncle Chimmy,' he repeated with his arm affectionately round my shoulders.

A crowd of our children and Tarbert children had gathered round and to argue was going to cause a scene. He turned to the spectators and began to dance for them. He was light on his feet, though he wasn't a young man, and was naturally a bit unsteady. The children were obviously delighted. The pleats of his kilt flared and he yelled and twirled and wobbled. We caught and steadied him and he again held out the note.

'Give three cheers for Uncle Chimmy!' he called. 'Come on now, for Uncle Chimmy! Hip hip!'

By this time the children were really enjoying the fun and given the opportunity none can cheer louder than ours.

'Hooray!' they shouted. 'Hooray, HOORAY!'

There was nothing else I could do but accept the money with dignity and graciousness. A normally kind man, made more benevolent and generous by whisky, cannot be easily dissuaded from his purpose.

'What'll we do with the money?' the surprised children asked.

'We'll see,' I said. I really am a very normal adult.

A few days later we went to Stornoway and I used the fivepound note to half pay for fish and chips, always a very expensive treat when we are fifty. The bus was parked alongside the harbour and when Margaret and I handed round the portions on cardboard plates we announced,

'Uncle Jimmy bought these.'

There was sudden pandemonium in the bus.

'Three cheers for Uncle Jimmy,' they yelled and the hoorays rocketted out of the open bus windows and echoed across the harbour.

On Harris it is the Highland Games which draw us like a magnet every camp. On Tiree we go the the Regatta.

'What time will it begin?' we asked John Lachie. We knew we had four miles to walk along the beach to Scarinish and we had to plan accordingly.

'Well, and I'm not sure at all if it begins at eleven or twelve o'clock,' he said, 'but it won't begin until two anyway and I don't believe there will be a Regatta at all today. Och, the weather is too poor.'

We often marvel that we ever get anywhere at the right time. The right time is certainly not the scheduled time, on Tiree, at any rate. We have waited hours for a Barbecue to start and now know that the right time may be hours after the billed time and can be a day or two later on occasion. I honestly do not know how the message gets round that there has been a postponement. I am willing to accept that it doesn't come at all. That Tiree people intuitively know whether the Regatta is that day or not and that, by a sixth sense, they all converge in the right place on the right day.

The next day the crofter said with conviction that there would be a Regatta that day and, as he knows better than we about these things, we decided to go. We were late leaving the camp site and arrived about three o'clock but we were in time. There were not many boats and I believe they would be mostly local. I remember little about it except that Calum won. This indeed was enough excitement for one day. The children were nearly falling in in their enthusiasm.

It must have gone somewhat to Calum's head too, for he and his one man crew were still fastening the boat onto the back of their old lorry when we had finished our Scarinish shopping, had our picnic and spent a long time playing on the beach. Margaret and I were bringing up the rear with a few 'hangers on' when we noticed the men still happily putting ropes round the champion boat.

'Would you be wanting a lift at all?' shouted Calum.

That is just what we did want, for as usual we had been left with more than our share of the picnic things and the slowest of the 'hangers on.'

'Come on.' I had no need to urge them. 'We're going to get a lift. We'll be back in time to have a meal ready for the others when they come.'

There was a mad rush towards the lorry.

'Och, there's plenty of room with her,' said the crew, helping the younger fry onto the lorry beside the wet boat.

There was a sudden clatter as two bottles shuttered onto the grass. They were pint sized, dark bottles with an unmistakable label. Betty caught them and broke their fall so that they landed less heavily onto the ground. I remember the amused look that passed between Margaret and me when Betty remarked innocently, 'Phew Calum, you nearly lost your squash bottles!'

They were empty and we were soon left in no doubt as to who had consumed the contents. The two men had great difficulty in getting into the lorry but they were in great spirits.

'Do you think we are safe?' laughed Margaret.

'Dunno,' I answered. 'I don't think the lorry can do more than fifteen miles an hour, anyway.'

Now the roads on Tiree are flat and straight, and the land on either side of them is as smooth as a well kept lawn. Passing places are unnecessary because almost anywhere on route a vehicle can pull off the road on to the grass. Tiree is the only place where Margaret will cycle for just that reason. Whenever another wheeled vehicle comes she pulls off the road. In spring the grass is studded with millions of daisies and there is no more beautiful land anywhere.

At intervals a trickle of water flows down a dyke, overgrown with yellow water flags. Where the ribbon of road crosses these seepages there is a little level bridge marked only by small walls on either side which indicate to the driver the presence of the ditch and advise him not to pull off the road at that particular place.

The lorry began a slow zig zag journey home. The driver was weaving first to port and then to starboard as if he were still sailing and obliged to tack against a head wind. We could see the marks of his lorry wheels on the grass on either side of the road behind us. The first time we saw a bridge approaching Margaret and I stopped breathing. It did not seem possible that the meandering wheels of the lorry could straighten sufficiently.to pass through the walled bridge safely. But just as we approached the tricky bit the lorry appeared completely in control, as if some guiding hand steadied the wheel, and we negotiated that and every other bridge excellently.

Between bridges the lorry was all over the place. It was going very slowly, but had a film been made of it and quickened, it would have made an excellent sequence for the Keystone Cops in the early days of Cinema. The lorry was perpetually leaving the road and in front of us was the long straggling line of Yorkshire kids. Every time the noisy, wandering lorry approached we added yells of 'Get out of the way' to the backfiring. Ahead of us children continually leapt to safety and stood well back on the grass shouting sarcastic remarks about the driving and our laziness and calling for food to be ready on their return. They stood with their eyes popping and their hair on end as we swerved before each bridge and then steered accurately through and they were falling on the grass in mock faints as if the shock of seeing the miracle, and the danger averted, was too great for them.

We were commenting on our hair-raising ride next day in Effie's little thatched cottage where we get milk.

'You've not heard the half of it,' said Ellen, her daughter. 'It took Calum two hours to milk his cow last night!'

It was the only time we ever saw Calum unnaturally merry.

The smell of the fire permeates all our clothes and our hair, especially if we are using wood. The peat is not nearly so pungent but the resinous bark strippings we have shipped annually from Killiechronan Estate on Mull (because Tiree has no fuel other than driftwood) are very scented indeed. The smoke clings to all our belongings. In camp we seldom notice it, but unpacking rucksacks at home the stale smell is unmistakable.

We have tried to take some entertainment to the islands for the people who so kindly entertain us. Joan had a cine camera with her for many years and was able to capture some of the beauty and quite a lot of the fun. We guessed rightly that the islanders would like to see the films as quite a number of them were photographed. The Salum children were all active on the screen and our small piper had a beautiful shot silhouetted against the sky, on the hill above Happy Valley.

Someone on the island owned a projector and the hall was packed with islanders and summer holidaymakers. There was a shot, on one of the films, of a fire of crackling logs and dancing flames leaping into the night sky. Above it rose a steady ribbon of smoke. It was one of those lucky shots an amateur sometimes takes. Children are very poor photographers and Joan was quite exceptional.

The film was very well received and because it was silent everybody was able to talk, comment, voice amazement and approval as well as laugh. They were very vocal about the lovely fire and quite distinctly I heard a visitor behind me saying, 'That fire looks absolutely real. I do believe I can smell the woodsmoke.' So could I. The evening was chilly and I had put on a sweater I had worn by the fire and the fire and I have a very personal and close relationship whilst together we do the cooking. Surreptitiously I buried my nose in the thick wool. I don't make that mistake nowadays. Even if I am late I have a complete change of clothes before I go anywhere!

One of the most spontaneous films we have ever had was taken by the father of one of the girls who came with us year after year to Harris. Her parents began staying at Horgabost and liked it so much they returned annually. He filmed the children unawares and used up several spools. We wondered anxiously what the result would be but could not predict. He did it so slyly we seldom saw him with the camera. We were quite unprepared for the final film which needed no editing. It was one of the happiest films we have seen and it gave us a chance to look objectively at what we do. We could just sit and watch, a thing we so seldom have time to do when we are actually on the job.

The film could have been set to music, for it was almost dance. We count it as one of our most valued indications that what we do is worthwhile. Mr Whalley has shown it in houses galore on the island, to crofters sitting round their own peat fires and at céilidhs and dances; and we have watched it again and again at home and annalysed each bit of it.

On it we saw relaxed children, forever laughing, forever eating. We saw an inter-relationship which delighted us. There was a friendly movement from group to group, a cosmopolitan mixing of boys and girls and adults and children were seldom seen with the same friends. We sat back in our easy chairs and watched the healthy adult-child relationships, the individual and group behaviour patterns unharrassed by daily chores and essential jobs. We loved the spontaneous desire for energetic activity and the occasional thoughtful immobility leaning on the deck rails, standing on the shore or just watching from a distance.

We saw tolerance and amusement flit over their faces and we saw social inter-change and shared wonder at beach treasures found. We watched children dealing with their personal equipment, writing letters, assuming responsibility and carrying out chores. We laughed at their gay abandon, the leaps and sommersaults and their enjoyment of food in the D'abri. We thrilled at their laughter and gaiety and we can never thank the photographer enough.

Each individual has contributed to campfire in some way. Even Nellie, now in the Women's Army, whose singing resembled that of the corncrake in Dolly MacLeod's corn. Those who put the orchestra in discord are often good at stunts and are always excellent at cheering.

A few have given so much to campfire that each generation is unknowingly indebted to them, for it is upon their singing and playing that foundations were laid and traditions built.

Ann was with us at our first Tiree camp in 1957. To sing, to Ann, was instinctive. She sang for personal pleasure and her repetoire of Scottish songs grew year by year. No campfire was complete without her singing 'The Road to Dundee,' 'The Hiking Song' or 'The Thistle of Scotland.' Later she sang for us 'The Waters of Loch Tay' and 'The Spinning Wheel,' and learned the Gaelic words to 'The Tiree Love Song,' 'Callin Mo Ruin Sa' and 'Morag of Dunvegan.' She sang on the shore and in her tent and frequently over the rails on the deck of the 'Claymore' or the 'Hebrides.' One of our first children, she became the first of generations of seniors. She wandered the islands with us in June when Margaret and I went in search of new places and she sang most of the way. The music lovers amongst us loved Ann, especially Julie who was destined to sing and play for us on her guitar and, later, to take Ann's place in the affections of all of us. On qualifying as a physiotherapist Ann sought a job in her beloved Scotland, later married a Scot and is rearing a family in Aviemore.

Another of our singers was Dorothy. We lost her from our campfires at sixteen when, as a trained member of our Sea Ranger Service Team, she began to give devoted help at the Diabetic Children's camp in Suffolk and dates began to clash. As a Nursery Nurse she began work in the Sunshine Homes for Babies, and later married one of the Diabetic Camp helpers. She visits us annually.

Fiona and Sarah have taught us songs from their native island, Jamaica. Prue brought her accordian; Rachel, Chris, Julie and Jenny their guitars. Recorder players we have had in plenty. It is a poignant moment when Alyson pipes our

140

'Taps' at the end of the day.

The film is precious but equally rewarding was a twenty-four page essay written by ten year old Robert. He could not stop writing until it was finished and, when it was, it contained no criticism, no hint of anything he had not enjoyed. And children's written work is extraordinarily honest at ten years old.

But we are not complacent. We dare not be. We know that harmony takes years to perfect but can be lost in an hour. We know that it is necessary to sing together for some time before we sing in unison. We know we have worked together and played together for a very long time to achieve this unity, this mutual understanding and this affinity. To keep it we must be watchful. We may slumber but not sleep, be weary but never too tired, frightened sometimes but never disturbed. We must never stop loving and liking children, never stop giving and sharing and working together. The responsibility is great and peace and happiness are fragile things. We know that things can go wrong, that tranquility and serenity have to be worked hard for. We are dealing with children who are very human and vulnerable, and so are we.

Campfires were born on Tiree where Calum piped us across the machair after the last campfire on the last evening of our first camp. If I close my eyes I can still see the dark silhouettes of the piper and his following of children, black against the lighter sea and the evening sky.

The hour we spend singing, almost every night of camp, we affectionately call 'Campfire!' The burning logs with their crown of peat are called, quite simply, 'the fire.' We say, 'Let's build a fire on the beach and have Campfire.' Therefore we can have Campfire in the D'abri without a fire. We did for years before we discovered the luxury of calor gas fires. Now we have two and they turn our tent, on a cold windy night, into a snug sitting room. They make an immeasurable difference to our comfort and ensure that every child goes to bed warm, which is so essential to a good night's sleep.

Our Campfires have endeared us to the islanders who frequently join us for the hour of fun and song before bed; that hour when we are together in closeness, friendship and warmth, beneath the lighted lamp and the steep roof of the tent. The spirit of Campfire is infectious and uniting, and by the end of the fortnight there is such spontaneity and sensitivity to mood and atmosphere that no discipline is needed, no leader required.

Few of us have not been tremendously moved at a Campfire and the final one has often brought tears. Coming to an end, as all things must, the singers have gone carolling back to their sleeping tents. The lovely songs have been on their lips for a long time and tune after tune has drifted away into the night, sweeter than the corncrake whose monotonous note is perpetual.

We sing, usually without pause. Little ones nod sleepily within the curve of an older camper's arm and bare toes peep beneath the gaily embroidered blankets which add warmth and colour and wrap us together. One song follows another, beginning with noisy action songs, yells and silly ditties passed down through the years. We journey from the ridiculous to the sentimental. The songs reflect all these moods in the space of an hour. When the Campfire spirit has really taken hold everyone is of one accord and pandemonium is never chaos because all are alert and all are responsive.

I remember Annie arriving from Strond in the middle of an indoor Campfire. She was weighted down with goodies for all of us in her spacious shopping bag. Even I find it difficult to walk down the D'abri when it is full of children and blankets and all the paraphernalia they deem necessary; the guitars, recorders, homemade percussion instruments, torches, song books and their favourite mascots. But on this occasion the sea of children divided like the Red Sea to allow her passage, and somehow we got the large lady de-coated and seated on a skip. She opened up her bag like a veritable Father Christmas and brought out sweets and crisps and fruit and pop and biscuits. Every child was leaning forward and making appreciative noises that ended in a cheer and a noisy rendering of 'For she's a jolly good fellow.' Annie was so overcome she rose and hugged and kissed everyone she could reach.

By the laws of cause and effect the tent should have fallen down, the blankets should have caught fire and arms and legs should have been broken, yet there was instant reverence as someone began to sing her favourite song, 'Amazing Grace,' and order was there because it had never been lost.

Don't ask me why! I was only a spectator. The lump in my throat and the tears in my eyes prevented me from having any share in it. In any case an adult could only have spoilt things. Unfortunately neither Margaret nor Hazel were there to share the moment with me and I looked round for some understanding adult. I turned to Ishabel, one of the islanders, and saw that she was moved.

'Now isn't that chust great!' she said.

It was one of the most memorable Campfires of the two hundred or more that we must have had.

The last Campfire of every year, weather permitting, is on the beach and at it little gifts are exchanged and Campcraft Ribbons are awarded. These are heavily embroidered with the emblems of over twenty-five camps and are now heirlooms of very great value. The evening is always a little emotional for one is pronounced Best Camper and one Personality of the Year.

There is no need for a little homily, no need to leave them a message to take home, no need for a hymn of praise or a simple prayer. Each is left to take his or her own memories back to everyday life on the Mainland, each is left to find God in an individual way. The tremendous ocean and the wild clouds, the peace of evening and the glow of the sunset on the shore, human friendship and endurance, kindness and love speak for themselves – to each differently but to all unmistakably.

Come along, come along, let us foot it out together;
Come along, come along, Be it fair or stormy weather,
With the hills of home before us And the purple of the heather,
Let us sing in happy chorus. Come along, come along!

143

Chapter Twelve

A HILL is to climb, a road to walk, a bend to see round and a beach to explore and whilst we are young and fit we will venture. We are not habitually early risers for the evenings are full, sleep comes late and the morning is usually old when we awake.

But not when we walk. Then we are up at daybreak. Our feet feel strangely heavy in unaccustomed socks and hiking shoes but the air is lovely and cool on our bare legs and there is a strong feeling in every limb.

Not everyone likes walking long distances and there is no compulsion to do so, but many delight in putting miles and miles behind them, looking and walking far into the awaiting distance. We need to have most of the miles behind us before noon for the easiest ones are the early ones. When the normal fatigue of evening is added to the tiredness of walking, enjoyment is lost.

Walking on the Mainland can be very rewarding but we have walked for many long miles along the shores of seemingly endless lochs. We have walked over vast stretches of moorland without seeing a house or a crofter at work. We have wandered twenty miles looking for a telephone kiosk so that we could phone home before we bivouacked for the night and we have walked on roads when we would have preferred footpaths because roads took the only way through the mountain passes.

Distances on the smaller isles are never too great to be interesting and are much more suited to children's gayer footsteps. The scene changes as often as it does in the Yorkshire Dales and the roads are infinitely quieter. A bay, or a loch, a mountain, or an island is round every bend of the narrow road. Dotted here and there are crofts and people at work so that every walk is full of brief encounters and friendly 'good-days.'

We have a compulsive urge to take any boat to any island and walk on it. It is, however, advisable to make sure that the pier marked on the map is suitable for landing from a small chartered craft. We made this mistake a long time ago when beginning a walking holiday on Mull. We asked the weather beaten, capable, lady skipper of the 'Island Queen' if she would take us to Croggan. She did not demure about the request and we were trusting of the map, believing that if the Ordnance Survey say pier then one will be able to land there.

What we required was a jetty or at least a pier with a landing stage for small boats. We did not bargain for arriving at Croggan pier at low water and finding it enormous, built only for large cattle boats and coal puffers. We found that the only way to land was by climbing ten feet of barnacled pier struts, wet and splintered by the impact of big boats bouncing against them in rough weather. There is a similar one at Salem and we have seen a boat almost broken being crushed against it.

Not being particularly keen on heights I only enjoyed the experience in retrospect but the landing gave us a beautiful walk round Loch Spelve, at rhododendron time, before bivouacking at Loch Buie. Next morning we walked all along the shore to Carsaig Bay and there are few places to compare when the yellow water flags are in bloom. It is more tranquilizing and rejuvenating than anything the doctor can prescribe.

Some islands are small enough to walk round in a day and these please us most of all. Nothing can be more varied than a day's tramping on Barra with its western coral beaches, the Tràigh Mhòr where the plane lands, the sandy spit of Eoligarry and the rocky bays and the lazy beds of the more populated east.

Our first introduction to Tràigh Vais is unforgetable. We were staying at North Bay at the house of the Choddie, regretably soon after he died. It would have given us great pleasure to meet him and hear his stories. On our first evening we walked as far as the Tràigh Mhòr, the two mile cockle strand where the orange air sac billows out as bravely as the ones over Heathrow. The tide was in and the Tràigh Mhòr looked like one huge lagoon, as still and peaceful as it is possible for the sea to be. We could not understand, therefore, why there was the thunder of nearby surf and wondered if it were an illusion, some lingering roar escaped from the whelk shells the children are always holding to their ears.

Obsessed by the noise we hurried across the dune and caught our first glimpse of Tràigh Vais with its great Atlantic rollers, turbulant and white, pounding incessantly on the shore. We have had the same experience travelling from east to west near the Butt of Lewis and seen the Atlantic giants sending up their white spray at Europie. Yet again at Sollas, on North Uist, where the Sea was as calm at Malaclett as the lake in Studley Royal though the din of it pounding on the long strands towards Veilish was a continuous background noise. To walk from Sorobaidh to Balephuil, on Tiree, is to witness the same sea change and from Scalasaig to Kiloran or Tobar on Colonsay or from Arinagour to Cleat on Coll but nowhere is it as dramatic as on Barra where the separating dune is less than a quarter of a mile wide. The narrow line of sand dune between tranquility and great turbulance is a lesson one might do well to remember.

Though islands differ so much from each other there are certain characteristics constant throughout the length of the Long Island, which is the collective name for the Outer Hebridean archipeligo. Down the west there are miles and miles of white coral beaches and down the east there are rocky bays and safe anchorages where crofters survive by farming lazy beds and lobster fishing. The lazy beds are incredibly small, often no bigger than a table cloth.

Because we camp on the sandy shores we delight to walk the eastern roads. From Tangasdale the road round Barra is only thirteen miles. From Luskentyre to Rodel in the south east of Harris is about twenty miles. It has been known for the stoutest walkers of our tribe to complete the journey right round South Harris, returning via Leverburgh and the west coast, a total of over forty miles. More often we take it easy and finish the journey comfortably at Rodel where excellent coffee can be bought from the hotel. It pleases us to know that the Queen and the Duke of Edinburgh were there before us. They landed from the Royal Yacht and a plaque commemorating this is on the front wall of the hotel. Their signatures are in the same visitors' book, in St Clements' Church, as all those of the Yorkshire children.

We were enjoying the excellent coffee in this hotel, one somewhat cloudy afternoon, when a young fellow came to the door merely to enquire about the possibility of transport. He was Youth Hostelling on the island and had come via the west coast from Tarbert. Having put some thirty odd miles behind him he wondered if there were any possibility of getting a lift northwards, along the eastern road, to the Youth Hostel at Stockinish.

He was fortunate. Someone would be going that way in an hour so the boy was told he may wait by the peat fire in the lounge where we were drinking our coffee. He was an interesting boy, a student, knowledgeable about maps and able to tell us some interesting facts about some very early maps on the lounge wall.

Shortly after his arrival the girl brought him an afternoon tea he hadn't ordered but he accepted it graciously, aware that his gratitude for their courtesy could best be expressed by taking some refreshment there. We dawdled over our coffee, relaxed and warm and pleasantly entertained and when the girl came with our modest bill for the coffee the young man took out his wallet to pay for his.

'Och, well, no,' said the girl with some embarrassment. 'There will be no payment. You didn't order it.'

The road along the eastern bays of Harris is extravagantly called the Golden Road, so named, we are told, because of the colossal building cost. This we can appreciate for few other roads will be more propitiously cut out of rock for such a straggling and struggling community. It is a most beautiful road and could have been called golden for that reason too. Its scenery is quite unpredictable and in the early morning mists it is like wandering through an illusionary land of mountain and sea, of fresh water lochs covered with clean water lilies and of lazy beds scattered among the rocks; of tethered cattle and brave little houses balancing on the edge of nowhere.

We set off at six, usually on a very misty promising morning, well clad against the cool air and the dampness hanging over all. Where the River Laxdale flows into the estuary at Luskentyre there are acres of sea pinks, the flower which looks so beautiful beside the turquoise of the sea. After heavy rain the River Laxdale pours water into the sea the colour of strong tea and turns the turquoise into gold.

We always take the old road from here. It skirts the southern shore of an attractive, fresh water loch before it climbs steeply up the rock. No one uses this road, since the new one was blasted out of the rock, except the residents of a small cottage now used only as a holiday home. It is becoming more and more overgrown and the frost has broken up what was left of the tarmac and made it unsteady underfoot.

The first three miles along the Luskentyre Road are easy and we scorn those who groan when twenty miles are mentioned.

'We walked more than forty to Loch Scourst,' we boast. 'We saw eagles hovering over Strone Scourst, remember? Anyone can walk twenty!'

But when we begin to walk the upward trail of the old road we are not so sure. There are those who begin to envy their friends still in bed and wonder why they were so foolish as to get up at six. Seniors instinctively take the hands of the little ones and urge them on. Reaching the funeral cairns, which mark the official resting places of the coffin bearers of not so many years ago, we appreciate their necessity to stop frequently for it is a gruelling journey across the bare rock and peat bog of the interior of Harris. It is all too obvious that the only suitable burying grounds are on the west and the pall bearers would find it a long and difficult carry.

Once the Golden Road is reached new energy seems to flow. Though the road is never flat there is as much downward as upward trail and there is always the element of surprise as one comes on the lovely fresh water loch at Plockrapool, the expanse of water lilies at Stockinish and the unexpected steepness at Geocrab.

The road is well signposted and every township named. Meavag, Finsbay, Lingaby, all jewels in the Golden Road. Margaret and I have walked this road many times, mostly with children. Once we walked it alone on one of the hottest days of spring when the mist hung cold and wet on the old road and disappeared in the heat of mid-morning on the Bays Road.

We stopped the travelling shop for a chat and a bottle of lemonade, for it was thirsty work walking. We should have been satisfied with the peat streams running down the rocky crevices for we soon found even the small weight of the bottle too heavy. Eventually we found a convenient hole for losing it down and we said goodbye to it gladly but with a twinge of guilt. We do not like leaving litter even though it is well hidden and cannot reappear.

We sat on a hillside looking across the Minch to MacLeod's Tables on Skye, feeling the sun burning into us. A crofter's wife, in a cottage below us, suddenly opened her windows wide and started carrying things out of her door. Out came her mats and rugs for a shaking, then her stools and chairs. Finally she began to sweep out the dust of winter inspired, no doubt, by the beautiful spring morning. I felt akin to her. I know the spring cleaning feeling and we live in a house where you can hurl things out of the door and do the job properly. I felt that she and I were very fortunate indeed and that those who lived in streets and flats or in suburbia where such things are not done were poorer than we. We waved gaily to the woman. I'm sure she was having 'a ball' as our Canadian children would say.

Very soon our anoraks and sweaters and cagoules were too heavy to carry. There was a little cottage under the bank of the road and a few pairs of Harris socks were displayed at the gate. Naturally we expected to find a Harris woman there but instead we found only a relative of hers home from the New World. Our request to be allowed to leave a haversack of clothing until the following day developed into a long and interesting conversation. The road from the cottage wound round the bay and our friend was still waving to us twenty minutes later as we began to climb the steep hillside on the other side of the water.

We had intended, that day, unencumbered by children, to walk the whole of the way back up the western coast but we gave up after thirty six miles, somewhat footsore. It is true but we don't like to admit it. We are not quite so young as we used to be.

We climbed the three hills on Tiree, with thirty children, on a lovely windy day. We had French girls with us that year for the first week of camp. They enjoyed it so much they were very emotional when they left. Marie was a strong walker and her long legs set too fast a pace for me. Unfortunately I was battling with a stubbed big toe. During the pitch I accidentally walked too fast into a tent peg and had bad language been a habit, mine would certainly have been unfit to record. I managed quite well barefoot but with shoes on I was in considerable pain. The toe was beautifully purple, for which I was grateful for no-one could then dispute the agony I was in or criticise my somewhat poor performance on the thirty mile walk. When I returned home I went to the hospital for an X-ray and was told that it was broken. The young doctor who told me this went home and told his wife he'd had to attend to the broken toe of a Guider who'd had all her Guides on Tiree. Ray did not know then, and neither did his wife, that she was to become a loved and indespensible member of our team and that, one year he would accompany us and learn what it is in the islands which is so attractive to us,

I digress too often. There are too many things to remember and I am writing for Vivienne who wants nothing forgotten which can possibly be remembered. It saddens me to think that so many of our experiences with children and with islanders must have been lost else this collection would have run into several volumes.

There are friends wherever we walk, be it Mull or Barra, Tiree or Harris, the Uists or Skye. We talk to them working in the fields, making hay, or on the peat bogs lifting their winter supply of fuel and we wave to them wherever we go. We find them on the hillside scraping the crottal from the rocks for dyeing their wool, at the fank and leading home their cow for milking.

With a large party of children we were passing a friend's house many years ago. It was a very small house on the edge of the sea and it had not been modernised like most of the island houses have. Our friend insisted that the adults in our party should come into the house for a strupag. We decided it would be a suitable place for the picnic and opened up our food sacks on the rocks below the house whilst our friend put on her kettle.

Whilst we were having tea there was a knock on the door and one of the older girls, Julia, asked if she might use our friend's toilet. We were naturally a bit embarrassed but the good lady took her into the bedroom without fuss.

A short time later small Julie came to make the same request and when Chris arrived five minutes later my embarrassment was unbearable and I made a feeble excuse to go outside where I ordered anyone wanting the 'loo' to find one behind a rock. There was nothing wrong, as a Hebridean friend of ours once put it, 'in putting one's backside to the sea.' On no account, I insisted, was anyone else to come to the house to use the toilet.

No one did and I controlled my curiosity for as long as I was able but could not resist the temptation to ask each one how she had coped at the 'loo.' I was glad I'd asked for their answers were unforgettable and have given us much pleasure for many years.

Julia, at fifteen was gentle. 'Aw, Skipper,' she said with such a kind smile, 'she was so sweet.' No more.

Julie, at eight, was honest and aghast. 'Auntie Jean,' she whispered, wide eyed, 'It was only a potty!'

Chris, brusque with twelve year old embarrassment said, smilling, 'Mind your own business.'

We have climbed Ben Luskentyre on many occasions, always with great delight and a sense of achievement for it is a stiff climb. We are careful to climb when the cloud is high for we have no wish to be caught up there in a mist. Not everyone reaches the top.

We have potterers who set out with no real intention of getting any further than the first ridge. Those who are perfectly happy looking for flowers and ferns between the rock crevices. They find gentian and thyme and wild orchids and hunt for butterwort and sundew. They are also the ones who like to sit with binoculars looking, first of all, down on the camp, commentating on all the familiar activities of those left behind. Then they look out into the distance and over to the rocks where the sea birds fly and train their spyglass on the hardy little ringed plover calling its chicks to safety. And lastly they look to St Kilda on the horizon.

There are, at the other extreme, the tearaways who race to the top far too quickly. They glue their eyes on the summit for as long as they can see it rising in the sky above their heads. They have a one track mind until they reach the top. They set a pace far too impossible for the majority and fill me with fear for their safety. Their thrill is in saying that they got up in record time. They are the ones who carry the annual flag to plant fluttering in the cairn on the summit. Nearly always they are boys, very sarcastic and big headed.

There are always the too timid who do not know how to plant their feet firmly. They fear to cross the boggy places in case their feet sink in the mire and sit on top of walls, not knowing how to get down. They seem incapable of helping themselves. They tremble in case they put their feet on an adder or meet a wild cat face to face. No one has ever done either nor is likely to. They seldom reach the top.

The ones who test our patience and endurance most are the 'I'll climb this mountain if I die in the attempt' breed who struggle slowly up the hill, panting because they have too much weight for such sport or because their legs are too foal-like and spindly to attempt such a gradient.

One of the former was Alison, a very plump child who was bringing up the rear with Viv, in the days when she was thin enough and light enough for the wind to have blown her off the mountain. They looked like a comedy act, the one so fat and the other so small and thin and when Alison began to perspire with the unaccustomed exertions and gave Viv, who was shivering, her enormous anorak the difference in their vital statistics was emphasised to the point of ridicule. The anorak was so voluminous that had the wind succeeded in getting underneath it Viv would have become airborne.

The successful climbers reached the top, signed their names on the flag and bedded it well into the cairn with innumerable small stones. We spent some time recovering from the climb, eating the biscuits and chocolates I always try to remember, and generally enjoying the view. The wide panorama is truly magnificent.

Because most humans are self centred and home orientated we generally spend our first minutes looking down on the camp which has become like small grains of salt spilled on the edge of the sand dunes. Sometimes silently, sometimes orally we wonder at the incredible smallness of human life and our relative unimportance in the scheme of things.

'Down there,' I said, one blue and white day, 'in one of those almost microscopic specks of white, Mrs Belsey is making sandwiches for our tea.'

Nothing could seem more impossible. Everyone should climb to a great height and look down. It helps to get things into perspective. It does us all good to feel very small sometimes.

On clear days St Kilda can be seen on the south westerly horizon and, beyond Berneray and Pabbay, can be seen the hills of North Uist. Skye always looks very near, especially the flat tops of the MacLeod's Tables and, if the weather is particularly clear, the Cuillin lift their rugged, black granite heads into the sky.

Looking north there is the most impressive view of the North Harris mountains. Clisham, the highest mountain on the island, guards the road to Stornoway and rising perpendicular above Loch Scourst stands Strone Scourst or Eagle Mountain as we have always called it.

When we have looked our fill towards the sun and followed the flash it creates on car headlights travelling towards Seilebost, and when we have named all the bays and townships on the Northton road, Horgabost, Borve, Scarista and Nisabost, and turned westward to gaze on Taransay and north westward to pick our Bunaveneader, Amhuinnsuidhe and Husinish and the island of Scarp, we climb the last few hundred yards to the Grid Point. We feel as if we have been on a world tour, our eyes have visited so many places.

From the Grid point we can see Tarbert and if we have timed it well we can watch the, 'Hebrides' sail smoothly up East Loch Tarbert and tie up at the pier. How small she looks, like a toy to sail on the bath-water. We know her intimately. She is a very good friend.

All this takes time and unless we begin to shiver on the high altitude we are never in a hurry to descend for we are always excused tea making when we climb the mountain. Imagine our surprise, therefore, on the day when on the way down we met Alison and Viv still climbing. They still had about a third of the way to go. I groaned inwardly for I know the 'I'll climb this mountain if I die in the attempt' breed. They are seldom to be dissuaded from their purpose.

However one can but try. My tactics were experienced.

'OH, WELL DONE YOU!' I said knowing that flattery sometimes works. 'Next time you'll manage it right to the top.'

'Next time be blowed,' puffed Alison, 'Ah've cum so far and Ah'm off t' top.'

'But it's an achievement to get so far,' I knew I was losing but I am not noted for giving in easily. 'You'll get to the top easily next year if we come back to Harris.' I brought out my final bribe knowing how much Alison liked her food. 'I bet Mrs Belsey has tea ready for us by now.'

'Nowt o' t' sort,' said Alison. 'Ah'm off t' top.'

There was nothing I could do but send the others off to enjoy their meal and laboriously climb back with them to the summit. It is an impressive climb for the slope of Ben Luskentyre is etched against the sea and the sky and is at least 40 degrees. Below the sea is deep and green and all the underwater rocks and seaweeds can be seen.

This was not the only time I have had to climb the mountain twice in one day. Jenny was the proud owner of a camera and she had carried it all the way to the top on a cold day, most unsuitable for long distance photography. It had turned cloudy after a mini-heat-wave but the cloud was high. It was bitterly cold and we did not eat the biscuits and chocolate at the cairn but hurried to the semi circle of wall which shelters the Grid Point. We all sat very close together behind the draught proof wall and ate all but one small piece of chocolate which could not be shared.

We were half way down the mountain on our descent and crawling under the barbed wire fence which the crofters have erected on the common grazing to divide the lower slopes from the steep cone. Suddenly Jenny realised she had something missing.

'I've left my camera at the top,' she gasped in dismay.

'You can't have,' I said with conviction. Children seldom lose things. More often than not the lost article is soon found. It is invariably in some duffle bag or haversack, a coat pocket or even down a coat lining. Nine times out of ten it is still at home never having been brought.

We tried all possibilities without success and eventually we believed Jenny that it really was still on top of the mountain.

'I know where it is,' the eleven year old insisted. 'It's at the Grid Point. I put it down when we sat behind the wall to eat the biscuits.' Any other child would have cried but Jenny was very brave always.

There was no alternative but to climb to the top and get it. We could not throw away an article costing several pounds and ruin a little girl's holiday. We are fairly philosophical about these things. A child had not been lost, only a camera and we had to be thankful for small mercies. There was no mist dropping and darkness was hours away, Ray Belsey was with us so he was able to take the others down while Jenny and I reclimbed the mountain and collected the camera from behind the wall. Hand in hand we leapt down the hillside singing songs from the 'Sound of Music.' I am indebted to Jenny. She has drawn the line drawings in this book.

Our reception was all that we could wish. Everyone was falling over each other to serve us, eager to untie our shoes and help us off with our anoraks. It would have been nice if I could have accepted it all with dignity for royal attention comes seldom and it was appreciated. I spoiled everything by sitting on an insecure skip lid and falling ignominiously within, among the dried onions and the gravy browning. It was rather unfair of Prue to record it on her sketch pad and offer it to Mrs Belsey for her camp log.

Adding small islands to our list is always popular whether it be Kerrera, or Iona or Scalpay. We went to Kerrera on a beautiful evening when we had a long wait in Oban before the boat came in. The walk to the ferry is no more than two miles and the crossing is short. The island is small enough to walk from east to west before it is necessary to return on the boat and we found it a very peaceful island.

The weather was so uncertain, the year we went to Scalpay, that we were in two minds whether to venture there at all. There seemed little point in getting fifty people deliberately wet. The ferries are infrequent and shelter for so many is hard to find. However there was one day when we decided to risk visiting this busy little island for the first time and it proved very kind to us. We found it the friendliest of islands where everyone waved to us and stopped on the road to talk to us. We would have loved to have been there when the fishing fleet was in for the island owns a flourishing fishing industry.

Children seem able always to smell out the places where food can be had. They immediately found the shop and then came with a most unlikely story that they had found a cafe where coffee and biscuits cost only five new pence. The cafe was the front room of a small house owned by a couple who had retired there from England. They liked meeting people so began offering cups of coffee and biscuits (at what surely must have been cost price) in order to do so. They were quite undaunted by the sudden arrival of dozens of children and were happy to feed them all, providing we staggered the party and lent a hand with washing the cups inbetween. It was a most pleasant and memorable encounter. I will never get used to, nor take for granted, the tolerance shown to the swarms of children I take to the islands every year. I am sure that it must be unequalled anywhere in the world.

It would be interesting to know how many miles we have walked with children in the Hebrides. We must have put hundreds of miles of island road and shore, footpath and heather behind us in the twenty years of our wanderings. All have offered beauty and challenge but none more so than the green footpath to Rheinigidale. I believe it to be the most spectacular I have ever walked.

Not one of us was prepared for the precipitous, winding footpath and even the youngest of those who walked it must remember it forever. We are told that it is less than five miles from the Kyles Road to Rheinigidale but it took us two hours at least, each way, to walk it.

We had first heard of Rheinigidale several years ago from a party of boys who were coming off the boat in Tarbert on the night we were leaving. They looked a very well organised group, all adequately dressed with sensibly packed rucksacks and healthy, smiling faces.

We were therefore astonished to see them begin to carry off tins of food, billies, custard powder, lamps, toilet rolls, everything you could think of, loose.

'The deck looks like our site when the skips are unpacked,' someone observed.

'They'll never get everything off,' said Hazel. 'Come on everyone. Let's help!'

We could not imagine why they had not even packed in cardboard boxes. Unloading the stuff was ridiculous.

'Where are you going?' I asked with my arms full of baked beans, squash and frying pans.

'Rheinigidale,' I was answered. 'They say it is fourteen miles from here and five of those are footpath. But we are going by boat.'

The food stuffs and equipment were indeed being handed down steps at the side of the pier into a little boat.

'We don't usually pack like this,' he hastened to inform me. 'It was all packed into the landrover and when we got to Uig there wasn't any car space on the boat for it. There are dozens of cars left behind. We had to unpack in a hurry. Cor,' what a shambles!'

We'd like to meet that party again. I hope they liked Rheinigidale when they finally got there. It was a wild night and the weather was unsettled.

When we walked there the day could not have been more perfect. For that reason and because I had never walked it previously and was ignorant of the actual nature of the walk, I arranged for the bus to take us all to the beginning of the footpath. But only half our number walked the whole way to what must be one of the most isolated and most remote villages in the United Kingdom. It can only be reached by footpath or by sea and the one is balanced on the edge of the sea and crossing mountains of bare rock and the other is the Minch which can be very stormy indeed.

The bus driver stopped on a passing place at the start of the green trail. We lifted out our two picnic skips which we left a few yards off the road. We left them labelled, 'Picnic for the Guides.' It was still there, untouched when we collected it five hours later. The beginning of the trek leaves the Kyles Scalpay road a few miles out of Tarbert and persists in a determined manner right on up into the hills.

These grassy footpaths can be found all over the east side of Harris. We walked a number of them when we joined a sponsored walk in aid of the new Harris Hall. They link the townships by shorter routes than the Golden Road and they are comfortable and easy underfoot. But being direct they climb steep hillsides and cling to the rocky coastlines. They may be difficult in places but they are never dull.

The track from the Kyles Road can be seen as a long green ribbon threading its way through rocks and heather, way into the remote distance and every yard we climbed we rose higher into the mountain air and saw a greater panoramic sweep of mountain, loch and sea. The only habitation we could see was so distant, so many miles away as to merge into the rocks whose camouflage is complete. It was such a hot day we kept leaving sweaters and anoraks by the wayside for recovery on our return.

The summit of the track over Beinn Chaolais is reached at about a thousand feet and from it we looked down on Loch Trollamarig and beyond to Loch Seaforth and the hills of Lewis. I have seen no more magnificent view. At this point the track levels out and then begins to fall gradually about a hundred feet until the coast is reached and the sea is seen nine hundred feet below. The path then begins a zig zag descent called the Scriob which would alarm lone walkers let alone a leader responsible for innumerable children. The curving ribbon of it clings tenaciously to the almost vertical hillside and I clucked, at the top, like an over anxious mother hen afraid for her large brood. I insisted over and over again on sensible spacing and extreme care and told them in no uncertain terms what would happen if they crowded and one fell or if they started to run. It was an adventure to thrill the most precocious of children and frighten the most placid of leaders.

Not everyone went down for, on a footpath to Rheinigidale, what is climbed down on the outward journey must be climbed up on the return. Those whose slowness had put them way behind on the route over Beinn Chaolais, were content to remain, sitting, chatting and sunbathing at the unrivalled vantage point. They amused themselves by watching our progress for the green ribbon was like a well marked footpath on a physical, three dimensional map and the patches of blue and white, that were our shirts, moved like sheep along it.

At the very bottom of the zig zag we came to a bridge over the burn which rushes down the steep sided ravine between Beinn Chaolais and the majestic Toddum, rising seventeen hundred feet into the sky. The burn flows more sedately under the bridge and pours itself into the little bay at Loch Trollamarig.

Here again some were content to stay. There was plenty to amuse them in burn and waterfall, shore and sea. We buttered several packets of cream crackers and ate them with cheese and apples. Thus refreshed the rest of us, twenty four in all, set out to complete the strenuous journey. All the while we were well aware that, to those who live in Rheinigidale, this journey must be part of the facts of life, ordinary and necessary when stores have to be brought from Tarbert. Children walk it a weekends when at school in Tarbert and the postman walks it three times a week with Her Majesty's Mail.

There is not one bit of track without excitement and interest. It appears, in places, to leap suicidally into the sea, zig zagging like a migration of lemmings and then hurtling crazily over the cliff. But it is only teasing. It continues steadily and purposefully towards Rheinigidale, the sleepy little township at its journey's end, a cluster of six or seven little houses and a school, sheltering in a natural harbour.

They will see many walkers in the summer time, these residents of one of Britain's remotest villages but in the winter time they will see no one for weeks on end. Twenty four Yorkshire children did not even wake them. Not even when they made a bee line for the bay and taking off shorts and shirts baptized themselves in the icy water of the Minch, in the flimsiest of underwear. We shared our sweets with some children sitting on a doorstep but they did not follow us to the beach. We made a phone call from the simple number Rheinigidale 1 and talked to the crofter's wife but our presence did nothing whatsoever to disturb the peace. A few men calmly carried some bales of hay through the village and over the hill. There was very little movement apart from the activity of our own children. It was a lazy afternoon and we felt part of it.

So we waved 'goodbye' and turned our footsteps south westwards, swinging quickly drying underwear in the sun.

'I wonder what they think of us?' said Jackie. 'We walk in in shorts and shirts and leave fluttering our bras and pants in the sun.'

It was a very hot summer's day, one of a long line in a blue and golden heatwave, and each one of us was privately thinking about the nine hundred feet climb ahead of us. We collected the potterers by the burn and they were full of the fun they had had exploring the narrow ravine and hunting for treasures on the shore. They were far more garrulous than those who had reached their Mecca. These had had an experience they couldn't quite put into words. The others found it easy to talk about the ordinary things they had done because they were known activities. The pilgrims who had gone all the way had been into a world they had not known before and were tired by the heat and satiated with remoteness and peace.

We climbed the incredible path with frequent stops feeling, when we eventually reached the top, that a major manoeuvre was successfully completed. Those who had not even descended from the heights waited until they saw us reappear in the distance and then they went back to the road to prepare our picnic. It was lovely to find it all ready for us when we arrived.

Much later I was having a strupag with Katie. 'Oh, I have never been to Rheinigidale at all,' she said.

Few of the islanders have. They do not walk for pleasure like we do. For us a hill is to climb, a road to walk, a bend to see round and a shore to explore and whilst we are young and strong we will venture.

13

Dance, dance, wherever you may be,
I am the Lord of the Dance said he,
And I'll lead you all wherever you may be,
And I'll lead you all in the Dance said he.

156

Chapter Thirteen

AFTER ALL these years I am still asked the unanswerable question. 'When is the Cèilidh, Skipper?' 'Are we having a Barn Dance?' 'Can we have a Barbecue?'

How do I know! I do not plan these things and am not responsible for days and times. Seldom do we know in advance. They happen quickly and spontaneously and are all the more fun for that.

When is it? Will we? What night? What time? My answers can only be vague. When the weather is right. When Calum, or Neil, or Charlie or Lachlan can play. When the hall is free. These are unsatisfactory answers to give to children but they ought to know by now how incapable I am of predicting the islanders.

Céilidhs are not planned at all unless they are formal evenings in the Island Hall. Even so we seldom know about them in advance.

'Are you going to the céilidh (or the concert, or the dance) tonight?' we will be asked and suddenly we have to plan accordingly. 'There's a dance outside on the pier tonight, Skipper,' I am told by excited youngsters. 'Can we stay for it?' We have to be ready to change our routine at a moment's notice because it would be unthinkable to miss these highlights of our island days.

"You will be going to 'Whisky Galore' tonight," we were told in the late afternoon, one idyllic day on Barra, seven miles away from Castlebay.

'Tonight!' we gasped. 'How could we get there?' We need not worry there is always someone who is 'going that way anyway.'

The céilidhs we like most happen when Julie wanders up to Annie's comfortable cottage with her guitar accompanied by Joanna and Janice, Viv and Christine and one or all of the many Donald Johns happen to be there. The right time for a céilidh is when Toots and Janet and Ann and Judith call on Mrs MacLean and Lachie is at home.

'Where have you been?' I asked them when they came back late.

'We've been to Mrs MacLean's and she asked us to stop and sing songs and she told us to show our sunburnt legs to Lachie.'

'And what did you do?' I laughed.

'We showed him them of course,' they grinned.

Our Barn Dances began many, many years ago in Calum's barn and now all our children expect to dance as they expect to eat. A camp without a dance is like Yorkshire apple pie without cheese or a kiss without a squeeze. Now Calum is gone and things will never be quite the same but his memory lingers for us in every 'Strip the Willow' and every 'Eightsome Reel.' Unfortunately our youngsters are not the world's best dancers but all get up to try.

The date of the dance in Calum's barn, was never planned ahead. I would go to the shop for groceries, one morning, and himself would be sitting at his half of the dining table, the half which was not piled high with what he affectionately called his 'deep litter,' and he would have the tea pot poised in his hand to pour me a cup.

'I've been trying to clear out the barn, Chean,' he would say. 'Ellen was down asking about the Barn Dance.'

I would be enthusiastic at once. There were forty eager dancers back at camp continually nagging at me to ask him about the dance of the year.

'When would be the best time to have it, Calum?' I would ask. I have learned not to stampede islanders. That is their perogative.

'Och, chust any day at all, Chean,' he would say vaguely, 'Except Saturday of course,' (dances go on long past midnight) 'and there'll be a dance in Crossapol on Friday.'

'I'll ask when would be the best night for an accordianist,' I would say. 'What time do you think we should start?'

'I think it would be best to be starting airly,' Calum would say as if he knew what the word meant and had respect for it. 'We'll start at nine o'clock this year.'

Having got so far I would dash along to the nearby crofts to ask the MacInneses and the MacLeans and the Clarks, the Lamonts and the Browns when the best night would be for them and they would all come up with the decision that, if something is worth doing it is worth doing at once.

'Och, we'll have the dance tonight,' they would say emphatically. 'But not at nine o'clock. Och, there'll not be anyone at all who will come before ten.'

'Tonight!' I would gasp in a panic. 'But who'll know to come tonight?' My question was as ridiculous as those the children ask. People on Tiree always know when to come. What I really meant was, 'How can we cope with a dance at such short notice? We who come from Yorkshire and are a bit slow in our reactions?'

'Och, there's plenty of time, chust.' I would be reassured.

That being so it was foolish of me to run all the way back to camp as if the train was due out. Plenty of time, they said! Where would I find plenty of time? The barn was to clean for a start. There would be plenty of help for that but everyone would want time for a 'hair do,' to wash underwear, to brush skirts and press blouses and ties with an enamel mug filled with hot ashes. There were refreshments to think about and life in camp had to go on, children had to be fed and normal chores done. Plenty of time indeed!!!

But I would get no support for a later date from the youngsters. The answer they always most prefer when they ask, 'When?' is, 'Now!' The announcement that the Barn Dance would be that night would set them prancing like a troop of circus horses and for the next few hours activity would be perpetual.

The barn was always in a terrible state. It was a lovely barn with a concrete floor and held a lot of dancers. But it only received its annual clean on the afternoon of the dance. Calum would oblige by driving out the old tractor, if it was capable of being driven out under its own steam. If not, we would all push and shove and roll it out with brute force. We would stack the bales of straw and pile the loose hay in a corner, brush up the hen droppings and sweep down the cobwebs.

Poor Calum! He always knew where everything was when it was untidy. We wondered if he'd ever find anything after our vigorous spring clean. We tidied the working surfaces of his benches and stowed things away underneath but he was never complaining. We cleared out the cardboard cartons and the litter of a year and scattered clean sand on the floor as a sweeping detergent. It brought up the oil and dirt and polished the floor fit for the bare feet which would dance on it until the early hours.

Everything about the Barn Dance was fun. Every available bath and bin and billy was filled with water and put on the fire for the ablutions, which traditionally must preceed a Barn Dance and the annual camp 'hair do' for which the small packet of shampoo had been brought. Hair washing cannot be done in sea water so the electric pump in Calum's kitchen had to work overtime and everyone had to carry a bucket across the sands.

It has been known for observant mothers to discover that the bar of soap taken to camp has come home so little used that LUX is still written plainly on it. This may be so, for the islands are clean places and bathing in the sea often replaces the daily shower. Nevertheless there are always plenty of soap bubbles around on the night of the dance.

There is no more fun anywhere than getting dirty, cleaning Calum's barn, and then standing in a bowl of water on the edge of the sunset; a bowl in which several others have previously stood and wafting soap bubbles into the night air, then cleaning teeth in a long smiling row beside the water bin.

Providing plenty of hot fresh water is on supply for the outdoor salon, the hair washing goes on apace. It is so much fun I have actually seen children standing on their heads in the bowl whilst a friend has helped with the squeezing out of the shampoo and the lathering of the curls. Hot water being in short supply, when so many heads need attention, of their own choosing they usually rinse with cold. It is fun to pour cold water over someone else's head and, strange as it may seem, it is fun to scream with the sudden shock of its icyness and leap around groping for a towel, then try to rub more vigorously than anyone else.

And all the while we would be busy packing the picnic skips with packets of biscuits, the huge tins of coffee, hot chocolate and tea bags. We collected every mug in camp and sorted out big billies that would fit on Calum's stove. Eventually the children were all ready in their pressed blouses and gay red ties, their groundsheets had been laid and beds left ready to unroll when we returned in the small hours. They hurried along the beach in glad anticipation, flushed and smiling as if they had just risen. We followed after a quick wash and complete change, looking as if the first dance would finish us off completely.

The islanders were right. No one ever came before ten and even so Charlie had played several tunes on the accordian before Calum appeared, inspite of his nine o'clock prophesy. He was usually sitting by his stove when we arrived, tinkering with his bagpipes. They were invariably in pieces. Salum house is the only place where I have seen bagpipes indecently dressed. You cannot rush a Hebridean nor hurry him into manipulating the naked bladder into its tartan bag.

We always entered the barn via the byre, whence cats and poultry had fled from the unusual happenings in their bedroom. The hens balanced warily on their unac-customed perches and the green eyes of the cats gleamed suspiciously from dark corners. Someone would invariably be singing in Gaelic when we squeezed past the island men who stood shyly just inside the doorway at the beginning of every Barn Dance. It would be Hugh or May or John Lachie or Mary and the song would be 'Morag of Dunvegan' or 'The day we went to Rothsea O' or 'The Tiree Love Song!' There would be a poignant silence, pierced only by the one clear singer until the chorus came. Then two or three would join in and foot tapping would begin. Gradually everyone would be singing and we, ourselves, would be trying to put the strange words to the catching melody.

As soon as they were aware that Calum had joined them the children would crowd round him and, full of pride, he would blow up his pipes and begin to play and everyone would dance. We danced to the piper and we danced to the accordian and we sang our songs and tried to join in theirs. When exhaustion threatened to reduce the numbers on the floor we hurried through the dimly lit byre into the kitchen for the hot drinks and biscuits and we carried in every mug we possessed and every cup in Calum's kitchen but there were never enough and we had to collect and wash the empties and begin all over again.

Each year we saved the stoutest of our pine bark strippings and balanced them on empty petrol cans round the barn. Sitting on these somewhat irregular and rocky seats the youngsters contemplated their dusty, healthy feet and hoped the dance would go on until morning.

Every girl from Yorkshire looks beautiful at a Barn Dance, every boy is hand-some. On Tiree they always danced barefoot. The very nature of the sandy islands ensures cleanliness. They are always so browned by the sun and so flushed by dancing, so happy and gay that even the plainest child is lovely. Completely uninhabited they all dance, some well, some clumsily, many will sing if asked and if we have a guitarist she will always play. There is no false modesty.

Our memories of Calum's barn are among our most precious and most vivid. It was traditional for the islanders to sing, 'Will ye no come back again,' and all our children's voices would shout in answer 'Yes we will come back again, Better lo'ed we'll never be.' Then there would be 'Auld Lang Syne' and cheering fit to raise the roof.

Sleepy heads would nod and many would stumble as we filed through the dim byre into the warm kitchen. There we would collect our billies and mugs and put on warm jackets. We would organise ourselves into groups for the dark journey back to our home on the machair. Some of the little ones would be carried pick-a-back, many would stumble sleepily, vaguely proud that, like their older companions, they had danced until two o'clock in the morning. How dark an island is after being in a lighted barn, how cold the night air, how welcome the grey squares, in the small valley, that are our white canvas homes.

Once our feet started to dance they would not stop. We danced nightly round the cooking fire with the help of Donald Brown's tape recorder. We danced in Scaranish Hall and more recently in Crossapol Hall and we thought nothing of walking the four miles home from Scarinish. I remember the tears Barbara shed because we were offered lifts and she wanted to walk. They were very happy days and they set the standard for the many years that followed.

No other barn but Calum's is spacious enough for a Barn Dance. Our numbers are already big before the islanders arrive and when everyone wants to dance a confined space is useless. A Dance in an island hall needs a couple of days' warning. This gives the island shopkeeper his chance to write out a notice and display it in his shop window.

COME AND JOIN THE GIRL GUIDES

at their Dance,

on Wednesday, 9 pm to midnight.

Where on the mainland would such a notice bring the response that it does on an island? For these dances we have to thank Duncan and Margaret MacInnes, Hector and Mairi Campbell and their piper son Lachlan.

'I believe you were dancing yourself,' said John Lachie when we were both at the butcher's van on the morning after one such dance.

'Well,' I parried 'I'm not a dancer but I was dancing last night, right enough.'

'Och, well,' laughed John Lachie, 'you'd better be careful. What you don't do when you're young it's dangerous to do when you're old!'

If we had little warning of a Barn Dance we once had even less of a Barbecue on Harris. The weather was so fine and settled I was asked by the seniors if we could have a Barbecue and Dance on the machair, in the quadrangle enclosed by the tents.

'Well,' I was non commital, 'I'll see what I can do.'

I asked one of the young men in the township if his brother would play for us if we had a Barbecue in camp.

'Yes, yes, och, he'll play,' said Donald John 'I'm certain of that, Chean. Och, It'll be quite all right. I'll tell him but I know the answer already. He will play, yes.'

Feeling rather pleased that things were going to be as simple as that I told the clamourers that there was no problem. Neil would play for the Barbecue.

'When?' they shouted.

'I'll know tomorrow,' I said. I ought not to have been so definite for tomorrow came and my friend had not contacted his brother but he was confident that there would be no problem.

'Yes, yes, he'll play for you that's certain,' he reassured me. 'I'll be 'phoning him tonight, anyway. Don't worry at all.'

I enquired again next morning.

'Yes, yes, I was 'phoning him last night but I wasn't speaking to him at all but I left a message. I don't think he will be free on Monday but any other night I'm sure he will play.'

I immediately ear marked Monday night for an important visit we all had to pay on a friend. We were all filing into her living room when the young man drew up in his car. Hazel brought me the message inside.

'Donald John's just been. He says the Barbecue is tonight and he's just going to pick up his brother and he'll be back in an hour!'

That was true! His van was just disappearing over the hill. It was already nine o'clock and we could not, nor did we wish to, hurry our important visit. I determined not to think about the rush we were going to have so that nothing would spoil our immediate visit. I cannot count the number of times we have sat, relaxed, with friends, as if we had indeed plenty of time, that illusive commodity in which all Hebrideans are so rich; when all the while a bus was waiting, a boat due, visitors expected or merely a fire needed stoking so that children could be fed. It is discourteous to be always in a hurry and we are guilty of it so often.

So we sang songs leisurely and made no haste to go. It was only when we were on the road to the shore, some considerable time later, that urgency accelerated our feet and we began to run. Some deviated from the road to tell friends in the township and holidaymakers in the caravan to come and join in the fun.

We had no rolls but we had plenty of sliced bread and I opened large tins of sausages and hamburgers and stoked up the fire until we could hear a healthy sizzling in the frying pans. It was already too dark to see properly. Everyone was dashing around with a torch. Everyone had a job to do. We removed the flagpole from the centre of the quadrangle and placed it near the D'abri. From it we hung our one gas lamp, high above the cleat out of danger.

Many people came and we danced and sang beneath the stars until one o'clock in the morning. We danced until we thought we had found the secret of perpetual motion and when I said, 'This must be the last dance, our accordianist played another and another until we thought he would not stop until we dropped. Finally we persuaded him to play 'Auld Lang Syne' and we thanked him heartily and said, 'Goodbye,' to all the visitors. Exhausted, but happy, we crawled into our sleeping bags.

The accordianist had not gone home. He just could not stop playing. He sat on the dunes above the shore and played for a long time. His repertoire of Scottish and Gaelic melodies seemed never ending. Finally we saw the headlights of the car as it went up the hill and there was only the noise of the sea on the nearby shore. Above us millions of stars looked down on the sleeping camp.

One year we had the unique experience of dancing on the pier to a full pipe band. We had been attending the Sports in the afternoon and some of the older ones found out that there was to be a dance on the pier that night. Of course they wanted to stay and they would not be put off by the thought of a considerable wait. Providing they have food and the bus to sit in if they get tired, they are seldom difficult to entertain. Our driver was agreeable that we should stay and so we did. The weather was warm and balmy and the pipe band arrived early and played for a long time on the tarmac of the car park. We had a grandstand view from the bus and the children encircled the pipers and obviously enjoyed themselves. In this pleasant fashion the time on our hands did not drag too much.

Only Jonathan did not want to go the dance. It was his first and at eleven he was 'agin' all dances everywhere.

'Never mind,' we consoled him. 'It's lovely in the bus and you can watch. No one has to go.'

Just when the children began to think it never would, and that they could not wait much longer without bursting, the band went over to the pier and one of our most exciting and best remembered dances began. It was already dark.

Fortunately the night air was warm and dry. The darkness was pierced by innumerable dancing lights from pier and boats and reopened shops. Light falling on the restless water around the pier was shattered into hundreds of reflections.

'Keep away from the edge of the pier,' I warned constantly. I was in perpetual fear lest one of them should prance over the edge or be pushed unceremoniously overboard by the dancers. The splash would have gone unheard, lost in the screel of the many pipes and the infectious gaiety of the accordian.

After a while Hazel went to keep her unsociable son company. He, who in later years would wait long hours in Tarbert after other Sports Days or beg to be allowed to return in a car that 'happened to be going that way anyway',could not be coaxed out of the bus on the occasion of his first dance.

It was long after midnight when we decided we ought to go home. There were many miles between us and the welcoming tents, the warm sleeping bags and the oblivion sought by our exhausted limbs and drooping eyelids. I found our patient and accommodating driver. There had not been one word of reproach that we had stayed so long. There was however uneasiness in the elderly gentleman's mind about the last three miles of our journey.

A single track road bravely branches off the main Tarbert to Leverburgh road just before it begins to turn south and follow the west coast. The road to Luskentyre continues westwards, zig zagging precariously and keeping very close to the shore. Before it was re-routed to cross the River Laxdale at a less acute angled bend, and before the new stone bridge was built, the road was tricky to negotiate even in day-light. Small though the bus was its inflexible length could not take the bend without making a three point turn. We used to pile out onto the rocky verge to lighten the load but even so the wooden structure used to groan and creak and give alarmingly.

Now we remain seated and only the older ones among us have memories of the old bridge and say a little prayer of thankfulness to the County Council as we cross the new one in complete safety. The road is still narrow and appears many times as if it is going to plunge into the sea but the improvement at the bridge is impressive.

'Oh, whell. Chean, and I've been wondering,' said our driver as a seemingly endless queue of children packed itself into his bus. 'Och, it's a terrible bridge chust. Och and I don't like the Luskentyre road at all. It's terrible dark now. Would you be minding at all if I chust put you all down at the road end? I'll not be wanting to have an accident at all after such an enchoyable evening.'

'That's quite all right,' I agreed at once, half glad that we were to be spared the frightening journey and half horrified at the thought of propelling forty tired children the last three miles along the road.

A night journey across Harris, since the new road was laid, resembles a ride along a lighted street. Every Passing Place, alternately and sometimes precipitously pitched on each side of the road, is marked by a pole and a diamond plate of flourescent paint. These catch the headlights right into the distance and mark the road as efficiently as street lamps. There are thousands of these poles in the Western Highlands and Islands.

Therefore it must have been a very dull or unobservant ten year old who once staggered me by calling out in wonder as we returned across Skye by bus.

'Hey,' she said. 'Skipper, there's a village here with the same funny name as one on Harris. It's called Passing Place.'

It takes all sorts to make up our little community!

There will be groans, I thought, when I have to tell this lot that they have to get out of the bus and walk the three miles home. The night air is warm until you have enjoyed the bliss of a warm and crowded bus. Then it is incredibly cold. I put off the unpleasant task until we neared the road end. Some were singing, some were nodding drowsily and others had already slipped into the depths of first sleep.

I always underestimate our children. Far from being shocked or distressed by the summons to alight, far from habitation, at 1.30 am; far from being alarmed by the prospect of walking for at least another hour before bed, our inexhaustable children thrilled at the thought of a midnight hike, leapt out excitedly, linked arms five or six abreast and singing gaily disappeared into the night ahead of us.

On Harris we had Angela and Morag and Maggie to thank for the great times we have had in Leverburgh Hall and when Angela died two island Guider friends Mary Stewart and Margaret MacLeod took over and gave us many happy evenings. They were dances and céilidhs combined. At one of these socials Doreen was presented with her Queen's Guide Award. It was appropriate that it should be handed to her by our good friend and benefactor, John Morrison of Northton.

I went early to his home to make sure that he had not forgotten. It had been a busy day for him as the Sheep Dog Trials had been held that afternoon. He was still at his table eating salted mutton. He would have me join him. The meat tasted remarkably like boiled ham. We sat chatting as if the dance and the presentation were later in the month. No host is more courteous, hospitable and entertaining, than he. Like Calum he can hold children spellbound with his tales of his monkey and the interesting people he has entertained in his house. He and his wife have been our good friends for many years.

We have had many gay evenings in the Leverburgh Hall followed by sleepy sing-songs on the eighteen mile journey home. We will each treasure our favourite memories. For Doreen and her mother it may be the presentation of the Award, for some it will be the laughter Stuart and Liz, both eleven, caused when they won the elimination dance by successfully holding a penny between their foreheads for an incredible time. Tim will remember the chocolates with which Mrs Belsey bribed him to dance with her and Christine will remember the forfeit she had to pay and the public proposal of marriage she had to make to Jonathan. Some will remember the pipes and some the singing. Few of us will forget hearing Mary Sandeman who has recorded many Gaelic songs.

My favourite memory is quite clear and definite. It links the old and the new and both our most loved and frequented islands. Long, long ago at, a dance in Calum's barn, a visitor to the island came to play her guitar and lead the singing. She sang folk songs mostly but the Beatles were all the rage at that time and the song which really set the Yorkshire children singing was one which announced, 'I need somebody to love.' How they all loved it!

Julie was still very small, no more than nine years old. She never took her eyes from the singer and followed every movement of her fingers on the strings. She had eyes only for the musician and she sang every word. Her admiration was complete and she crept nearer and nearer to the front.

'I do wish that I could play like that,' she whispered.

Ten years later, in the Hall at Leverburgh, Julie was our guitarist. I had warned her that she would be asked to play. We had been dancing for some time and the atmosphere was alive and everyone was responsive. The cold hall had become warm and the windows were all steamy. The faces of the children were flushed and bonny and everything was just right. We had listened to the pipes and the Gaelic singing and there was a great bond between us.

'We will now hear from the young lady with the guitar,' said our Master of Ceremonies and the accordianist made room for her on the stage.

There were encouraging cheers from the islanders. Julie picked up her guitar and every Yorkshire eye was on her. She smiled and nodded her head, unobtrusively but definitely as if it were a pre-arranged signal. I was quite unprepared for almost every child to follow her up the steps and onto the stage as if they and she belonged and could not be separated.

'We're all going to sing.' she said simply.

They grouped themselves closely and naturally round her, heads turned towards her, loving her and her skill and the songs they were about to sing together. She began to play and then to sing and they were all involved and together, and I thought I had never seen anything more moving. They were looking at Julie as she had looked at the guitarist on Tiree, a decade ago, and my cup was full.

It overflowed a few days later when we were all safely back home. Margaret, Joanna, Hazel and I were having a Yorkshire céilidh in the farmhouse sitting room when Mr and Mrs Whalley arrived with their daughter Chris and Margie, the American Girl Scout who had been in camp with us. She had brought a poem she had written about the fortnight she had spent with us on Harris. In this way we receive our rewards.

> T'was to a place of rocky moor,
> And a shore where rolled the waves,
> With sand-dunes capped in golden sand,
> To this haven my love I gave.
>
> But this my love doth enshroud
> More than just the physical splendour,
> For here I had an experience
> Which for all my life I'll remember.

There was a deep feeling of brotherhood
In this community that I knew
Where love blossomed like a flower
And charity and joy thrived too.

And the perfect fellowship
In singing round the fire
And working for each other
With a love that never tired.

And neither shall I e'er forget
The games played on the sand,
The swimming in the ocean
And walking hand in hand.

And the sound of joyous laughter
Which always filled my ears,
Along with singing voices
And I knew that God was near.

And I'll always praise my Father
For the lessons I had learned,
And the peace and love found with my steps
And true beauty at every turn.

Margie Ricards (14 years old) USA

Now the Harris Camp is over,
It is time to say 'Goodbye,'
We must leave the fields of clover
And I feel like I could cry.

14

From the sand dunes silver soaring,
From the deepening, wide, blue sea,
From the bright dew-spangled morning
We must wander, you and me.

We must leave our rugged island
With its hills so heather clad,
We are leaving for the Mainland
And that parting makes us sad.

For our Harris Camp is over.
And it's time to say 'Goodbye.'
We must leave the fields of clover
And I feel like I could cry.

Written by Chris, Paddy, Julia and Mandy.
Set to the tune of The Carnival is Over.

Chapter Fourteen

I HAVE been writing for a great number of hours over the past weeks and my unskilled fingers may not want to touch my typewriter again for quite some time. They have bounced clumsily over the keys, trying to record an experience shared by a great many people.

I have had no difficulty in remembering what is so much a living part of me but I sincerely doubt whether I have been able to do justice to the great beauty, the friendship, tolerance and resourcefulness which have been my inspiration. A gentleman has just visited my home and delayed the final pages of my book. On leaving he made the profound statement that tolerance and resourcefulness are today's most essential virtues. To them I would add mirth. It is a dull life without that! And we, personally, need faith. Ours has grown over the years and weathers all storms.

I have tried to record honestly. Those who have been with me will vouch for the fact that I have not embroidered the beauty nor exaggerated the kindness. If anything I have not been appreciative enough of the children who have given us so much joy and so little trouble. Neither have I given enough credit to the Guide Movement in my endeavour to take our ideals into a wider world.

I have tried, inadequately, to convey my respect and affection for the two who have been with me as sister and friend; who, between them have taught our children to give generously of time and strength and possessions and to love all living things, plants and animals and fellow human beings. Through example Margaret has taught a respect for animals no one could equal and Hazel's contribution has included that of being a good wife and mother. Their presence has been my security, my consolation, my only hope of relaxation. Each has been with me right to the end of every demanding job, impervious to extremes of weather, undaunted by work and watchfulness. They have never been too tired to listen to children nor wearied by their boisterousness.

I hope this spillage on the pages from my overflowing memory will, in some way, be meaningful to those who have not been and seen and known. It has been without order or plan because it has been about things which have happened spontaneously. It has been about a lot of children with many names and many differing personalities.

There is a tendancy to think that the children of today want something different from their forebears and that the wind of change must be perpetually blowing. I do not think it so. Children need security more than anything in their formative years and the opportunity to have a place in the whole family with its several ages and ideas. There needs to be understanding between the generations. Children need the same homes, parents and schools, the same family holidays, the same traditions, the same adult leaders. Within the framework of the known they feel free to adventure and we must not take too lightly our great responsibility.

I have recently been asked wherein lay the secret of our success. I think it is hidden somewhere in the fact that we have never tried to segregate the age groups. Into our age range of from ten to twenty five we have absorbed the infants, juniors and seniors of every island. We have mixed with the working adults who have made our journeying so simple and pleasant, with the crofters and with the elderly. We have been a family.

A great deal is said, in the field in which I work, about the children of today, their lack of discipline, their laziness, and their precociousness. It offends me. I believe it is their environment and adults who are against them which make them so. I do not believe that the grand boys and girls who have wandered with us are unusual. They are ordinary children whose good fortune it has been to see great beauty and know fine people.

I am sure that there are thousands of children everywhere who would be just as happy, tolerant and sensitive; just as considerate and aware as ours; just as inventive and resourceful if they were given the same opportunity and the same simplicity.

If I am wrong, and by some unfair twist of fortune, we have indeed had the best of Britain's children, for over twenty years, then Hazel, Margaret and I have been singularly blessed.

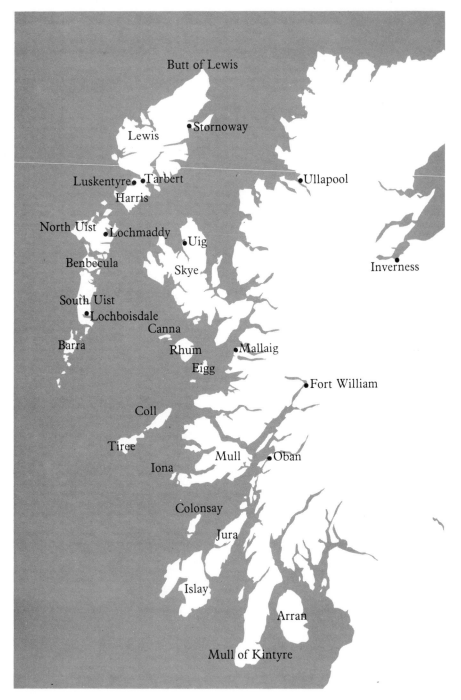

Western Islands and Highlands of Scotland

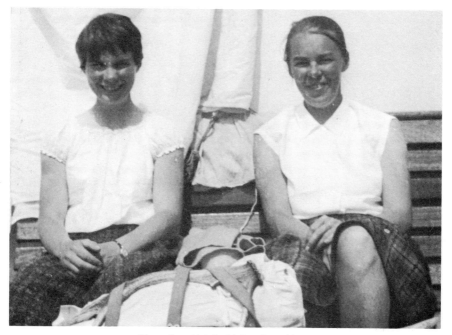

The author, (right) with her sister, Margaret.

Hazel with her husband, Dr Ray Belsey.

Paul.

171

Angus and Katie Morrison and family, Harris.

Rachel MacLeod, Harris.

Annie MacLeod, Harris.

Calum MacLean, Tiree, with the author's father.

John and Donald Alick MacDonald, Harris.

With Marion MacLean, Tiree.

Happiness on a Tiree shore.   Joanna.

Linda and Julie.   Lexy and Dolly MacLeod, Harris.

In camp at Luskentyre, Harris.